I Married
Wyatt Earp

Josephine Sarah Marcus Earp, c. 1880

I Married Wyatt Earp

The Recollections of
Josephine Sarah Marcus Earp

Collected and Edited by
GLENN G. BOYER

The University of Arizona Press
Tucson, Arizona

About the Editor . . .

GLENN BOYER, as a youth, was captivated by the dramatic portrayal of Wyatt Earp in Stuart Lake's popular book. The desire to discover the true man behind his boyhood hero embarked him upon more than thirty years of library and field investigation regarding the facts of the life of Wyatt Earp. He became a close friend of the descendants of Wyatt's second wife and the family of the lawman's sister. Eventually these associations led to his obtaining the two Josephine Earp manuscripts upon which this book is based. Glenn Boyer is author of two additional volumes, *The Suppressed Murder of Wyatt Earp,* dealing with the evolution of the Earp myth, and *An Illustrated Life of Doc Holliday.*

Third printing 1981

THE UNIVERSITY OF ARIZONA PRESS

Copyright © 1976
The Arizona Board of Regents
All Rights Reserved
Manufactured in the U.S.A.

I. S. B. N. 0-8165-0484-9 cloth
I. S. B. N. 0-8165-0583-7 paper
L. C. No. 76-4673

For Betty

Wheresoever she was, there was paradise.

Contents

Illustrations

Introducing
Josephine Sarah Marcus Earp

A neat, gray-haired old lady, characteristically dressed in black, sat in a well-known Los Angeles restaurant, critically picking through her salad. Meanwhile she chatted with her captive luncheon partner, a somewhat reluctant teen-ager. It was evident that the self-conscious girl was becoming uncomfortable, and the reason soon was revealed. The woman called the waiter, then pointed at the perfectly fresh, crisp lettuce. She wrinkled her nose delicately. "This salad is not good!" she told him. Apologetically, the poor man brought another salad.

The same transaction was repeated with the steak — it wasn't done right; the coffee was cold; the pie wasn't perfect. Patiently the waiter replaced each item. Josephine Earp was a regular customer, a good tipper, but her barrage of complaints was a dreaded ritual both for restaurant employees and her young companion.

This peevishness was undoubtedly calculated; it amounted to a perverse delight in commanding attention from others. It had been a part of Josephine Sarah Marcus Earp long before the day she ran away from home, a voluptuous eighteen year old with huge, lambent brown eyes. In her youth, men had fallen all over themselves for her. Now, in her old age, what beauty could no longer command, craft could.

Josie's biographers, Mabel Earp Cason and Vinolia Earp Ackerman, encountered her imperiousness again and again as they sought the truth about the old woman's younger days. Jeanne Laing, Mrs. Cason's daughter, confided a revealing remark made by her Uncle Harold Ackerman after a 1937 research trip to

[1]

Tombstone with Josie: "No one could convince me that Wyatt was a killer — he lived with Josie for fifty years!"

But this sometimes domineering old lady could be utterly charming as well. In her waning years, she dined with such personalities as Gary Cooper and Cecil B. DeMille. They sought her, not her them. When she decided to turn on her charm, her conversation could be simply delightful, spiced with hilarious stories, often at her own expense.

Even Jeanne Laing, the girl who had suffered that youthful embarrassment when her distant relative snapped those illogical complaints to the waiter, remembers Josie's "dignity, charm and even playfulness." One of Jeanne's anecdotes is particularly revealing:

"I recall having seen *HMS Pinafore* one time while Aunt Josie was staying with us. The next morning I was telling her about it — especially the little cabin boy dancing the sailor's hornpipe. She said 'Oh yes!' and got up and repeated the dance for us. She must have been well past eighty — she was very secretive about her age. At any rate, I still remember vividly the little elderly woman with her long-gone youth flashing from her eyes. She would never say exactly what part she had played, but we felt sure it must have been the cabin boy. It would have suited her."

This vivacity was undoubtedly the quality that had attracted Wyatt Earp when he first saw Josephine Sarah Marcus in the bloom of her youth. His good sense must have cautioned him that this beautiful, spirited creature would never become a conventional, quiet, deferential wife. But Wyatt was not a conventional man — he felt he was more than a match for her, and she acknowledged that he was right.

Wyatt Earp never tamed Josie — no one could — but he captivated and held her with his flair for constantly finding adventure. Shrewish his wife occasionally may have been, but she gladly embraced their challenging life — the sanguinary Tombstone vendetta, the bitterly cold arctic winters during Alaska's gold rush, the insecurity of an itinerant life of gambling and sports. At well past fifty, this dauntless woman met with relish the demands of a prospector's life of camping throughout the Mojave Desert.

The belle of Tombstone had learned to adapt to whatever her husband might ask of her. He loved good food; she became a gourmet cook of his favorites, such as dutch-oven cornbread. He did not like displays of emotion; she was able to conquer her terror of desert electrical storms and even learn to delight in the rain's refreshing aftermath — the pungent smell of wet creosote.

This was the Josie who lived these memoirs — a strong-willed woman filled with intense, loyal love for Wyatt Earp. Her zest for life, her daring, adventurous spirit sparkle through this tale, despite her "little-old-lady" attempts to tell only the decorous and proper. In her earlier life with Wyatt and before, she never had cared a fig for propriety. It is well that her story of adventure deceived her intent, conveying Josephine Earp as she really was — a fiery, delightful contradiction.

GLENN G. BOYER

1

I Run Away From Home

The need to write this story has seemed to grow greater with each passing year after the death of my husband Wyatt Earp. It is, if not an attempt to vindicate, at least an attempt to explain him. And in such an enterprise I need take a backseat to no one. I lived with him for almost half a century. That should be time enough to understand something about the man I loved — and still love, for that matter.

This book is probably the first and may be the last rendition of the Tombstone story as it really happened. It's a dreadful memory for me. I know it was painful for Wyatt. But so much speculation and dramatization have surrounded the Tombstone vendetta — it's high time all that malarkey got a firsthand going-over.

Looking back over Wyatt's lifetime of almost eighty-one years, his twenty-seven months at Tombstone seem so short. There is no question that those months were important — what happened then irrevocably changed our lives. Still, the events that filled our forty-seven later years together seem far more real to me.

For this reason I had once thought of telling about our years after Tombstone first. Then I realized that such a course would be nothing more than putting off the inevitable. Everyone wants to know about Tombstone, and I might as well grit my teeth and get that overplayed story told once and for all — at least this time the true motives on both sides will be made public.

Next to questions about all the shooting, I guess what people ask me most is, "How did you and Wyatt meet?" To make it short and sweet, we were introduced by my fiancé at that time,

Johnny Behan.[1] It happened in Tombstone in 1880. I have to laugh at the response that answer usually gets. If the questioner knows who Johnny Behan was, I generally see his jaw drop.

For those who don't know, I guess you'd call Johnny Behan Wyatt's arch enemy in Tombstone. He was surely as much the author of most of the Earp trouble as anyone. And no one was in a better position to know that than I was. Plans to marry Johnny were what brought me to Tombstone in the first place.[2] At that time Johnny and Wyatt were on friendly enough terms. Both had been lawmen, so they had something in common.[3]

The first Earp I was to meet was not Wyatt, however. It was his brother Morgan. Morg was riding shotgun guard on the stage-coach between Tombstone and the railroad at Benson some twenty miles north.[4] He was the guard on the stage that first took me into Tombstone. I don't hesitate to say that I noticed him because he was a very handsome man. He greatly resembled Wyatt. In fact they were sometimes mistaken for each other.

In my opinion, an even better question than those I'm usually asked is, "What was a strictly raised girl not yet nineteen and from a prosperous German Jewish family doing putting her dainty feet down from a train in a place like Benson?"

Southeastern Arizona was only a few years away from being a howling wilderness. It was still the stamping ground of the Apache. People, I soon discovered, were sometimes picked off by stray renegade bands within a few miles of Tombstone.[5] Wandering from the beaten path unarmed was simply asking for it; I had a close call a little later myself.

But back to why I was getting off a train at Benson, all ready to board a stage to Tombstone to marry Johnny Behan. A girl raised as I was would normally never be allowed to meet a man like Johnny, much less one like Wyatt. They were both frontiers-men who had seen hard sights. Both were boomers, which means they were the kind that gravitated from one boom camp to the next, whichever was then the big news in mining. Wyatt was more of a mining man and speculator than Johnny. Johnny was a sure-thing gambler. He always managed to wangle some sort of political appointment or other.[6]

I liked the traveling sort of man better than the kind that sat back in one town all his life and wrote down little rows of figures all day or hustled dry goods or groceries and that sort of thing. I can see the need for solid citizens such as those, but they were never my type for a husband. My blood demanded excitement, variety and change. I sensed that fact before I was very old. In the late 1860s my parents had brought me and my two sisters, Edna and Henrietta, from Brooklyn to San Francisco to make our home there. I must have been about seven. We came by way of the Isthmus then went up the coast by ship. When my young feet touched the well-known San Francisco Embarcadero, I wanted to investigate everything about this glamorous new place. The gold rush was not yet twenty years past. San Francisco was still a miners' town above all else. Between stampedes the boomers fell back to San Francisco to wait for the next big excitement to break. That's how we heard of Tombstone. The name may seem strange to some people, but it didn't seem that way to me, being familiar with others equally unique, such as Hangtown, Shoot-Em-Up, and the like.[7]

I don't know where I got the adventure in my blood. Certainly not from my parents, who were the soul of middle-class, solid respectability. My upbringing was all directed toward taking my place some day as a proper matron in a middle-class setting. I probably would have fulfilled this destiny if it hadn't been for Gilbert and Sullivan.

In 1879 the *H.M.S. Pinafore* craze swept the country. Tunes from the Gilbert and Sullivan operetta were sung, hummed and whistled everywhere. The sailor's hornpipe became a dance familiar to almost everyone. I don't know how many times I sneaked off with some girlfriend to see the *Pinafore*. In my room I secretly practiced the sailor's hornpipe and could do it very well, if I do say so myself. I was then eighteen, and was I ever stage-struck!

My downfall came because of two girlfriends, Dora Hirsch, daughter of my music teacher, and a music pupil named Agnes.[8] Somehow Agnes had landed a part in the Pauline Markham *Pinafore* troupe then playing at the Adelphi Theater in San Francisco. She persuaded Dora to run away from home and join them when the group went on the road.⁹ I suppose this was because some regular member of the cast didn't want to leave San Francisco. Pretty soon that's all Dora could talk about. She had been practically my inseparable friend for years. The prospect of life in San Francisco without her appeared to me then as a pretty lonely outlook. We had, of course, always confided in one another.

Apparently Dora was thinking somewhat along the same lines. Maybe she needed moral support. At any rate, one night when I stopped at her mother's for my music lesson she met me on the porch all excited. "Josie, you've got to come with me!" she insisted.

I knew where she meant. The thought wasn't a new one to me. Envy over the seeming luck of Dora and Agnes had fairly eaten me up. But I couldn't act or sing very well, a fact I was quick to point out. "What will I do?" I protested, but not very strongly.

"You can dance," Dora said. "They need someone to play the cabin boy, Tommy Tucker."

I did a lot of moralizing with myself over what I was about to do. But I always wanted my own way. The thought of hurting my family was not as compelling as the thought of missing out on a chance for adventure and applause. You can guess what I did.¹⁰

I left home one morning, carrying my books just as though going to school as usual. My mother may have wondered at the fervent kiss I gave her, rather than a dutiful peck. Tears were very close, but I fought them back.

I can remember exactly how I was dressed, in a plaid worsted dress, a blue Normandy cap and my raincoat. My hair was in two braids wound Dutch-fashion around my head and fastened over the ears with plaid ribbon bows. I have kept one of the ribbons to this day.

It rained all day and was pouring when we boarded the boat for Santa Barbara. Dora and I went to our cabin and immediately fell into each others arms crying. We were pretty scared, but also happily excited. We were on our own with no families to shelter us. Soon enough we found out what that could mean.

Our itinerary from Santa Barbara had us scheduled for a few days in Los Angeles, a one-night stand in San Bernardino, then a stint in Prescott, Arizona, and finally a few performances in Tombstone, which was then the big news in mining boom towns.[11] We had two stagecoaches for the members of the troupe and a heavy transport wagon for the stage props and luggage. There were twenty-six of us in all.[12]

My first appearance before the footlights with a live audience was probably like everyone else's, but I'll never forget it. Scared stiff isn't the word for it. I was numb, head and all. I seemed to be floating around without even touching the floor.[13] It's a wonder I managed to get through it without falling over my own feet. After that it went better.

Pauline Markham had a good, kind heart, even though the theater might be expected to harden a person. She looked after me and Dora. I remember how one day she put her arm around me and said, "You're a good, sweet little girl!" I loved her for it. She must have seen that I was pretty blue and homesick. When she said those words I thought of my poor mother probably worrying herself half to death over me. I'm afraid if I were a good girl I'd have never gone away from home and my mother. But we are what we are and might as well face it early as late.

We were getting close to the Colorado River on our trip from San Bernardino to Prescott when we met another stage headed the other way. We saw it coming and thought it would break the monotony of an otherwise pretty boring ride. It certainly did that. "You're headed into trouble!" the driver on the other stage yelled over to us first thing after he stopped. "The damn Apaches are on the fight again!"[14]

I felt like I was a goner already. Indians, just the thought of them, terrified me. It's been a lifelong dread. The words of one of our drivers, an old hand on the route, were probably intended to keep everyone like me from panicking; he said, "Hell, it ain't very likely! There ain't been any trouble since General Crook got 'em all down to San Carlos in '74."

But his bland assurance didn't do a thing for me. At every turn of the wheels from then on I expected to see a cloud of redskins materialize from behind some clump of sagebrush. I hoped we'd turn back, but when someone suggested it Miss Markham scotched the idea. My heart sunk. Young as I was, I thought, "She's either got a lot more grit than the average or a lot less sense."

We stopped at Ehrenburg to change teams. "Better keep your guns handy, boys!" the hostler at the stage station warned us. His good advice didn't do a thing to help my chicken heart. I just knew we were going to end up in trouble up to our ears, and sure enough we did.

Within the next couple of days we saw smoke signals several times, coming from both sides of our trail. I recall someone who was trying to be funny saying, "That fellow over to the north is probably telling his friends down south to sneak up on that side while they get us on the other!" Nobody laughed much.

A few hours later one of the men riding outside yelled, "There they are! Indians!" I was paralyzed. You can't imagine this kind of fright unless you've experienced it. You wonder, "How can this really be happening to me?" I gave up right then and there, hoping it would all be over quickly and not hurt too much. I actually felt relieved at this sense of resignation and got brave enough to look out the window.

I could see a line of riders strung out to the north riding parallel to us and maybe a half mile away, keeping out of good rifle range. They moved at a lope, keeping even with us as the drivers whipped our horses to a lumbering gallop. The urge to push to make us go faster was pretty strong, I can tell you!

Then someone yelled, "There's another bunch on the other side of us!" I looked over there. We could see this new threat bouncing in and out of arroyos, angling toward us. Lord, was I relieved when someone said, "Hey this new bunch ain't Injuns! They got hats on!"

Sure enough, even I could make that out through the dust. They crossed our trail and pitched into the real Indians. We could see the puffs of smoke from their guns and hear the distant pops.

Our drivers rested the horses by slowing them to a walk, and we all waited expectantly for the outcome. We could see for ourselves that the riders had got the Apaches on the run. In about twenty minutes our rescuers came trotting back, their horses all wet with sweat.

The men were a fierce, grimy-looking set, with long hair and unshaven faces, to say nothing of guns and knives belted all around them. They'd have scared me as bad as the Indians if I didn't know they had just saved our lives. I learned their leader was called Al Sieber, a name that meant nothing to me then. Later I learned of Al Sieber's fame in Arizona as a great scout.[15]

One of the riders rode close to our coach, looking inside. When he saw women, he raised his hat politely. "How do you do, ladies!" he greeted us. "No cause to be afraid now. We got the jump on 'em!" He was far neater than any of the others I'd seen, with a carefully trimmed black moustache and piercing brown eyes. When he looked at me he inclined his head ever so slightly in a polite little bow, which I found very flattering. To my eyes he was a romantic, dashing cavalier. I wondered if I'd ever get to meet him. That was the first time I laid eyes on Johnny Behan.[16]

We were escorted to a ranch that served as a stage relay station.[17] It was made of thick adobe with a large, high-walled corral. People from the neighborhood were converging on this small fort in buggies, in wagons, on horseback and even afoot, banding together for mutual protection till the Indian trouble blew over. Several posses of armed men were also coming in from other parts of the territory.

When we pulled into the ranch, the moon was just rising. Al Sieber came to help the ladies down. I noticed he was absent-mindedly humming "Darling Nellie Gray" under his breath, which strikes me as funny when I look back on it. When he got to me he stopped and said, "Whoops! I thought you were a boy for a minute! What is a little girl like you doing out here?"

I was still too shook up to give him much of an answer, but he must have found out from someone. Later he came to me and convinced me I should give him an address of relatives so he could let them know in case anything happened to me. I have no idea to this day why he took an interest in me, unless the word was out in Prescott to be on the lookout for a couple of runaways. At any rate, I gave him my name along with my married sister Edna's name and address.[18]

After we got to the ranch, it didn't take my cavalier long to find me. He introduced himself as Johnny Behan, deputy sheriff of Yavapai County. He was a lot older than I was,[19] but all I noticed was that he was markedly handsome, with dark, flashing eyes and a ready smile. He managed to be alone with me on the moonlit porch that first night. His attention made me forget my bad scare and how tired I was.

We had to practically camp out at the ranch for several days, but everyone was cheerful and cooperative, all pitching in to do whatever needed to be done. The posses would leave at daybreak on scout and return at night.

I noticed such things as the fact that Johnny always washed up as soon as he got in from those scouts. He kept his hair neatly combed and cleaned the dust off his boots as well. He was a lot more particular about his appearance and manners than any of the other men.

We managed to see a lot of each other during the week the troupe was cooped up there. Before the end of that time Johnny had made his desire to marry me perfectly clear. Although I'd had the usual school-girl romances, this was something else. I knew my heart and was sure of what I wanted.

You can imagine then what a shock it was when Pauline Markham drew me aside shortly before the end of our enforced stay and told me, "Honey, Johnny is an attractive man, but I've been told he's married and has a child. You'd better be careful."

I was crushed! Then I got mad. I made up my mind to give Johnny a piece of my mind the next time he came near me. I got up a first-class "hate" for my suitor.

It wasn't long before he came around. Even his smile I'd liked so much looked different to me. "Let me alone!" I told him. "I know all about you, and I hate you for your deceitfulness. You ought to be ashamed of yourself!"

My remarks hardly ruffled Johnny. "Someone's been talking to you. I expected as much. But believe me," he said reassuringly, "I am perfectly honest about wanting to marry you." He sounded convincing, and, oh boy, how convincing Johnny could sound when he wanted something!

Johnny Behan in his mid-forties. An obvious Dapper Dan, he was sensitive about the baldpate.

"What about your wife?" I shot right back at him. I was watching him for the effect of that thrust.

He looked genuinely surprised, but not nonplussed. "Did someone tell you I'm married? I've been divorced for over four years!"[20] He let out a sort of relieved laugh. "Is that what's been bothering you, sweetheart?"

There wasn't anything to do but confess that it was. But I still had my doubts.

"I'll let you find out for yourself when we get to Prescott," Johnny told me. And sure enough, I did. He was not lying. Someone had misled Pauline or deliberately lied out of spite.

After clearing the air of that, Johnny and I reached an understanding. He was going to the new boom camp of Tombstone. As soon as he prospered he would send for me from wherever the troupe was then, and we could get married.

Unfortunately for our young plans, the first morning we were in Prescott I was greeted by a message that a Mr. Jacob Marks[21] wanted to see me. I couldn't imagine who in the world he was.

The name wasn't at all familiar. I soon found out. Al Sieber had wired my sister. Her husband wired back to Mr. Marks, one of his business associates, to tell me that my folks and Dora's wanted us to return home. I was actually a little relieved. So was Dora. We both recognized we'd got in over our heads. In a couple of days Mrs. Marks was accompanying us back to San Francisco.

Before I left, Johnny promised to come and win my folks over to our plans. He told me to write him as soon as I felt the time was ripe.

Fate threw another monkey wrench into our plans, however. I got a case of Saint Vitus dance. Maybe the strain of all the things I had just experienced was too much for my nerves. At any rate, I burned with impatience to recover so I could have Johnny come meet my folks. As soon as I was well I wrote him.

He came at once. Between his persuasiveness and my wheedling he won my parents' consent to our eventual marriage. They were both real softies; they could never say no to anything their daughters really wanted. I'm afraid I took unmerciful advantage of them.

Our plan remained the same: as soon as Johnny was securely prospering in Tombstone, I would join him and we would get married. My parents wanted the wedding to be in San Francisco, but Johnny argued that while he was just getting started in the community his business wouldn't permit him to leave. My businessman father could see the sense in that, even if my mother couldn't. Johnny's new enterprise was to be a livery stable.[22]

Looking back on these events, I can see that my father must have had serious misgivings about the whole thing. But he was wise enough to know me, and, recognizing that I could learn only by sad experience, he hoped for the best.

Johnny gave me a diamond engagement ring before he left. There was now no question in my mind that I'd answer his call to come to Arizona to marry him. All in all, I thought his long journey to ask for my hand was the most romantic thing that had ever happened to a girl my age. Little did I know!

But the fat still wasn't out of the fire. My mother was sure I'd be prey to either Indians or desperados. Happily Johnny found just the right person to convey the word that he was ready for me to join him. This was Kitty Jones,[23] who soon became one of my best friends. She was married to a young Tombstone lawyer, Harry Jones, and was visiting her folks in San Francisco. Her white lie assuring my parents that Tombstone was by now a budding metropolis smoothed over my mother's misgivings. Kitty promised to accompany me to the boom town and give me a home until the wedding.

So now I was on my way to Arizona again, and that's how my "dainty" feet stepped down from the train at Benson. It was the railroad's point of deposit nearest Tombstone, where one changed to the stagecoach.[24] When I had traveled the route on my first trip, the railroad had hardly touched Arizona, and the *Pinafore* troupe had had to make the whole trip by stage. Now nearly a year had passed since that exciting adventure. Soon I would be nineteen, and I thought of myself as rather grown up and worldly.

My meeting with Kitty Jones was a fateful one that was to have a significant bearing on my knowledge of the inner workings behind later bloody happenings in Tombstone. By coincidence another individual I met on this trip was to have an equally important role. She was a timid young Mexican girl who boarded the train at Tucson and took the seat opposite Kitty and me. In a matter of moments, despite a slight language barrier, we found ourselves gossiping away like lifelong friends. The pretty little newcomer was named Marietta Spencer.[25] She told us she was on her way to join her husband,[25] who was working in the mines near Tombstone. I remember that Kitty shared a bag of gumdrops, and we rode happily along, all innocent of what the future might bring.

HISTORICAL NOTES AND EDITORIAL COMMENTS

1. John Harris Behan was one of fourteen children of Peter and Sarah Ann Harris Behan. Sarah came from a rather famous border family; her father was Colonel Jack Harris, who built and operated the well-known

Harris House at Westport (now Kansas City), Missouri. John Behan was born in the Harris House October 23, 1845.

John's father, Peter Behan, born in Ireland on December 18, 1809, was educated to be a priest at Trinity College, Dublin. He came to the U.S. in the 1830s and enlisted in the army to fight Indians, eventually ending up on the Missouri border. Once out of the army, he married Sarah Ann Harris at the Harris farm at Westport on May 16, 1837. Thereafter during his life he was variously a carpenter, freighter and veterinarian. He died on June 10, 1889. Sarah Ann died on April 24, 1898.

In 1863 their son John came by way of San Francisco to Prescott, Arizona, where he subsequently became prominent in local politics. He held the county offices of deputy sheriff, under-sheriff, sheriff, county recorder, tax collector, assessor and deputy clerk of the district court. He was also a member of the Seventh Legislative Assembly in the House, from Prescott (Yavapai County) and the Tenth Assembly, also in the House, from Mohave County. He married Victoria Zaff March 1869 in San Francisco and had two children, Henrietta, who was born in 1869 and lived only five years, and Albert born July 6, 1871, who died in 1947.

John and Victoria were divorced in 1875. (Number 275 Judgment Roll, District Court of Yavapai County, Judgment Book 234–5–6, June 2, 1875; see Chapter 2, note 5, for details.) Victoria remarried September 22, 1881, to Charles A. Randall.

John did not remarry. As Josie has indicated, he moved to Tombstone sometime in 1880 and started a livery stable there in partnership with John Dunbar, became deputy sheriff of Pima County, then first sheriff of newly formed Cochise County in February 1881. Subsequent to his Tombstone years he was deputy superintendent of the Arizona penitentiary at Yuma, a U.S. Customs agent at El Paso and, in the Spanish American War and the Boxer Rebellion, a commissary officer for the army. At the time of his death he was the favored applicant for superintendent of the soldiers' home in Prescott. He died on June 7, 1912, in Tucson. (Cason notes in personal collection of the editor; hereafter cited as Cason notes; Mary Coe to the editor, September 16, 1974; Mrs. Behan W. Meeker to the editor, August and September 1974; Jay J. Wagoner, *Arizona Territory 1863–1912, A Political History,* pp. 511–514; recorder of Yavapai County to the editor, March 20, 1975.)

2. Although Josie does not here specify the month she came to Tombstone to marry Johnny, in Chapter 2 she tells us that she arrived shortly before the shooting of Fred White, which occurred in October 1880. However, the register of the Cosmopolitan Hotel in Tombstone records the arrival of a J. Marcus during the week ending May 12, 1880, five months prior to the White shooting. (*Tombstone Weekly Nugget,* May 13, 1880.) If this J. Marcus were indeed Josephine, the old woman was obviously wrong about

her arrival date when she dictated her manuscript many years later. Whether she was being deliberately evasive or merely the victim of a failing memory is impossible to determine. Josie was certainly capable of circumvention when she felt the circumstances called for it, but in this case it is difficult to find a motive for her lying.

3. Wyatt Earp was elected the first constable of Lamar, Missouri, in November 1870. (*Lamar Democrat,* September 6, 1957, Centennial Edition.) He was appointed policeman in Wichita, Kansas, April 21, 1875, and served until April 3, 1876. (Nyle Miller and Joseph Snell, *Why The West Was Wild,* pp. 147–151.) In May 1876 he was put on the police force at Dodge City, Kansas (*Wichita Weekly Beacon,* May 24, 1876), and by October 14, 1876, he was listed as deputy city marshal. (*Dodge City Times,* October 14, 1876.) Wyatt Earp was periodically listed in the Dodge City newspapers as either a deputy marshal or policeman until he resigned in September 1879. (*Ford County Globe,* September 9, 1879.)

John H. Behan is listed in Yavapai County, Arizona, records as deputy sheriff, October 8, 1866, and December 2, 1867; and as sheriff December 31, 1870, and August 5, 1871. Strangely, no bond is listed for under-sheriff, but on November 6, 1867, a bond is recorded revoked as under-sheriff for Behan. (Bonds and oaths file, Recorder's Office, Yavapai County.)

4. If the J. Marcus on the hotel register in early May was in fact Josie (see note 2), then she is also incorrect regarding the end of the railroad line. Regular train service had not yet extended to Benson by May 1880; Josie instead probably would have taken the stage from Tucson or Pantano. By June of that year, however, regular train service had been extended to Benson. (*Weekly Nugget,* June 24, 1880.)

5. It is apparent that some renegade Apaches could have been encountered off the reservations at any time during the 1870s and early 1880s; John G. Bourke wrote, "The Chiricahuas . . . led a Jack-in-the-box sort of existence, now popping into an agency and now popping out. . . ." (Bourke, *An Apache Campaign in the Sierra Madre,* p. 8.) When off the agency, they would make their way to join the hostiles in Mexico, and Tombstone was surrounded by their preferred routes. Dan Thrapp refers to "gloomy and little-known mountain corridors . . . the Dragoons, the Mule Mountains, the Whetstones, the Chiricahuas." (Thrapp, *Al Sieber, Chief of Scouts,* p. 222.)

6. See note 1, this chapter, confirming this assertion.

7. Josie's familiarity with the names of the various mining camps probably came from overhearing conversations of the mining crowd who made San Francisco homebase.

8. This was probably Agnes Sterns. (Cason notes in editor's collection based on a letter from the California State Library to Mabel Earp Cason, June 9, 1937.)

9. They were known as the "English Opera Company," or, when they went on the road, the "*Pinafore* on Wheels," and were booked into Tombstone the first week of December 1879. (Pat M. Ryan, "Tombstone Theatre Tonight," p. 50.)

10. Josie's account of how she came to join the *Pinafore* troupe is one of the most dubious elements in her story. In the first stages of their collaboration, Josie actually told Mrs. Cason and Mrs. Ackerman a wild tale in which she met with the Pauline Markham company when they rescued her from Indians! Later she came up with the more believable version involving her stagestruck girl friend Dora.

Still, considering young Josie's weakness for men, one cannot help but wonder if a romance with some member of the theatrical troupe was not the true cause of her unconventional departure from home. Such a circumstance might have prompted her equivocation on the subject during her proper old age. Additionally, the fact that she knew her biographers were strongly religious may have tempered her frankness with them.

11. Again Josie is misleading. After leaving San Francisco on October 19, 1879, the ports of call of the Pauline Markham players, in order, were Tucson, Tombstone, Prescott and Phoenix. (*Arizona Weekly Miner* [Prescott], December 12, 1879.) Prescott was third on the actors' itinerary, not first as Josie indicates. From the known evidence we cannot determine whether she was deliberately trying to conceal something that may have occurred during the stop in Tombstone or simply befuddled in her old age.

12. Casts apparently sometimes varied in different locations, probably due to the practice of using some local talent to save traveling expenses. Therefore, although there may have been twenty-six actors at some time during the tour, the number probably fluctuated. (*Arizona Star* [Tucson], November 16, 1879; *Arizona Weekly Miner*, January 2, 1880.)

13. Exactly which part Josie was playing during this first-night trauma is not entirely clear. Although she says she was the cabin boy, there are hints that the young runaway may have occasionally taken another part. The Cason notes suggest that she was Little Gay during the San Francisco run, but the information is not positive. Another source asserts that Josephine was using the alias "Miss May Bell," and playing Cousin Hebe. (Pat M. Ryan, "Tombstone Theatre Tonight," p. 50.) In view of the fact that Josie insists that she could not sing or act, and considering her neat execution of the sailor's hornpipe when she was almost eighty (see "Introducing Josephine Sarah Marcus Earp" in the beginning of this book), it seems most likely that her role in the company was in fact that of the cabin boy, as she asserts.

14. Josie is once again confused or deliberately adding color to her story. It is certain from lack of mention in the newspapers that there was no Indian outbreak when the Pauline Markham troupe was en route from

Tombstone to Prescott in December 1879. Josie's realistic description of her fear suggests that she probably did experience such an Apache scare, but historically it has to be placed at some other time, possibly in March 1882, when Apache renegades from Mexico were out in force to persuade Loco to jump the reservation. Josie and Wyatt may have innocently chosen that unfortunate time for her to attempt to leave Tombstone undetected, and, without leading his enemies to him, join Wyatt in Silver City, New Mexico, where he had at first planned to remain while the heat over his Arizona killings died down.

It is probable that Josie would have made the initial part of such a trip surreptitiously by private buggy, piloted by one or more of Wyatt's trusted associates. The route most likely would have taken her across the Sulphur Springs and San Simon valleys, right into the path of the band of renegade Apaches. This is largely speculative. But such an itinerary would certainly account for Josie's mentioned meeting with scout Al Sieber, who was definitely after Apaches in that locale at that time. (Sieber to Willcox, June 8, 1882, Adjutant General's Office Letters, U.S. Army, 1882, in National Archives.)

15. Al Sieber was by 1879 probably the most famous Anglo hired by the army to supervise groups of Apache scouts employed in hunting their own raiding tribesmen. (Thrapp, *Al Sieber, Chief of Scouts.*) Josie could have met him on her 1879 trip as she relates, for he and Bob Paul (who is mentioned in Chapter 2) were searching the area for three Mexican stage robbers at that time. (*Arizona Weekly Miner*, December 5, 1879.) Josie may have met him again in March 1882, as indicated in note 14 above.

16. Josie probably did meet Johnny Behan almost in the manner she claims. While the Markham troupe was en route from Tombstone to Prescott, Johnny was out from Gillett, Arizona, with a posse scouting for the three Mexican stage robbers mentioned above in note 15. (*Arizona Weekly Miner*, December 5, 1879.) When they encountered the stagecoach full of attractive actresses, the posse probably abandoned their fruitless chase to escort the girls into Prescott.

17. Considering the fact that there was no Apache outbreak in December 1879, one can surmise that the real beginnings of Josie's romance with Johnny Behan actually occurred at Prescott, not at some beleaguered stage stop. If in fact the girl had originally run away with the Markham troupe due to a romance with one of its members, the affair had obviously cooled enough by this time to allow Johnny to take over as number one in her affections.

18. Josie did not mention her sisters by their married names in either basic manuscript, probably due to a desire not to draw her still-living family into the limelight. Obviously by Josie's intent, they were not even aware that she was doing her memoirs. The girls' parents were Hyman (called

Henry) and Sophia Marcus. Josie's older sister was Edna, her younger sister Henrietta. She also had an older brother, Nathan, whom she did not mention at all in her memoirs — for what reason I don't know. His death is reported in the *San Francisco Examiner*, May 19, 1906, p. 10. Survivors were reported as mother Mrs. Sophia Marcus and sisters Mrs. Emil Lenhardt, Mrs. A. Weiner, and Mrs. W. Earp.

19. Behan was thirty-four and Josephine was eighteen.

20. Records of the Clerk of the District Court of Yavapai County contain the following entry: "Victoria F. Behan vs. John H. Behan, Number 275 Judgment Roll: Entry in Judgment Book 234, 235 & 236 in Judgment Docket 2, Time of June, 2nd 1875, Judgment Decree of Divorce and allowance $16.66 per month. Cost satisfied. Filed June 2, 1875; Wm. Wilkenson, Clerk."

21. Jacob Marks was a Prescott liquor dealer who had come to the town around 1872 and died there August 19, 1907. (Sharlott Hall Museum to Mabel Earp Cason, undated; Cason notes.)

22. As indicated in note 1 above, Johnny was a partner with John Dunbar in the Dexter Stables in Tombstone. City of Tombstone Assessment Rolls, 1881, contain the following entry: "The Dexter Stables, Block 3, lots 6 and 7 and parts of lots 16 and 17, Dunbar and Behan."

23. Kitty Jones had probably been acquainted with the Marcus family before this time, though I have been unable to confirm this definitely. It is quite possible, if this prior connection existed, that Josephine initially met Behan at the Jones home in San Francisco, perhaps early in 1879, at which time the Prescott *Arizona Daily Miner* comments that Behan was visiting that town. It is an interesting speculation that Josie's incentive for running away actually may have been the knowledge that the Markham troupe was going to Prescott, Arizona, where she may have known Johnny resided. (Cason notes.)

24. See notes 2 and 4 for speculation regarding the date and manner of this trip to Tombstone.

25. Josie's memory again may have deceived her, or else Marietta did, for this girl's wedding to Peter Spencer is not recorded until the next year. (Recorded August 13, 1881, by A. O. Wallace, Book 1, p. 9, in Marriage Records of Cachise [sic] County, Arizona.) It was common in the West for a woman to cohabit with a man without the formality of a marriage; the unusual thing about this case is that a marriage actually followed. Apparently Josie had an arrangement of convenience with Behan for as much as a year, and Wyatt's ceremonial marriage to Mattie, who lived with him as Mrs. Earp in Tombstone, never has been confirmed by documentation.

2

A Feud Is Born

Just as the agent from the Benson office[1] gave the signal to pull out, a tall, slender, blond young man carrying a shotgun came out of the station. He was the Wells Fargo shotgun messenger. He glanced inside the coach at us and tipped his hat.

A passenger who obviously knew him said, "I'm glad Morg[2] is on the box. We can be sure of a safe trip." This, you recall, was my first sight of an Earp. Kitty said, "That's Morg Earp. His brother Wyatt is our deputy sheriff."

Recollection of the trip to Tombstone is chiefly of dust. The road was crowded with ore and freight wagons. The driver whipped up the horses rapidly past those going our way. The air was filled with fine powdery grit.

We changed teams once, then went right on. In a few hours Tombstone came into view on its hillside. I could feel my heart beating painfully fast as Johnny, who had ridden out to meet us, drew alongside the coach. He sided the coach for the last mile, occasionally grinning and saying something I couldn't make out. The driver whipped our horses to make a smart dash to the post office. This was a common show-off stunt of drivers; they almost all did it.

A throng converged on the stage, mostly friends and relatives, but it also contained one element I miss today at train stations.[3] The crowds that met stages had among them merely curious idlers who showed up for the entertainment because there was nothing better to do. Maybe they would hear some up-to-the-minute outside gossip. Kitty's husband Harry was there, of course.

Johnny leaped from his horse, grabbed me and kissed me right in front of everyone. He was never bashful.

Even in all the excitement I remember that Morg was met by a man who could have been his twin. Right away they got into a private discussion over to one side. The other man, of course, was Wyatt.[4] It was the first time I saw him. A little later Johnny spoke cordially to both Earps. They were all on good terms then.

Johnny had hardly finished my introduction to Kitty's husband when he told Harry, "We'll walk out; your buggy'll be full with Kitty and the ladies' traps." To me he explained, "It's only a little ways." Harry was promptly left to be drayman as well as to lead out Johnny's horse tied behind the buggy.

Johnny wanted to be alone with me, but I think he also wanted to show me off to the town. He was practically strutting with me on his arm. He made me feel important. His intimate ways were nice till I found out he used them on every good-looking woman.[5]

In those days it seldom occurred to men to take women out to a restaurant after a tiresome trip. Kitty and I were expected to make supper as soon as we got to their little house. By then it was growing dark. I was dog-tired. After we ate we soon got rid of the men. Impatient as I'd been to see Johnny, now all I wanted was a bath and bed.

The next morning I awoke with a tremendous sense of well being. I told Kitty, "I think I'll go look the town over."[6]

My friend had a fit over that. "Don't you dare go down there alone, *ever!*" she warned me. "I'll go with you. Better yet, we should have a man along."

Her advice was as good as gold. An unescorted woman in Tombstone was fair game for the drunks loafing around the streets. My mother would have fainted if she knew what sort of place Tombstone really was.

When I finally did look over the town I found it a mixture of adobe and frame structures with a good number of tents here and there. The streets were often crowded with freight and ore wagons, buggies, drays, ranch wagons, horses, burros, dogs and even a few chickens that the coyotes hadn't got yet.

Wyatt Earp, 1885, very similar to the way he looked during his Tombstone days. The dark-appearing hair was actually russet blond.

Editor's collection

Morgan Earp, c. 1880, probably photographed in Tombstone. His oft-noted resemblance to Wyatt is readily apparent. Morg was also blond.

N. H. Rose photo,
University of Oklahoma

The hill south of town was crawling with mining activity. The sound of machinery came from there day and night. By then there were even regular shifts, with whistles to signal the start and end of them.

Tombstone was getting to be a regular city in outward appearances. People were comparing it to Virginia City in its heyday. Big men from the financial centers of the world had money invested here. That sort of capital looked for law and order.

But it didn't get it. Tombstone's "citified" appearance was all on the surface. Beneath that veneer a political and economic volcano was ready to erupt. As a young girl in love, politics and business were far from my mind. I've learned plenty since.

It seems strange to me that there could be anyone who hasn't heard of Tombstone, but undoubtedly lots of people haven't, so a bit of history is probably in order. It was a silver-mining town. Ed Schieffelin had discovered the first ore there in 1877.[7] He had come over from Fort Huachuca to prospect the hills east of the San Pedro River. My old acquaintance Al Sieber had kidded him, "All you'll find over there is your tombstone, Ed." I suppose Ed remembered that when he struck it rich, so he called his discovery the Tombstone District. Even the hills there came to be called the Tombstone Hills.

When news of Ed's discovery got out, the usual stampede started. That was in 1878. By my time there were thousands of people in the district; some estimates run as high as 15,000. It was beyond doubt the largest settlement in Arizona then.[8]

The Indians were the principal danger around Tombstone at the time Ed Schieffelin discovered his bonanza,[9] but very shortly there were others running for first place. You must remember that I didn't have much idea of the hidden currents of affairs in those days when I was only a rather silly young girl in love. But now, looking back, it seems like a good idea to sketch the big picture behind those events that eventually affected my life so drastically.

The advent of Tombstone gave birth to the dependent communities of Charleston, Fairbank, Contention and Benson. The first three bordered the San Pedro River and were located in that order on it from south to north (the San Pedro flows north out of Mexico). They grew up as silver-milling towns, since Tombstone then had inadequate water to support mills. Just north of Contention was the Mormon village of Saint David, which had been there before Tombstone and played but little part in its history. Benson was yet a ways further downstream north, just west of where the Southern Pacific mainline crossed the San Pedro. It was a freighting, not a milling town.

The lay of the land around these little settlements was conducive to the growth of a thriving stock rustling industry. Several river valleys formed broad, natural, adequately watered cattle trails. Up these, stolen cows could be readily driven from Mexico. For convenience of delivery, there were a lot of level passes between these valleys.

Markets for cattle had previously existed at Fort Huachuca and populous points considerably further north. Now the four river towns and Tombstone were added to the list of buyers.

As if to further sweeten the situation for potential rustlers, the three side-by-side legal jurisdictions of New Mexico, Arizona and Mexico greatly facilitated evasion of the law, since there was practically no cooperation between officials of the three. How could the numerous footloose freebooters who roamed the Southwest during the decades following the Civil War be expected to resist such a ripe temptation? It is small wonder that the country around Tombstone was overrun by cutthroats and riffraff!

The worst ones in the group were already there when the town got its start. They had a profitable organized business going in rustling and freebooting. The rustling was natural enough, since the settlements and forts in Arizona created a large demand for beef, yet there was almost no native cattle industry.

There were three ways to import cattle: from Texas or New Mexico by a long, dangerous drive such as John Slaughter made;[10] from California with comparable hazards; or from nearby Mexico, up the convenient trails I just mentioned. I suppose the odds are that there must have been *some* legal importing of herds from Mexico. But rustled cattle, of course, sold cheaper than legally purchased animals on which duty had to be paid. Soon the Rustlers had two ready sources of clientele: buyers of fresh beef and a host of pioneer ranchers who were starting their herds on the unsettled virgin grazing land in Arizona Territory.[11]

The Clanton family of Fort Thomas was an example of a little of both. On their ranch they kept borrowed stock to restore its weight after the brisk chase up from Mexico. The boys were tutored by their father, who I never heard called anything but Old Man Clanton.[12] He was chief of the Rustlers who, by my time, were also known as the Cowboy gang. His sons were Ike, Billy and Phin, all apt pupils in law-breaking. So apt were they that Ike was killed in 1887 for rustling, Phin went to the pen for ten years in 1887 on the same charge, and Billy was killed while resisting arrest by the city police of Tombstone in October 1881.

By the time I came to Tombstone in 1880, the magnetism of that new and biggest market for rustled stock had enticed the Clantons to establish a new ranch about twelve miles west of town at Lewis Springs along the San Pedro River. It was centrally located almost midway between Tombstone and Fort Huachuca. With their presence, the new town of Charleston a couple of miles downstream (north) was soon transformed into the Rustler headquarters that Fort Thomas formerly had been.

In addition to his three sons, Old Man Clanton controlled a large gang whose best known members were Curly Bill Brocius, John Ringo, Frank Patterson, Joe Hill, Frank and Tom McLaury, Frank Stilwell, Pony Diehl, Pete Spencer, Johnny Barnes, Jim Crane, Harry Head, Dixie Gray, Hank Swilling and perhaps ten times that number of lesser lights and hangers-on with small ranches throughout the area. As Tombstone developed, this group added highway-robbery to their list of attainments. It is not hard to see why they and those they illegally supplied with beef at cut rates would be interested in lax law enforcement in the new mining district. When late in 1880 my Johnny announced his intention to become sheriff of the new county soon to be formed around Tombstone, this group enthusiastically supported him. He made sure that they knew he was *their kind of man*.

Naturally, at first I was all for Johnny's aspirations. The position of sheriff, like all other offices in the new county, was to be filled by governor's appointment. Territorial Governor John C. Frémont was a Republican, while Johnny was a Democrat, but my fiancé counted on getting the job anyway by pulling various political strings.

The only fly in the ointment was Wyatt Earp, an able Republican who had also applied. To make sure that Republican Frémont wouldn't be tempted to choose along party lines, Johnny courted Wyatt and presented him with a deal. One unplanned outcome of this was that I met Wyatt and in Johnny's company saw quite a lot of him. A more contrived result was Wyatt's agreement to withdraw his application for the sheriff's job with the assurance from Johnny that after he got the office he would make Wyatt under-sheriff. Johnny, of course, later double-crossed him, but I am getting ahead of my story. All this happened months after I came to Tombstone.

If under-the-table political deals were being made during those first days following my arrival, they didn't bother me in the least. I was blissfully unaware of almost everything but getting better acquainted with my man. After all, when I got to Tombstone we really didn't know much about each other.

Right after I came, Johnny gave me a big rush. But he didn't talk about a wedding date. Instead he squired me somewhere almost every day and night. In addition to the variety theaters and restaurants, Johnny took me to many homes, where his smooth politician's ways made him welcome. He was then politicking like crazy for the sheriff's office. He would have switched parties if the Republicans had let him.

In addition, Johnny was teaching me to ride a horse, one of my fond ambitions, since the swells had done it on Sundays in San Francisco. I was not a very apt pupil. We had our first tiff over my awkward timidity. I refused to see him for a few days. He was soon around with apologies, smiles and gifts. The riding lessons were back on. This was when I had my next close call with the Apaches.[13]

While we were riding east of town on the road to Antelope Springs, Johnny spotted several horsemen on a nearby ridge. "I think they're Indians!" he cautioned me rather tensely. "Pretend we haven't seen them and start for town slow. Don't act scared."

Strangely enough I wasn't scared, probably because I thought he'd protect me. The Indians were soon after us at a gallop, yelling like crazy. "Run for it!" Johnny shouted to me, sinking his spurs into his horse. Happily mine followed at a dead run. How I stayed on I can't imagine. We did outrun the little Indian ponies.

Johnny never looked back. I could have been lying unconscious in the sagebrush from a tumble off the horse for all he knew. Nonetheless when we got back to the Jones', he told the story so it sounded like he'd saved my life.

Love wasn't as blind as they say. Right there a big doubt entered my mind about Johnny. I must admit though that he showed real *leadership*. But other things took my mind off of such problems.

The grimly humorous phrase about our town was that Tombstone had "a man for breakfast every morning," meaning someone was killed every night.[14] My first man for breakfast occurred not long after I reached town. I was lying awake in bed when the noise of a lot of shooting cracked through the air. It lasted quite awhile. Harry got up and went out on the porch with a pistol, but didn't go further to investigate. It was just as well to mind your own business in a place like that. When Harry came back in, he said, "It sounded just over in the next block."[15]

The next day Harry came home with the full story. He told me, "A bunch of the cowboys tried to shoot up the town. They shot Marshal White when he tried to stop them. Wyatt Earp cracked the fellow that shot White over the head with a pistol and took him in. After that the Earp boys ran in the others too. They weren't gentle about it either! Those Earp boys are hard as nails! It's a good thing the town has them around!"[16]

This happened before Johnny introduced me to Wyatt, but it nonetheless recalled to mind the time I saw Morg Earp meet the man wearing a star when I first got to town. That was also the first I'd ever heard of Curly Bill Brocius.[17] He was the man who shot Marshal White.

But such violent events disturbed my own days very little. I was more concerned because Johnny's talk hadn't once turned to the subject of a marriage date. Finally I brought it up point blank.

He was very apologetic. He told me in rather an injured manner, "The fact is, I've been rather heavily invested in some things that didn't pan as quick as I hoped. We can't afford to get married yet."[18]

This admission put me entirely on the defensive. I felt horribly forward. "I'm sorry, Johnny," I told him. "I didn't imagine! Why don't you let me help? We can get all the money we need from my father."

Johnny protested a lot, but he let me go ahead. My father sent the money and an understanding letter showing that he knew what was going on even though I didn't. He ended by writing: "We pray that we will soon hear of wedding bells there, but if things don't work out, you are always welcome in *your* home."

I gave the money to Johnny. With it, the pawning of my engagement ring and what he could borrow, Johnny built a small house. He brought his son Albert down to live there with him,[19] but still the marriage was put off. I continued to live at the Jones' but took care of Albert during the days. I came to love him as my own. He was the only child I ever had in any sense of the word. We are very close to this day.[20]

Though I sought to avoid admitting it to myself, I was becoming less concerned about whether Johnny married me or not. The community offered a lot to keep me occupied and happy.[21]

My diminishing concern about marriage was also traceable to finding out more about Johnny. He wasn't the fastidious young cavalier of our early acquaintance. Furthermore, his amoral obsession with self-advancement was repugnant to me, for my family had pounded notions of ethics into us. Although I'm not a very good example of their success, all of us girls had a strong sense of right and wrong. Johnny had almost no such scruples. Right to him was what made him the most money, which explains his alliance with the Rustlers and stagecoach robbers. I could never condone that. I began to think of marriage to him with a degree of panic. Suppose he couldn't be reformed?

The crowning blow came when he deceitfully told me he had to be out of town for a few days and induced me to stay a couple of nights with Albert at the house — I always before stayed at Kitty and Harry's. The second night Johnny came home in the wee hours drunk. At first I was relieved to discover that the noise that startled me was only Johnny. That was a short-lived relief. He tried by force what all of his effort short of marriage had failed to gain for him. He wasn't brutal, in fact he actually alternately laughed and swore as he tried to paw me and I fought him away. He finally went to sleep in what I now know was a sort of drunken stupor. I ran home to the Jones' half hysterical. It took both Kitty and me to persuade Harry not to go back up there with a pistol.[22]

Looking back in the light of what I've learned since, the episode is merely funny. I must have shed a river of tears over what really was trifling. But the whole experience was worth it. In the eyes of many people, Johnny, the pompous little dandy, could do no wrong, but I found him out good. He did me just one favor. Through him I met Wyatt Earp.

I wrote a long letter home, recovered the house my father's money had purchased and looked around for a job. It wouldn't do to go home like a whipped puppy.

When Wyatt heard of my falling out with Johnny, he sought to court me for the first time. I knew he was married, but it was no secret that his marriage was on the rocks.[23]

Wyatt's interest in me alone would have been enough to set Johnny at odds with him. Johnny was both jealous and possessed of a pronounced dog-in-the-manger attitude. But something else had already assured a rift between them. When Johnny was made sheriff of the newly formed Cochise County early in 1881, he had appointed a strong machine Democrat as under-sheriff. Typically, he assured Wyatt that it was only a matter of temporary political expediency, that their previous deal to make Wyatt under-sheriff still held. Wyatt accepted this, and the two remained friendly. Wyatt, although no longer deputy sheriff, still had plenty to keep him busy, since he had been appointed deputy

Celia Ann Blaylock, probably shortly before meeting Wyatt. Photograph taken at Fort Scott, Kansas, c. 1872.

Editor's collection

Wyatt Earp, age twenty-one, at Monmouth, Illinois. He undoubtedly appeared much the same when he met his second wife, Celia Ann.

Turner-Oster collection

U.S. marshal and was also working for Wells Fargo both as a detective and as a shotgun messenger when required.

The rift between Johnny and Wyatt actually started with a now-famous stagecoach robbery on the night of March 15, 1881. The story is told in the article that appeared in the *Tombstone Epitaph* of March 16, 1881:[24]

"At about 11 o'clock last night, Marshall Williams[25] received a telegram from Benson stating that Kinnear and Company's coach, carrying Wells Fargo & Co.'s treasure, had been stopped near Contention and 'Budd' Philpot, the driver, killed and one passenger mortally wounded.... [Soon] Williams, the Earp brothers, and several other brave, determined men were in the saddle, well armed, enroute to the scene....

"... As the stage was going up a small incline ... a man stepped into the road from the east side and called out 'Hold.' At the same moment a number of men — believed to have been eight — made their appearance, and a shot was fired from the same side of the road instantly followed by another. One of these shots struck 'Budd' Philpot, the driver, who fell heavily forward between the wheelers carrying the reins with him. The horses immediately sprang into a dead run. Meanwhile Bob Paul, Wells Fargo & Co.'s messenger, ... answered back shot for shot before the frightened horses had whirled the coach out of range. It was fully a mile before the team could be brought to a stand, where it was discovered that one of the shots had mortally wounded a passenger on the coach named Peter Roering.[26] As soon as the coach could be stopped, Paul secured the reins and drove rapidly to Benson....

"At Drew's Station the firing and rapid whirling by of the coach sent men to the scene of the tragedy, where they found poor 'Budd' lying dead in the road, and by the bright moonlight saw the murderers fleeing rapidly from the place. A messenger was at once dispatched to inform agent Cowan of the circumstances, and within 20 minutes after the news arrived Mr. Cowan had dispatched nearly thirty well-armed volunteers after the scoundrels. He then rode rapidly into Tombstone, when the party mentioned above started out to aid in the pursuit. This, with Mr. Paul's party, makes three bodies of determined men who are in hot chase. . . ."

The aftermath of the stage holdup is what put Wyatt and Johnny at odds. The motive for Johnny's actions, I think, can be traced to a remark Wyatt made to Johnny, partly in jest, regarding the under-sheriff job. Wyatt shrugged it off lightly by saying, "That's O.K., Johnny, I'll run fair and square with you for top dog in the next election." From then on, I think, knowing Johnny as I did, his every move was aimed at discrediting Wyatt as much as possible with the voters, just in case.

Wyatt, as deputy U.S. marshal, formed a posse to go after the stagecoach robbers. Since Wyatt still thought he was on good terms with Johnny, he placed his posse at the sheriff's disposal. Johnny and his deputy Billy Breakenridge[27] came out from the sheriff's office. The rest of the posse consisted of Wyatt; his brothers Virgil and Morgan; Marshall Williams; Bat Masterson, who happened to be in Tombstone at the time; and later Bob Paul after he returned from Benson.

The posse picked up the tracks of the highwaymen at the scene of the robbery and followed them for days. Eventually they led back to the lower San Pedro Valley and the Len Redfield[28] ranch. As Wyatt and Morgan, who were several hundred yards ahead, approached the ranch, a man leaped over a corral fence and footed it for the brush. Morg and Wyatt rode him down, placed pistols in his face and stopped him. The suspicious thing about him was that he'd been milking a cow in the corral, yet when caught his shirt bulged with many boxes of rifle shells inside and he wore two pistols. This was surely a strange way to be attired for milking a cow.

He admitted only to his name, Luther King, but protested his innocence of any robbery, claiming he'd run thinking the approaching men might be outlaws. Johnny Behan was all for letting him go. Wyatt wasn't too sure. He stalled a decision, hoping to get King alone, which he and Bob Paul finally managed to do.

Wyatt laughed whenever he explained how they got King to talk:

"We told it to King pretty scary about how the robbers had killed Doc Holliday's[29] woman when they cut loose with their rifles at the stage. That scared hell out of him because he knew Doc would be coming after whoever did it. He looked pretty scared and spilled the beans. He wanted to be damn sure we told Doc he'd only held the horses. He admitted his pals were Harry Head, Billy Leonard and Jim Crane.[30]

"About that time Johnny came up and smelled a rat. He wanted to know what we'd said. King told him and found out from what Johnny said how we'd actually trapped him. He tried to skin it back, but he'd already talked too much. Johnny still didn't want to run him in, so I told him I'd do it on a federal warrant for robbing the mail."

Wyatt's suspicions were aroused by Johnny's strange attitude. When the sheriff insisted on taking King to jail personally, Wyatt became so suspicious he sent Marshall Williams along to see that King actually got there. The rest of the posse stayed on the trail but eventually lost it several days later. Wyatt's suspicions about Johnny weren't unfounded either, as the following newspaper clipping from the *Tombstone Weekly Nugget* of 19 March 1881 attests:

"Luther King, the man arrested at Redfield's ranch charged with being implicated in the Bud Philpot murder, escaped from the sheriff's office by quietly stepping out the back door while Harry Jones, Esq., was drawing up a bill of sale for a horse the prisoner was selling to John Dunbar. Under-sheriff Harry Woods and Dunbar were present. He had been absent but a few seconds before he was missed. A confederate on the outside had a horse in readiness for him. It was a well-planned job by outsiders to get him away. He was an important witness against Holliday. He it was that gave the names of the three that were being followed at the time he was arrested. Their names were Bill Leonard, Jim Crane and Harry Head."[31]

This accusation of Doc was an obvious political manuever to smear Wyatt through his friendship with Doc. The Harry Jones, Esq., mentioned was of course Kitty's husband. Because of that I eventually found out the true story behind the escape. Harry later told me for certain that Doc had actually had no hand in the robbery or in engineering the escape of Luther King. I can't recall just when I heard the details from Harry, but it must have been subsequent to his falling out with Johnny, after which he became a friend of the Earps and a member of the Citizens Safety Committee. This is what he told me:

"I thought it was pretty raw. Besides, it was taking a lot for granted with me sitting there.[32] But they cooked that whole Doc Holliday thing up over a smoke and a pull from the bottle. King had mentioned how Wyatt wormed the truth out of him with his story about Doc Holliday's woman being killed on the stage. This got Harry Woods to thinking about Doc. He said, 'I wonder where old Doc was about the time that stage was being stuck up.' John Dunbar just happened to know Doc was out of town, since Doc had rented a horse from him the day of the holdup. 'He rented a nag from me to ride over to Charleston,' John told him. That was all it took. Harry laughed. 'He better have got there and have an airtight alibi or he's going to be in trouble. Nobody would believe him on a stack of Bibles.'

"About that time they looked around and noticed that King was gone. 'Son-of-a-gun!' Woods said. 'The prisoner escaped. Ain't that a real shame?' He looked out the door. 'No doubt his accomplice, Holliday, rented another horse for him to escape on so he couldn't squeal on him.'

"That's about the way the conversation went. I thought it was kinda funny in a way, but the more I thought about it the hotter I got under the collar. After all, a couple of innocent men had been killed, and there *could* have been women on that stage just as well as not. I didn't mention how I felt about it right then, because I thought it might not be too healthy with a crowd like that, and I've been keeping my eyes open ever since, believe me!"

It was months afterward that Harry finally told Wyatt this, but I had already repeated the story to him before then. All Wyatt had said when I concluded was, "Who would believe it now? Everybody knows that Harry had a falling out with that crowd. They'd just say he was making it up to get even with them."

More to the point, Wyatt called down Johnny personally regarding his deceitful maneuvering. He tried to eel out of it, of course, but he never forgave Wyatt. My later part in the affair simply deepened the rift.

This is the whole inside story of Wyatt's falling out with Johnny Behan. In addition to motives we can only suspect, it is obvious that Johnny didn't want Wyatt to get credit for catching the robbers. But a split between them was probably inevitable when one considers the fundamental differences in their characters. Men like Wyatt were a constant reproach to Johnny's type by their mere example.

The economic factions which they served probably would have made a split inevitable sooner or later on that account as well. Actually, these opposing groups were partially at the root of what happened, since it is now obvious to me that Johnny all along had been in with the group using the Rustler[33] element to do their dirty work.

Doc's implication in this robbery through the propaganda of Harry Woods and the *Nugget* led straight to the Earps' shootout with the Rustlers some six months later. The underlying cause was the fact that the Earp brothers were investing heavily in the community.[34] They intended to make their fortune and home in Tombstone, and they had to clear Doc's name in order to clear their own. Obviously the way to do that was to go after the bonafide robbers and bring them in alive so they could be made to confess. It was this enterprise that went so disastrously awry, as I'll tell in Chapter 5. Before revealing that part of the story, however, I think it's best I relate why Wyatt and his people came to Tombstone in the first place.

HISTORICAL NOTES AND EDITORIAL COMMENTS

1. As pointed out in Chapter 1, note 2, Josephine's arrival may actually have been in May 1880; if so this stage trip would have been from Tucson or Pantano, not Benson. The posted running time was seventeen hours from Tucson and the fare ten dollars. The company was the Tucson and Tombstone Stage Line, also known as Kinnear's Express (J. D. Kinnear, proprietor). It carried Wells Fargo's express and the U.S. mail. (John and Lillian Theobald, *Arizona Territory, Post Offices and Postmasters*, p. 44.)

2. The Earp family bible entry written in the hand of the boys' father, Nicholas Porter Earp, records: "Morgan S. Earp was born April 24 in the year of our Lord 1851." The N. P. Earps were then living at Pella, Iowa.

Biographical information on Morgan Earp is fragmentary and often unreliable. His early travels followed those of the rest of the family from Pella to California in 1864, with a return trip in 1868. Thereafter his record is blank for a few years. He does not appear in the 1870 census with the balance of the family at Lamar, Missouri. It is my guess he was then living with relatives in or near Monmouth, Warren County, Illinois.

Morgan next shows up in 1875 at Dodge City in the Ford County treasurer's warrants, having been paid for serving a process for Sheriff Charlie Bassett. (Thus Morgan was a lawman in Dodge prior to Wyatt, who arrived in 1876.) Morgan followed his older brothers to Tombstone, arriving a few days after the others, on December 8, 1879. (Fred Dodge, *Under Cover For Wells Fargo*, pp. 8 & 9.)

In Tombstone Morgan replaced Wyatt as a shotgun guard for Wells Fargo when Wyatt became deputy sheriff. (*Tombstone Epitaph*, July 31, 1880.) However, he must have at least visited California sometime during that year, since p. 52 of the 1880 census for San Bernardino County shows Morgan and his wife Louisa, age 25, residing with Morg's father Nicholas in Temescal. "Lou," as she was most often called, is indicated as born in Wisconsin, with both her parents born in Illinois. I have been able to discover very little else about this woman, except that she accompanied the Virgil Earps and Morgan's body to the parental home in Colton, California, for the funeral in March 1882. (Frank Waters, *The Earp Brothers of Tombstone*, p. 207, and testimony at Coroner's hearing into death of Frank Stilwell, by David Gibson, reported in *Arizona Daily Citizen* [Tucson], March 27, 1882.)

Morgan was, of course, a participant in the famous O.K. Corral shoot-out, being there as a city policeman. He generally was involved with his brothers Virgil and Wyatt in their activities as lawmen at Tombstone. According to Wyatt, he also dealt faro for him at the Oriental.

Morgan was murdered while playing billiards the night of March 18, 1882, by a shot fired from ambush through the glass portion of a locked rear door of Campbell and Hatch's saloon. He was initially buried near the parental home in Colton, California, in the so-called "old city cemetery" under Mount Slover. When the cemetery was moved in 1892, his body was transferred to the Hermosa Cemetery, where it rested in lot 8 and later was moved to lot 23. (Notes of U.S. Air Force Captain Melvin Gibson, in Colton, California, Public Library and Earp family recollections.)

3. Josie was unfamiliar with the bustle of the modern airport; "today" in this narrative refers roughly to the decade between 1930 and 1940, when her two manuscripts were being developed.

4. Wyatt Earp was born in Monmouth, Illinois, March 19, 1848. The family moved to Pella, Iowa, in 1850, where Wyatt's father Nicholas Porter Earp had purchased farmland. Wyatt told Stuart Lake that here as a youth he developed a lifelong sympathy for the hoeman, especially during the Civil War, when he and his younger brothers Morgan and Warren were charged with raising 160 acres of corn.

Wyatt drove one of the wagons when the family moved to the vicinity of San Bernardino, California, in 1864. (Lake collection and Rousseau diary.) The Earps left California in 1868, moving to Lamar, Missouri, where Nicholas Earp owned land. The family traveled by wagon to the Union Pacific railroad line in Wyoming, where Wyatt and Virgil Earp took jobs grading on the railroad right-of-way. Apparently Wyatt learned a great deal about the science of boxing during this period. (Earp family recollections.) See Chapter 1, note 3, for Wyatt's experiences as a lawman prior to coming to Tombstone.

Wyatt's first marriage, to Urilla Sutherland, took place on January 10, 1870, at Lamar, Missouri, the ceremony having been performed by his father N. P. Earp as justice of the peace. (Recorded January 24, 1870, by L. N. Timmons, clerk, Barton County Recorder's Files.) His young wife died later that year in childbirth, along with the infant. (Cason notes.) Shortly after her death, one Wyatt S. Earp (probably our man) had a true bill returned by the Grand Jury of the U.S. Court of the Western District of Arkansas at Fort Smith, not far south of Lamar, in May 1871 on the charge of larceny — "horse stealing in the Indian Nations." He skipped bail and was never tried. (Records for the U.S. Court, Western District of Arkansas, 1871, in the U.S. Federal Records Center, Fort Worth, Texas.) If this was in fact our Wyatt, perhaps he was footloose and desperate after the death of his young wife.

Sometime prior to his arrival in Tombstone, Wyatt married, or at least lived with, Celia Ann Blaylock, who went by the nickname Mattie. She came to Tombstone with Wyatt and publicly lived with him there as his wife. See note 23, this chapter, for speculation regarding the length of Wyatt's association with Mattie before he became enamored of Josie.

5. Regarding Johnny's proclivities where women were concerned, the following excerpt from his wife's divorce complaint is eloquent testimony:

"... The said defendant disregarding the solemnity of the marriage vow, has within the two years last past at diverse times and places openly and notoriously visited houses of ill fame and prostitution ... , and more particularly the said defendant in the month of December 1874 at a house of ill fame ... at which resided one [woman], commonly called Sada, a woman of prostitution and ill fame, did consort, cohabit, and have sexual intercourse with the said [woman] ... openly and notoriously causing great scandal ... all of which came to the knowledge of this plaintiff. ..."

Witnesses satisfied the judge of the justice of this complaint, and the divorce was granted. See Chapter 1, note 20, for more details on the divorce; see Chapter 4, note 1, for further evidence of Johnny's suave ways with the ladies.

6. Despite Josie's description of her newcomer's curiosity, this was probably not her first introduction to Tombstone. According to the Markham troupe itinerary she had played there briefly in December 1879. (See Chapter 1, note 11.)

7. Josie's dates and statistics on Tombstone were usually either provided by Clum or Mrs. Cason and are historically valid unless otherwise noted.

8. Tombstone was undoubtedly the most populous town in Arizona at that time. However there is quite a wide variance of estimates regarding its population, some running as high as 15,000. For a fair approximation I used the 1882 Great Register, assumed one quarter of the total population were males of voting age appearing on the Register, and reached a figure of 9,302. This also assumes that 65% of 3,578 total registrants actually resided in Tombstone itself — the 65% based on a sample including all people whose names began with A.

9. The Indian threat was a continuing problem in Arizona in the 1870s and until 1886; even when there was no general outbreak, the threat of small bands of renegades was ever-present. Parsons in his journal repeatedly refers to the Apache threat near Tombstone; I find nine references in 1880 alone. (George W. Parsons, journal.) See also Dan Thrapp, *Al Sieber, Chief of Scouts* and *Conquest of Apacheria*, as well as John G. Bourke, *Apache Campaign* and *On the Border With Crook.*

10. The Stuart N. Lake notes, in the Lake collection in the Huntington Library indicate that Slaughter imported more than cattle from Texas. Lake says that the future Cochise County desperados of note — John Ringo, Curly Bill Brocius, Frank Stilwell and Billy Claiborne — all came to southeastern Arizona as cowboys with Slaughter. It is certain that at least John

Ringo already had a record. (Dora Neill Raymond, *Captain Lee Hall of Texas,* pp. 131–132.) Raymond records that at the time that John Wesley Hardin was incarcerated in the Travis County, Texas, jail, other "notorious criminals, several of them as desperate as himself" were to be found there, among them John Ringo, as listed in the *Galveston News,* August 25, 1877.

11. The economy and convenience of rustled stock as a source of brood herds for Arizona's pioneer cattlemen would account for a fondness for the Rustlers among many first-generation small ranchers. Their bitterness toward the Earps, who killed some of their major cattle suppliers, can be readily understood. Their bias persists in their descendants, probably as a typical human family loyalty.

On the other hand, well-established ranchers in the Tombstone area were vehemently opposed to the rustling element. Colonel Henry Hooker of the Sierra Bonita ranch near Fort Grant, in fact, reputedly had a personal reward of one thousand dollars on Curly Bill Brocius' head (presumably dead). Although the Hooker offer is unconfirmed, it is certain that the Stockmen's Association did have such a reward. (*Epitaph,* April 4, 1882.)

Sentiment against Curly Bill's gang among the established Mormon ranchers of the vicinity was similar to that of Hooker. They held that the Earps rid Arizona of a curse when they killed the leaders of organized rustling and scared their followers out of the country. (Numerous personal interviews of editor with descendants of Mormon settlers of the 1880s.)

The total number of cattle in Arizona in 1880 is reported as 475,000 by Martin in *An Arizona Chronology.* This may seem like a lot, but actually it is equivalent to less than 500 ranches with 1000 head apiece.

12. His full name was Newman Haynes Clanton. Stuart Lake, who, like Josie, didn't know the old man's given names, has it that Clanton was a Texan who went to California during the gold rush of '49, then drifted back to Arizona. If so, this is not the full story. His son Ike indicated his place of birth as Missouri on the 1881 Cochise County Great Register and lists his age as thirty-four on November 26, 1881. We may safely deduce from this that the Clantons must have been Missourians in 1847. Apparently they had migrated to Texas by 1858, since the *Dallas Herald* of December 22, 1858, mentions N. H. Clanton in reporting the death of A. C. Kelso (probably the brother of N H. Clanton's wife, who bore the maiden name Kelso). The Clanton residence in California is confirmed by the William H. Frink ms. "The Old Martinez Ranch," copy of ms. in the editor's collection.

13. This story is completely plausible. Parsons mentions Tombstoners killed by Indians on June 20 and July 13, 1880. In May 1880, when Josephine first may have come to Tombstone to live, Parsons mentions the Indian threat, with entries on May 16, 19, 21 and 22. (Parsons' journal.)

14. In his journal Parsons mentions two fellows going for each other with guns (as rifles and shotguns were then known) and six-shooters on his first day in Tombstone, February 17, 1880. He mentions eight more shootings or killings between then and Fred White's murder on October 27, 1880, and five more before the end of that year. A casual survey of Parsons' journal for 1882 turns up eleven diary entries indicating shootings or killings, an attempted lynching, and three stage robberies, in contrast to one poetry reading. This more or less supports the "man-for-breakfast" theme, despite John Clum's latter-day playing down of such violence. (See Clum, *It All Happened in Tombstone*, p. 54.)

15. It is likely that Josie is deliberately altering the names of her characters as she relates this story, since in later years she obviously wanted to conceal the true depth of her relationship with Johnny Behan. However, it is almost certain that Josie did not stay chastely with the Harry Jones family upon her arrival in Tombstone. More likely she lived openly with Johnny, ostensibly as his wife. To support such a belief, the Tombstone Postal Receipt Books for 1881 in the possession of Mrs. Burton Devere of Tombstone list a receipt number 2298 on June 11, 1881, in the name of Josephine Behan for twenty-five dollars sent to Mrs. H. Marcus of San Francisco. In view of this, it doesn't stretch credibility to slightly revise Josie's story of the White killing so that she was actually living with Behan in their house half a block from the Jones' residence when she heard the shots. If this was in fact the case, the man who went outside with a pistol would have been Johnny Behan, not Harry Jones. Behan held lot ten, block forty-nine and Harry Jones owned lot four, block thirty-five, just across Safford south and four lots below. (Tax Records of Tombstone 1881.) The Jones house was still occupied in 1975; the Behan lot was vacant.

16. If it was also Behan rather than Jones who spoke well of the Earps in this matter, it simply shows that he and Wyatt were not yet enemies at that time.

17. In 1880 Curly Bill Brocius wasn't yet well known as an outlaw kingpin around Tombstone; in fact, the White killing may have been what raised him to the top level with the badmen. The *Epitaph* garbled his name as Rosciotis in the article on the White shooting, a sure sign he was not then famous. (*Epitaph* October 29, 1880.) However, within less than a year it was a different story. When one Jim Wallace shot Curly Bill in the neck in Galeyville, the *Arizona Weekly Star* of Tucson on May 26, 1881, captioned the story "*Curly Bill. This Noted Desperado* Gets It in the Neck." Tombstone old-timer Billy Breakenridge — who should have known — wrote, "[Curly Bill] was notorious as a leader of the rustlers and cattle thieves. . . ." Parsons' journal entry for April 1, 1881, bears out Breakenridge, referring to Curly Bill as "our chief outlaw at present."

However, despite all this smoke, no one seems to have known much about Curly Bill's background. There are rumors that he was active in New Mexico's Lincoln County cattle war, but if this was so he must have gone under some other name. He also is rumored to have hailed from Texas. The White killing is the only confirmed information on what could be described as Curly Bill's outlaw activities up to the time Deputy U.S. Marshal Wyatt Earp killed him in self-defense in March 1882.

18. The notion that Johnny couldn't afford to marry in 1880 may hold water, but after he became sheriff, the treasurer's warrant books for the county show that he collected a total income of almost $25,000 in 1882 alone. We may assume 1881 was an equally fat year, since the mines were booming. The 1882 "take" was as follows:

Warrant #	Date	Purpose	Amount
382	1-25-82	Sheriff's Fees	485.00
389	1-25-82	" "	3628.63
393	8- 4-82	Rent Jury Room	105.00
405	2- 7-82	Sheriff's Fees	1077.16
508	4- 5-82	" "	3729.17
521	4-10-82	" "	280.00
530	4-10-82	" "	1204.45
552	5-17-82	" "	2070.70
595	6- 2-82	Transporting Insane	674.00
596	6- 2-82	Salary as Assessor	700.00
613	7- 6-82	Sheriff's Fees	2773.38
629	7- 7-82	" "	1148.75
706	10- 6-82	" "	1310.00
824	12-23-82	" "	400.00
825	12-23-82	" "	3745.73
873	12- 3-82	" "	678.55
			$24010.52

Source: Warrant Register, Cochise County, October 1881–December 1892.

19. Perhaps Albert came to live with Johnny because his former wife was planning to remarry. Behan probably bore a genuine affection for his son, which was quite likely reciprocated.

20. We are justified in viewing Josie's allegations as to where she lived with reservations, but her life-long affection for Albert is unquestionable; she corresponded regularly with him up until her death. (Cason notes.)

21. If one were to believe all the writers' gossipy speculations on the subject of Josie's relations with men, one might conclude that the old woman was being slyly truthful here about having a lot to keep her occupied. For

example, Doc Holliday once openly antagonized Behan by telling him that he (Johnny) was gambling with money Doc had given his woman. (*Denver Republican*, May 22, 1882.) We can only guess what "woman" of Johnny's Doc was referring to, but we can be sure that in that time and place there was but one thing the gambling dentist was suggesting he had given the money for.

However, despite Doc's allegations and all the other rumors on the subject by various scandal-mongers, it is doubtful that the darkly beautiful Josephine was ever queen of the dancehall girls or a prostitute. She didn't have to be. Important men of the community avidly sought her company. If they hadn't, her well-to-do father would have gladly financed her return home at any time.

If Josie found diversions in Tombstone, they were probably not men, excepting Johnny and Wyatt. For so-called society women, Tombstone offered legitimate and amateur theater, restaurants, parties, outings, reading societies, shopping, sewing circles, riding, promenading and community betterment projects, to mention a few. For the poor miner's wife it was a different story, but Josie was a member of the social upper crust. Even her associations with gamblers and saloon-keepers did not hinder her acceptance as a "lady" in polite society of the day. Quoting the *Albuquerque Journal*, the *Arizona Weekly Star* on November 16, 1884, wrote that Josephine "... besides being very handsome, is certainly a lady anywhere." (Cason notes and interviews of the editor with old-timers from Tombstone.)

22. This story is almost indisputably nonsense. But Josie told it. It may be a fairly accurate description of an actual event, but not very likely a true depiction of the sequel to it. If Harry Jones ever had a desire to take a pistol to Johnny, it was probably much later and for a different reason. Josephine once hinted to Mrs. Cason that her final falling out with Johnny was really over a married woman with whom he was consorting. A most logical candidate for the other woman is Kitty Jones, particularly in view of the fact that Johnny's former bosom pal, Harry Jones, for some substantial reason jumped the political fence and became an ardent supporter of Johnny's enemy, Wyatt Earp. I pick about July 1881 as the date of the big falling out among Johnny, Harry and Josephine. However, this is all merely speculation on my part.

23. Josephine tried to keep the fact that Wyatt was married from the Cason/Ackerman team of writers, but Mrs. Cason eventually discovered the truth. (Glenn G. Boyer, *Suppressed Murder of Wyatt Earp*, p. 78ff.) Mrs. Cason got the impression from Josie that Wyatt and Mattie had been together for ten or twelve years. However, Wyatt's documented marriage to his first wife, Urilla Sutherland, at Lamar, Missouri, on January 10, 1870, rules out the twelve-year figure. I suspect that after his first wife died in late 1870, Wyatt probably met Mattie in Fort Scott, Kansas, near Lamar,

since I have a photo of her in that town in which she appears to be perhaps twenty years old. I have no information confirming Josie's bland assertion that Wyatt's marriage was on the rocks. However, when I asked Mattie's niece if that were likely, she said: "If Mattie had a temper like her sister, I don't blame him for leaving her." (Conversation of editor with Mrs. O. H. Marquis, Denver, 1965.) Mattie's sister was Mrs. Marquis' mother-in-law.

24. Note that in this case and almost consistently throughout her account of the events at Tombstone, Josie quotes John Clum's pro-Earp *Epitaph*. The *Tombstone Weekly Nugget,* which clearly favored the Rustlers and allied factions, often told a very different story, especially after Harry Woods of the County Ring became its editor.

25. Marshall Williams was the Wells Fargo agent at Tombstone.

26. This name is spelled Roerig in some sources. Stuart Lake said he was a beer salesman from Milwaukee, but the Milwaukee Historical Society could find no record of him there. (Milwaukee County Historical Society to the editor, July 22, 1975.) I have been unable to find out anything definite about him beyond the *Epitaph* article quoted by Josie.

27. Billy Breakenridge supposedly was one of Behan's principal deputies. However, the early files of bonds of office for Cochise County do not substantiate Breakenridge's having been a deputy continuously or for long. He appears to have been largely a tax collector and later a jailer. Wyatt Earp disdainfully called him a "process-server."

It is evident to one seriously surveying this area that recollections of old-timers are not always adequate indications of who was who. For example, Sol Israel, who lived in Tombstone in the early days, was by 1928 ready to concede that Billy Breakenridge was Behan's chief deputy — probably based on faulty recollection plus Breakenridge's 1928 self-elevating autobiography *Helldorado*. But he recalled the name as Blackenridge. (Israel to Lake, September 21, 1928, Lake collection.) In the same letter Israel wrote: "As to Johnny Behan, he was afraid of his own shadow. . . ."

It is my opinion from tracing its genesis that Breakenridge's reputation as "Tombstone's deputy" was largely self-generated over the years by his own windy stories. Nonetheless, he was probably a likeable old fellow.

28. Len Redfield appears to have been connected with stage robbers for a number of years. He was one of two men lynched in Florence in 1883 in connection with the killing of a popular stagecoach guard, Johnny Collins, in a holdup at the Riverside Crossing. (Joseph Henry Miller, *Arizona, The Last Frontier,* p. 216.)

29. It seems unlikely that many today are not acquainted with John Henry "Doc" Holliday; it will suffice here to say that his homicidal reputation alone, especially in Arizona, kept brave men home at night, especially if they were on Doc's "list." He was Wyatt's staunch supporter and lifelong

friend, also the cause of much of Wyatt's trouble at Tombstone. He undoubtedly had an extremely bad reputation, perhaps justified, including notoriety as a killer.

Holliday was a Georgian, educated as a dentist at the Pennsylvania College of Dental Surgery. (Mrs. Susan McKey Thomas to the editor, August 7, 1974; Albert S. Pendleton and Susan McKey Thomas, *In Search of the Hollidays,* Special Notes, p. 19.) Apparently contracting tuberculosis set Holliday adrift from a respectable professional life. By January 1875 he was in the West and mixed up in a shooting scrape. (*Dallas Weekly Herald,* January 2, 1875.) Perhaps the best book on Holliday's career despite a great deal of what appears to me to be inadequately supported speculation and psychoanalysis, is Pat Jahns' *The Frontier World of Doc Holliday.* Doc died of miliary tuberculosis on November 8, 1887, in Glenwood Springs, Colorado, where he was buried. I believe, as did many others, that Holliday's conviction that he was doomed to an early death by an incurable disease drove him to desperate conduct. This also explains the rather widespread fear of him on the part of those who would not be daunted by someone who harbored a normal distaste for dying young.

30. There is little information available on Leonard, Head and Crane. Notes in the Lake collection indicate Doc Holliday's conviction that his old friend Leonard, who had been a respectable jeweler in Las Vegas, New Mexico, when Doc was there, was a classic example of a good man influenced by bad company — in this case the Rustler gang at Tombstone. One wonders if their accomplice Luther King and a man named Sandy King, hung in Shakespeare, New Mexico, were one and the same. (See Walter N. Burns, *Tombstone,* Chapter 10.)

31. This article was undoubtedly written by Harry Woods, editor of the *Nugget* and the self-same under-sheriff who let King escape. One has to admire his cheek.

32. Perhaps as a bribe to keep him quiet, a commission as deputy sheriff was given to Harry Jones shortly after this incident on May 18, 1881. (Bonds of Office, Cochise County, 1881.)

33. It must be made clear that the term *Rustler* as Josie uses it was synonymous with *Cow-boy* as used in the newspapers of that time. On this subject John Myers Myers (*The Last Chance*) wrote: "Eventually its [the *Epitaph's*] columns made the term "Cow-boy" synonymous with criminal, not only in Cochise County but elsewhere in the West."

Confirming this judgment, the *San Francisco Exchange* of November 2, 1881, printed the following: "A cow-boy met the natural fate of all cow-boys in Camp Rice yesterday, being riddled with bullets. The Tombstone *Nugget* should send down a special reporter to weep over the remains. That journal is now recognized in Arizona Territory as the great obituary organ of all slaughtered cow-boys." The latter phrase refers to the fact that Clum was so successful in his campaign of derision that he succeeded in hanging on Harry Woods' *Nugget* the term "the Cow-boy Organ." Specifically, the *Exchange* reference points to the *Nugget's* obituary of the Cow-boys who had been killed in the so-called O.K. Corral gunfight a few days before.

34. The Earp mining holdings are listed in Chapter 3, note 20. In addition, they and their associates held many lots in the town itself. Examples of these holdings, as indicated by the 1881 tax rolls for Tombstone, are as follows:

Property		Taxpayer
Block	*Lot*	
29	22	Earp Bros. & Winders
V	3 lots	James Earp
Grasshopper Mine*		
10 acres		Earp Bros. & Neff
Mtn. Maid N.E.*		Earp Bros. & Winders
Mattie Blaylock*		" " "
Long Branch*		" " "
29	23	Earp, V. W. & W. S.
29	24	Earp, James
29	1	Winders, R. J. & Earp, V. W.
29	2	Earp, W. & J.
M	1	Winders, R. J., Earp, V. W.
M	2	" " " "
M	3	Earp, James
M	4	Earp, Wyatt

---

*These mining claims were taxed by the village of Tombstone.

3

The Earps
Come to Tombstone

The Wyatt Earp who arrived in Tombstone on December 1, 1879, was a very different man than the one who left as a fugitive in March 1882. He was not, and never was a gunfighter in today's pulp-fiction sense of the word. He had killed no one prior to coming to Arizona, despite having been an officer in the Kansas cowtowns during their red decade. Yet, as John Clum has written,[1] Wyatt's merited reputation as a lawman had preceded him. For this reason Charlie Shibell, sheriff of Pima County in which Tombstone was then located, early offered him a job as deputy sheriff for the Tombstone District. Wyatt initially declined for a very good reason which was, he later told me, "I had my belly full of lawing." He was to get it a lot fuller before Tombstone receded into his past. Perhaps if he had known it then he would have gone elsewhere. I am almost sure of it.

Events drew Wyatt into a vortex of intrigue and violence from which a sense of duty prevented his escape unscathed. But one must not forget that in the first place he came to Tombstone only as a businessman. The aspirations of the Earps were to make their fortunes there in legitimate business enterprises.[2] They hoped to start a stage line, but finding that field already crowded, turned to prospecting. This provided no immediate income either. As a last choice they turned to saloon-keeping and gambling,[3] which in those times were respected professions, a fact seldom appreciated today.[4] Then, of course, Wyatt and Virgil both finally turned to lawing, as they called it, as an additional source of needed income. Before Wyatt did so, he tried his hand at other alterna-

*James Cooksey Earp, c. 1880, old-
est of the five Earp full brothers.*

*Warren Earp about 1888, photo-
graphed in Illinois. This is the only
known photo of the youngest Earp
brother, revealing him to be the
sole Earp with black hair.*

tives for several months before finally accepting Shibell's offer. Virgil had already been appointed a U.S. deputy marshal before reaching Tombstone.[5]

Notwithstanding, I want to strongly emphasize again that Wyatt, Virgil and Jim Earp[6] considered themselves businessmen, first and foremost.[7] Morg and Warren, the other two brothers, were not cut out for the business world.[8] However, they took a hand at whatever their older brothers were engaged in when they were needed. If one judged the part of the Earps in the community solely from their business connections, which far exceeded their "lawing" connections, then what I have emphasized here would be crystal clear — they were entrepreneurs, not two-gunmen. But unfortunately, as John Clum observed, "they all knew what six-shooters were for, and Wyatt had the big reputation."[9] In such case, if need arises, a community will eventually ferret out such unique talents and harness them.

It was also his "lawing" reputation that got Wyatt his first job in Arizona. I imagine getting some money coming in was important to him in order to prevent shrinking his capital. Therefore, he probably accepted whatever turned up first. If it hadn't been for a job offer from Wells Fargo, he may even have snapped up Shibell's offer. Who knows?[10]

I'll put Wyatt's coming to Tombstone in his own words as nearly as I can recall them. He told me, "I was the scout for the whole family. I got there three days before our wagons did, riding 'shotgun' for a payroll. Almost the first local man I met was Dick Gird. He was postmaster,[11] and the stage always went to the post office first. He was one of the big men of the town too, but you couldn't tell it by the way he acted. He was as common and comfortable as an old boot."

Wyatt's job as shotgun guard for Wells Fargo became a permanent thing. When he gave it up later to become a deputy sheriff, his brother Morgan replaced him.

At the time the Earps first reached Tombstone, the town was just growing out of the village stage, with some thousand people already there. When I got there the next year it was already a little city.[12] It was Western to the core. By that I mean the first-

Alvira "Allie" Sullivan Earp, the
third and last Mrs. Virgil Earp, in
Tombstone, 1879.

Virgil Earp, 1882, probably in San
Francisco. The date is specified on
the back in his wife Allie's hand-
writing.

comers, the boomers, were generous — tolerant to an amazing degree and a little on the wild side. The whole breed of boomers were generally self-reliant, inventive, industrious and able to take care of themselves in fast, hard company. The softer city breed came later as a rule. This also describes the case of all the boom camps I later went to with Wyatt.

Some of the boomers, of course, were ruthless and dishonest. These words certainly described the Rustlers, whom I have already introduced. However, very little of this Rustler element concerned Wyatt and his brothers at first. It was almost a year before any Earp interest brought them into conflict with Old Man Clanton's legions. When they did, they learned that the sly old outlaw had his minions spread out at strategic locations over some ten thousand square miles. As Billy Breakenridge states in his book *Hell-dorado,* his esteemed friends all "looked after" the Rustler interests; these friends were namely the Clanton boys and Pattersons in the San Pedro valley, the McLaurys in the Sulphur Springs valley, Joe Hill in the San Simon and Old Man Clanton as well as Curly Bill in the Animas.[13] But this is leaping too far ahead of my story. My intention has been, as they say in the theater, to set the stage.

My story regarding the Tombstone years of the Earps is probably as full and accurate as can be reconstructed at this late date. In addition to my own recollections and the fact that I intimately knew the participants in the drama on both sides — as perhaps no one else did — I have had the assistance of others in recent years who were there then. Most important has been John Clum, a dear friend of these many years,[14] who was Tombstone's crusading first mayor, and founder and editor of its famous newspaper the *Epitaph.* He fought the Townlot Company tooth and nail and almost paid for it with his life. Without his help, the Tombstone part of my story would lack many insights, things that in those early days went over my head.

John Clum in turn was assisted by George Parsons, who kept a daily journal. We are indebted greatly to this journal for many names and dates, as well as for recollection of forgotten incidents. Another great help was Fred Dodge, who posed as a gambler during my time in Tombstone but was secretly a Wells Fargo detective. I visited him at his Texas ranch and obtained significant information.

I will pull no punches, as Wyatt's boxing friends would say. The truth will out anyhow. For example, I didn't know Mr. Clum personally in Tombstone and hoped he really hadn't remembered me. But it was a vain hope. He had an elephant's memory. His journalistic standards of factualness may have led me to giving a fuller account of my own part in the Tombstone tragedy than personal inclination would dictate. He has persuaded me that only the whole truth conveys the convincing logic needed to vindicate Wyatt regarding the controversial Earp role in Tombstone's early years.[15]

Finally, to reiterate an important point regarding my sources, one must not forget that they included, before our falling out, Johnny and his fine feathered friends, including Curly Bill himself. There was also Billy Breakenridge,[16] the County Ringers, all the Earp boys, Doc Holliday, Mrs. Pete Spencer,[17] Addie Bourland (one of my best friends at Tombstone), Harry and Kitty Jones and many others I'll mention as I get to them. They are all gone now, but they are still very real to me; at times I even experience a recurrence of the apprehensive dread I felt so poignantly after Johnny became my enemy and Wyatt became my love.

Difficulties crop up on every side when writing in the shadow of the many tales already published about my dear dead husband. I know it weakens one's hand to always be defending rather than attacking, but I have found no other way. For example, readers of the fare on the market would be led to believe that Wyatt, his brothers and their friends pursued a constant merry round of gambling and carousing between gunfights and forays after outlaws. This is simply not true. In the first place Wyatt didn't drink hard liquor of any kind, to my knowledge, until long after our marriage.[18] In the second place, if he were in a saloon or gambling parlor, it was usually a matter of business. He operated and owned extensive gambling interests during his stay in Tombstone. Beyond obvious reasons of management, Wyatt, like most other men, saw the saloon as a social and business center. In early-day Tombstone

Knowles Ryerson

John Clum on his final trip to the San Carlos Apache Reservation, where he had been Indian agent 1874–76. Around the time of this picture, eighty-year-old Clum was spending a part of his time helping Josie prepare one of the manuscripts upon which this book is based.

there was almost no other accepted place to meet and converse with friends or business associates. There were no office buildings or country clubs. The equivalent of a business luncheon in those days took place in the gambling clubrooms or saloons.

Considering only the real-estate enterprises acquired by the Earps in such a short period,[19] it should be clear that they had little time for loafing anywhere. Wyatt and his brothers also spent a good deal of time in the hinterlands, finding and filing on timber, water and mineral claims. They were incorporated with both Bob Winders and Andrew Neff in various mining ventures.[20] In addition they owned large portions of the townsite itself.

As a matter of interest to some who picture Wyatt as traveling in the manner that Hollywood shows it today, solely on horseback, he preferred what was then known as a light delivery wagon. It's advantage was room to carry a camping kit. Since he and his brothers were often afield for days at a time, its convenience is fairly obvious. He also owned several fine riding and harness horses. His racehorses were frequently entered in events at the track west of town.

If all this has begun to develop a different picture of the Earps than that established in lurid tales of their exploits, I have made a start in achieving my aim here. Wyatt Earp was simply not the creation known to the public through literature available today.[21] He was a real warm-hearted, flesh-and-blood man, not gregarious but also not a cold-blooded killer as some have painted him; he was not a gunman.

Wyatt was above all a level-headed businessman with an eye on the future. The fact that he possessed an unflinching type of courage made him stand out from other men. It was a family trait. In Tombstone this courage was the factor that eventually opposed the Earps to all four of the contending elements plaguing the country — the Rustlers, the County Ring, the Townlot Company and the stage robbers.

The people found no other champions. They needed no others when the chips were down. The Earp sacrifice cleaned up the country, but ruined their fortunes in the bargain. If they had evaded the issue, the family might be known there today simply as pioneer businessmen, perhaps with children or grandchildren still running the local grocery, hardware or drug store.[22] But it was not their style to turn aside from their civic responsibilities — and with their talents, that meant a lot more than voting.

HISTORICAL NOTES AND EDITORIAL COMMENTS

1. Former *Tombstone Epitaph* editor John Clum wrote: "Among the newcomers to Tombstone were the five Earp brothers — Virgil, Wyatt, Morgan, Jim and Warren. Tall, gaunt, intrepid, they caused considerable comment when they first arrived, particularly because of Wyatt's reputation as a peace officer in Dodge City, Kansas. All the cattle rustlers in Kansas, Colorado, New Mexico, and western Texas knew and feared Wyatt Earp." (Woodworth Clum, *Apache Agent*, p. 259.)

2. See Chapter 2, note 34, for the Earp's townlot holdings. See note 20, this chapter, for the brothers' mining interests.

3. The first of the Earps to get a job at saloon-keeping was Jim, who worked as a bartender at Vogan's from shortly after his arrival in Tombstone in December 1879 until he opened his own Sampling Room at 434 Allen Street in 1881. In August 1880, shortly after the opening of the Oriental gambling concession by Lou Rickabaugh, Dick Clark and William H. Harris, these three sold Wyatt a quarter interest in return for his protection from a gang headed by Johnny Tyler, a small-time racketeer. Later, after the foregoing partners had trouble with Milt Joice, from whom they leased their clubroom, they moved their gambling layout to the Alhambra Saloon, in which Wyatt was a silent partner with Mellgren and Meagher. (Notes accompanying the first ms. of Josephine's memoirs, in the editor's collection.) Confirming this, Wyatt Earp, on November 16, 1881, testifying before Justice Wells Spicer (Document 94, Clerk of the Superior Court, Cochise County, 1881) answered in regard to his business and profession: "Saloon-keeper at present." Later in his testimony he referred to "...the Eagle Brewery, where I had a faro game...." The city tax records do not reveal Wyatt's saloon holdings, although they do record Jim's Sampling Room. It does not appear that Virgil, Morgan or Warren Earp owned similar enterprises, although Wyatt informed Adela Rodgers St. Johns in a 1928 interview that he had set Morgan up in a faro bank in Tombstone.

4. Referring to Dallas, a typical frontier town in the 1870s, Bat Masterson wrote: "Gambling was not only the principal and best-paying industry of the town at the time, but it was also reckoned among its most respectable...." (William Barclay Masterson, *Famous Gunfighters of the Western Frontier*,

p. 37.) In the same vein, Billy Breakenridge observed: "Most of the gamblers and card dealers were good citizens, and gambling was just as legitimate as dealing in merchandise or any other business." (Billy Breakenridge, *Helldorado*, p. 103.) Likewise, most old-timers, when interviewed regarding gambling (especially their own or that of their friends), explained to me, "in those days it was considered respectable. Everyone did it."

5. Virgil Earp, born in Hartford, Kentucky, on July 18, 1843, was in some ways an enigma. While sharing the peregrinations of his family to a large extent, he also went on independent forays that have created mystery about his life. For example, despite parental opposition, he secretly married Ellen Rysdam at Knoxville, Iowa, on September 21, 1861, using his middle name, Walter Earp, and listing her as Ellen Donahoo. They were both convinced the other was dead after he went to the Civil War with the Eighty-third Illinois Infantry. Ellen married John VonRossen and moved to Kansas City, then Oregon. However, she had a daughter by Virgil, a fact that he and the daughter, Nellie Jane, first discovered in 1888. After the Civil War and the Earp family's return to Lamar, Missouri, from California, Virgil married Rosella Dragoo at Lamar in 1870, a fact unknown to his third wife, Alvira, or "Allie." What happened to Rosella, or when Virgil married Allie, if he ever did ceremonially, are unknown. He probably met Allie in 1874.

In 1877 the Virgil Earps moved to Prescott, the Arizona territorial capital, where they stayed for over two years prior to coming to Tombstone. Virgil apparently worked as a lawman there at times. (Frank Waters, *The Earp Brothers of Tombstone*, p. 71.) Virgil himself referred to his service as a lawman in a September 1900 speech before the Republican Convention at Prescott, which nominated him to run for sheriff. However, Waters specifies that Virgil worked for a Sheriff Dodson, whereas Virgil referred to his boss as Sheriff Ed Rowen, and during the 1900 speech called to him in the audience, saying, "Do you remember that time, Eddie?" (*Arizona Republican* [Phoenix], September 26, 1900.)

Waters also quotes Allie as saying that Virgil wore a badge in Dodge City. If so, Miller and Snell in *Why The West Was Wild* found no record of such service. However, we may rather safely conjecture that Virgil was well acquainted with the U.S. marshal for Arizona, Crawley P. Dake, whose office was in Prescott. Virgil probably suggested his own appointment as deputy marshal to Dake, rather than vice versa. Since no salary was involved, only fees, the marshal was probably the less reluctant to choose a good man with a gun, and Virgil received the appointment. Virgil's motive was probably to secure a means to go legally armed in Tombstone, being familiar with the turbulence of such places. (Colyn/Earp genealogy in editor's collection; Illinois Adjutant General Records.)

6. James Cooksey Earp was the firstborn child of Nicholas Porter Earp by his second wife, Virginia Ann Cooksey. James was born June 28, 1841, in Hartford, Kentucky, and died in Los Angeles, January 25, 1926. He was

buried in the Mountain View Cemetery, San Bernardino, California. His travels followed those of his family until he enlisted in Company F, Seventeenth Illinois Infantry, May 25, 1861, (Illinois Adjutant General Records.) His pension record in the National Archives shows him wounded October 3, 1861, at Fredericktown, Missouri, and discharged for the disability on March 22, 1863, claiming he was unable to use his left arm due to a wound in the left shoulder. He drew a disability pension the rest of his life. His pension record shows him back at Pella, Iowa, on March 2, 1863, perhaps on convalescent furlough awaiting discharge.

James accompanied his family on the way to California in 1864, crossing the plains and mountains by wagon train. (Rousseau diary and N. P. Earp to James Copla, April 2, 1865.) However, Jim did not go all the way to San Bernardino, but turned off to Austin, Nevada, which was then a boom town. It is my opinion that he picked up gambling as a profession there and later taught his younger brothers. He did not return to Lamar, Missouri, with the family, being in Montana in 1868–69. However, his pension record shows him at Aullville, Missouri, in 1872, where N. P. Earp appeared for him as an identifying witness. Thereafter he can be found in the towns where Wyatt was located — Wichita, Dodge City, Fort Worth and Tombstone. The newspapers in those places identify him as a bartender, or saloon-keeper and/or gambler. He married Nellie Bartlett Ketchum April 18, 1873, in Illinois. She died in San Bernardino in 1887.

7. Their real-estate and mining holdings alone give validity to this assumption. See Chapter 2, note 34, and note 20, this chapter.

8. See Chapter 2, note 2, for background on Morgan. Baxter Warren Earp was born March 9, 1855, the youngest of the boys. He remained at home with his parents and did not share in the adventures of the rest of the brothers during the 1870s. When the N. P. Earps returned to the vicinity of San Bernardino, California, in 1877, their youngest son was with them. Although he was on a visit to Tombstone in 1880 and early 1881, he did not return to Tombstone until after the October 1881 shooting in which Virgil and Morgan were wounded. According to family recollections, he operated a small family grocery for his father until he finally went to Tombstone. He left Tombstone with Wyatt and wandered over the West with him, returning to Arizona in 1891, where he worked for Colonel Hooker on the Sierra Bonita Ranch. The 1898 Great Register of Cochise County lists him in Willcox as a bartender. He was killed by Johnny Boyett in Willcox in July 1900, as detailed in Chapter 15.

9. Josephine is merely paraphrasing John Clum here, not quoting him directly.

10. Apparently Wyatt took the job as deputy sheriff late in July, regardless of Josie's belief that he held it earlier. The *Epitaph* of July 31, 1880, congratulated him on receiving the job and mentioned that his brother Morgan replaced him as shotgun guard for Wells Fargo. Since Morg became

a guard after July 1880 and was on the stage Josie arrived on, she may actually have come to Tombstone in October, as she said, rather than in May. (See Chapter 1, notes 2 & 4.) The *Tombstone Weekly Nugget* of November 12, 1880, mentions Wyatt's resignation from the job.

11. Dick Gird was a co-founder of the Tombstone Mining District, with the brothers Ed and Al Schieffelin. Gird remained a lifelong friend of Wyatt Earp. (John and Lillian Theobald, *Arizona Territory, Post Offices and Postmasters*, p. 131; "John Vosburg's Account Concerning the Big Strike at Tombstone," given to Frank C. Lockwood, Arizona Historical Society; Cason notes.) Vosburg, on the advice of former Governor of Arizona Territory Anson P. K. Safford, grubstaked the Schieffelins and Gird.

12. See Chapter 2, note 8.

13. The Clanton ranch, operated by Ike Clanton and his younger brothers Phin and Billy, was located at Lewis Springs, a couple of miles up the San Pedro River from Charleston (south) and about a half mile west of the river. The ruins of the house were still visible in 1975. The Patterson ranch was on the Babocomari Creek about two miles west of the San Pedro River. The McLaurys, at the time of their deaths in October 1881, had their ranch about four or five miles south of Soldier Hole in the Sulphur Springs valley. Joe Hill's ranch was at the San Simon Cienega. Curly Bill and Old Man Clanton had ranches near Hachita, New Mexico, as did Mike Gray of the Tombstone Townlot Company. Maps of the area reveal the strategic nature of these locations for the Rustlers' purposes. (Locations of various ranches given to Stuart Lake by Wyatt Earp in Lake collection; locations confirmed by various old-timers in the Tombstone area in interviews by the editor, 1969/70 and 1973/74/75.)

14. John P. Clum leaped into prominence by his courageous action in bringing an injunction against the Townlot Company, restraining them from even setting foot on the lots in contention. This action propelled him into the political arena, replacing Robert Eccleston as Republican candidate for mayor. He was elected in what amounted to a landslide. (See Parsons, journal, December 1880.) It is my belief that the untimely demise of Fred White, a marshal who supported justice in the Townlot transactions, brought the Earps, particularly Wyatt, to the attention of the Republicans as a suitable replacement for the strong arm of White. He was pushed for sheriff by the group supporting Clum. Their first choice for marshal was Ben Sippy, who didn't pan out. He was forced from office and replaced by Virgil Earp. This is the situation that brought the Earps to power officially. Wyatt and Clum hit it off personally and remained lifelong friends. The old newspaperman visited Wyatt in Los Angeles the night before he died. (See Clum, *It All Happened In Tombstone*, p. vii; also Cason ms. and notes.)

15. Here Josie herself refers to her frustrating tendency to bowdlerize her story of Tombstone when she was relating it during her proper old age. As discussed in the back section entitled "How This Book Came To Be,"

Josie was forced into frankness with Clum because, as a participant in the events, he was already aware of the truth.

16. Josie invariably gave Billy Breakenridge the name Billy Blab, sometimes shortening it to Billy B., but never leaving doubt as to the name she had in mind. She was also known to imply that he had homosexual tendencies. (Cason notes.) Others shared her attitude: for example, Fred Dodge in a letter to John Clum wrote, "Billy was a nice young girl in those days, and undoubtedly today is a nice old lady." (Dodge to Clum, undated.)

17. The name Spencer often appears in writings as Spence, probably because people called him Spence as a nickname. For example, his wife referred to him as Spence in her testimony at the Morgan Earp coroner's inquest. However, on their marriage record filed at Bisbee, the name appears as Spencer. (Marriage Records, Book 1, p. 9, August 13, 1881, Clerk of the Superior Court, Cochise County, Bisbee, Arizona.) The name also appears as Spencer on the Tombstone tax records.

18. But sobriety was certainly not a virtue of Morgan Earp and Doc Holliday, a fact having great impact on the final outcome of the Earps' Tombstone saga. The subject of a marriage is also a moot question. At the very least Josephine was legally married to Wyatt by common law. No official record of a marriage has ever been discovered despite the many searches. See Chapter 7, note 2, for more speculation regarding Josie's marriage.

19. See Chapter 2, note 34 and note 20 below.

20. One example of other Earp holdings is the Holliday, Clark and Wyatt Earp Water Rights, filed February 3, 1881, and recorded in Millsites, Book 1, Cochise County Recorder's Office, Bisbee, Arizona. Other properties appear in the list below. This list is far from exhaustive; many leases and similar transactions are also recorded. The city tax records of Tombstone and the County Recorder's Office at Bisbee show the following Earp mining claims:

Date	Locators	Name of Claim
Dec. 6, '79	V. W., W. S., J. C. Earp & Robt. Winders	1st North Ext. Mtn. Maid
Dec. 10, '79	" " " " "	Earp
Jan 14, '80	" " " " & A. S. Neff	Grasshopper
Feb. 8, '80	VW., W. S., J. C. Earp	Dodge
Feb. 16, '80	W., V. W., J. C. Earp	Mattie Blaylock
Feb. 16, '80	Wyatt Earp & A. S. Neff	Comstock
Feb. 21, '80	W. S., V. W., & J. C. Earp & A. S. Neff	Rocky Ridge
Apr. 20, '80	Wyatt Earp	Long Branch
Nov. 4, '80	C. Billicke, W. Earp, Albert Steinfield	Ole Bull
(?) [Book 1 – entry 66]	V. Earp	Red Star

21. This is probably an oblique reference to the dramatic image of Wyatt presented in Stuart Lake's so-called biography *Wyatt Earp, Frontier Marshal.* Josie's hostile reactions to Lake's deification of her husband are described in the back section of this volume entitled "How This Book Came To Be."

22. Josie's speculations may be unrealistically rosy. It is unlikely that the adventure-loving Earps would have stayed in Tombstone after mining declined there in the mid-eighties. Certainly all the solid commercial entrepreneurs who had supported the Earp faction eventually left the waning town. These included the Schieffelins, Girds, John Clum, George Parsons, the Billickes, Tom Fitch, Wells Spicer, Vickers and McCoy, the Herrings, the Solomons, Dr. Goodfellow, Judge Lucas, Judge Peel and many more. (Great Registers, Cochise County.) The effect of their departure was to leave only Earp enemies or their descendants living around Tombstone, which accounts for the bitter bias against the family which has repeatedly misled various writers who interviewed Tombstone old-timers in the 1920s and 1930s into crediting some very one-sided accounts.

4

The Opposing Forces

Johnny Behan was a politician in every sense of the word. He was an Irishman, full of blarney, very likeable, at least on early acquaintance. Women fell all over themselves when he turned on the charm. This should be fairly obvious from the story of my infatuation. There were plenty of other ninnies.[1] In addition, men liked Johnny; even Wyatt was attracted to him at first, before he found him out. The only person I ever knew who took an instant dislike to Johnny was Doc Holliday, perhaps because they were much alike — good conversationalists, ladies' men, and amoral in many ways. They were also both good judges of character. Their dislike was mutual. The only difference was that Doc was not afraid of Johnny and openly showed it by seeking to antagonize him. Looking back I'm amazed he didn't eventually kill my first fiancé, in view of Doc's record along that line. He certainly thought he had justification.[2]

Perhaps this is as good a time as any to talk about Doc. In a few words he could be described as a well-educated, consumptive, frontier bum. His friendship was Wyatt's Achilles Heel, at least at Tombstone,[3] but Wyatt was intensely loyal to Doc for having probably saved his life in Dodge City when he was on the police force there. Doc had got the drop on someone or other who had Wyatt covered with his pistol and was threatening to kill him.[4]

Doc had been well educated as a dentist and was a good one. He liked the practice and pursued it on and off till the end of his days. Unfortunately for him, he also liked women, liquor and gambling. The latter he found more profitable than dentistry, since he was an even better gambler than a dentist. Inevitably, on the frontier, the combination of Doc's expensive tastes and his touchy personality led to trouble. He was rumored to have killed men prior to coming to Tombstone; if this was true, who they were I never knew, nor cared to discover. It is certain that he killed men at Tombstone and did it at least partially because of his loyalty for Wyatt.

Doc was good company to his friends and bad news for his enemies. He had a sense of humor and a sense of fun as well. I liked to be around him, and we saw a lot of him after Wyatt and I left Tombstone, when we were all in Colorado. Wyatt felt the same way I did about Doc. He was fond of him and treated him much as he would a younger brother. Doc and Morg were also very close, but in a different sense — as carousing buddies. They had the same tastes and shared the rollicking pursuit of them. Doc took Morg's death very hard, which accounts for my surprise that he didn't kill Johnny, whom Doc felt was one of those behind Morg's murder. I think Wyatt restrained Doc in that connection, but if the opportunity presented itself, I have my own idea of what Doc would have done. The intensity of mutual hatred when the vendetta finally broke into the open is almost unimaginable to one who has never experienced such a thing. Even I, who lived it all, can only occasionally re-experience my own emotions then, like an elusive refrain heard long ago.

Doc and Morg with their quick tempers, were directly responsible for the smouldering animosities breaking into the open. It may seem strange that such a remark comes out of me. But it is the truth. Without this knowledge, the happenings that eventually occurred cannot be readily understood, perhaps not understood at all. Doc and Morg's responsibility for triggering the bloodshed lay deep in the hotheaded characters of both men.

In addition to the traits just described, Doc was agressively quarrelsome at times and capable of bearing deep grudges. These grudges were never held passively; Doc always felt that they should be settled. Perhaps that was his hot Southern blood asserting itself.[5] But Morg was the same way. Although Morg possessed the intelligence and courage of his older brothers, he was more quick to

John H. "Doc" Holliday, c. 1882, probably photographed in Denver. The spectral eyes were accentuated by his advancing tuberculosis.

N. H. Rose photo,
University of Oklahoma

anger. I'll give an example that happened only a few months before he was killed.

At the time I'm speaking of I was still living in the house I'd bought for Johnny. Wyatt was out of town somewhere, probably prospecting for some water or timber rights.[6] About sundown the first day Wyatt was gone, Morg stopped by the house. How glad I was to see a friendly face! I've always dreaded being alone at twilight, the most lonesome hour of the twenty-four. I invited him to have supper to postpone the time when I'd be alone. After we ate he said a strange thing, but knowing of the Earps' troubles, I supposed there was a reason for it. He said, "I'd better get out now so people won't talk, but I'd like to sit on your porch awhile if you don't mind."

Late that night a sound outside woke me up. I was terrified! My first thought was "someone is trying to break into the house!" But you may have guessed what it was. Morg was still out there freezing in the cold winter night, harboring the notion that he was protecting me, knowing well my chicken-heartedness.

I can still remember what I said when I somehow found out who was outside. "Morg, you sweet simpleton, get in here this instant!"

I persuaded him to let me make him a bed in the small parlor. That's how he came to be there when I had an unwelcome visitor in the A.M. — Johnny Behan. Whether Morg had got wind in advance of Johnny's intentions I never knew. At any rate, Johnny had come, he said, to dispossess me, which he could, since like a nitwit I'd put the lot my money had financed in his name.[7] Johnny sweetly said, "You can move your house, of course, or move out."

We were arguing there on the front porch when Morg stepped out. Johnny's attitude had put Morg into one of his rages. Without saying a word, he hit my former sweetheart in the mouth and knocked him off the porch. When the stunned man got up, Morg hit him in the stomach, doubling him over and causing him to fall again. I was terrified, but somehow got between them anyhow. I suppose there were still some tender feelings in my heart for Johnny. He left bleeding from the mouth, but without saying a word. Later, Doc, who had heard the whole story, made the fatal mistake of giving Johnny the "ha-ha" about it in public. I think this public mockery is what sealed Morg's fate. In any case, the whole episode is certainly worth relating, for it reveals both extremes of Morg's personality, the sweet and the violent.

I am not giving a chronological account of events here, as you probably realize, but an insight into some of the characters, which is why I'm jumping around quite a bit. Morg's run-in with Johnny must have happened early in 1882, just before I moved to Mrs. Young's boardinghouse.[8]

I did not often encounter Virgil Earp at Tombstone but got to know him well in later years. Contrary to stories that somehow have circulated about Virgil's brooding and dangerous character, he was the most jolly and approachable of the Earp boys. He was a great one for teasing and laughed easily. He also loved children and animals. This sounds like a classic testimonial of some kind, but it's true.

When Virge discovered after some years of marriage that he and his wife could have no children, he tried to adopt one of his sister Adelia's but she told him she didn't have any to spare. The result was that, for all practical purposes, he adopted them all whenever he could borrow them. Adelia told me years later that one time when Virge and his wife came to see them at San Bernardino they had moved since he'd last visited them. Virge had only a general idea of where their new place was located on one of the outlying roads. Adelia said she could hear him coming a mile away, yelling her family nickname "Deelie" all the way down the road till she came out to meet him. This jolly extrovert hardly squares with the storybook myth of a brooding, dangerous man. He was dangerous enough when pushed, but he took a lot of pushing without getting ruffled.

As chief of police of Tombstone, Virgil helped a lot of trouble simply to melt away because of his calm, imperturbable nature. Many officers nervously cause more trouble than they can handle. That wasn't Virge. In addition, on a frontier which was notorious for fast and loose operators on the small-town police forces, Virgil was scrupulously honest. I recall Wyatt telling me of one night in Tombstone when Virgil relieved a falling-down drunk visitor of a thousand-dollar bank roll for safe keeping till he sobered up in the morning. Some of the town sharpies had had their eyes on the man when Virgil took him in tow. This fortunate fellow apparently couldn't believe it when Virge returned his money and refused a reward.

This concludes my description of the leading members of the Earp faction. As Johnny's housekeeper and Albert's foster mother I also had an opportunity to meet almost everyone among the Earps' antagonists. These included the Rustlers, also known as the Cowboys: John Ringo, Curly Bill Brocius, Ike and Billy Clanton, and Frank and Tom McLaury. Old Man Clanton, the leader of the Rustlers, was familiar to me only by sight; I never met him socially. I'll first describe the Rustler gang as I knew them before I touch upon the members of the corrupt County Ring.

Johnny entertained all of the Rustlers except Old Man Clanton at our house at one time or another, for political motives. He was always having a little poker get-together. In addition, Johnny was forever standing in our backyard, out of my hearing, having confidential talks with one or another of the gang. After their business became more widely known, the Rustler crowd were no longer invited to come around.

Curly Bill, who became the Rustler kingpin after Old Man Clanton was killed in 1881,[9] was the most likeable of the crew. I feel he might have amounted to something if he'd had the chance. Curly, whenever he visited, always brought Albert an old, unserviceable six-shooter to use to play cowboys and Indians (or whatever they called it then). It made me nervous, but Curly laughed and assured me it was safe. He laughed quite a lot, which relieved his otherwise dark, ferocious appearance. He always treated me as a lady, and I would not have been afraid in his company alone, which is a lot more than can be said for some of the others, Billy Clanton, for example.

Billy was always making passes at me when he thought Johnny wouldn't get wise — not that he was afraid of Johnny. Billy was a big, loutish boy for his age, which must have been about nineteen. He was taller than his brother Ike. I'd guess he was well over six feet, and he must have outweighed Wyatt by at least twenty-five pounds.

Billy's brother Ike was an entirely unlovely person in my eyes. What I found most offensive in him was his eating with his mouth open, smacking his lips. He also was messy about chewing tobacco. Beyond that he was a blowhard and personally not too cleanly, at least when I saw him. Of course, few of the cowboys were. John Ringo was the exception.

Ringo, about whom so much has been written,[10] seemed to me reserved and gentlemanly. The first time he came for poker he apologetically explained to me that he kept his hat on as a superstitious lucky charm. Cowboy-style, the others never took theirs off as a rule. I doubt, on my own observation, that Ringo was as wantonly murderous as some have tried to portray him, though he was admittedly a killer. Wyatt was mortally certain he was one of the men who ambushed both Virge and Morg.

A great amount of fiction has been written about Ringo challenging Wyatt and Doc to a duel, which they declined. There is a grain of truth in this! Ringo, of course, recognized that there

Joseph Isaac "Ike" Clanton, date unknown. He engineered the trouble that got his brother Billy and the two McLaury brothers killed.

was small chance of it coming off, since both Wyatt and Doc were already in enough trouble at the time. Ringo had a bad case of the whiskey shakes, which satisfies me that either Wyatt or Doc would have disposed of him in a classic Hollywood pistol duel (which, I might add, would have been a frontier oddity).

Frank McLaury was a little fellow, with a short man's cocky attitude. He regarded himself as a lady-killer. For my part, I never saw a little strutter like him who wasn't a trouble-maker. By contrast Tom McLaury was reserved and had a reputation as the hard worker in the family. He was quiet and pleasant toward everyone. It is my guess that his brother got him into the trouble that cost them both their lives. However, he had to have a great deal of nerve to run with the crowd he associated with. Both Tom and Frank had a reputation as gunmen,[11] but I can't say why from firsthand experience – I simply don't know.

Frank Stilwell was in a class by himself. As I look back on it, he acted like a daring, wild boy playing cops and robbers. Even Billy Breakenridge in his book *Helldorado* has admitted he caught Frank one night laying in ambush to kill Doc Holliday from a dark alley. (Notably, Billy didn't warn Doc.) Wyatt figured Frank as another of the parties involved in the ambushing of his brothers. Frank's partner in the highway-robbing business, Pete Spencer – Maria's husband – I never met, though I knew him by sight.

That covers the members of the Cowboy crowd whom I knew personally. I was also acquainted with most of the members of the County Ring, the clique of connivers to which Johnny himself belonged. It also included Art Fay, owner of the pro-Democrat *Nugget;* Harry Woods, Fay's editor and Johnny's under-sheriff; John Dunbar, the county treasurer; and Billy Breakenridge.

The County Ring was rumored to thrive on robbery and graft.[12] As you can see from the list of members, these men were all outwardly respectable and even prominent political leaders. Johnny Behan and Art Fay were in the Tenth Legislature together during Governor Frémont's tenure, while Woods was in the Eleventh, also under Frémont. When the legislature created Cochise County, all three of these delegates fixed themselves on the new county like vultures, ready to garner what they could in public funds and positions.

Thomas "Tom" McLaury, date unknown. The steadiest of the two McLaury brothers, he was liked even by Josie.

Arizona Historical Society

Newman Haynes Clanton, date unknown. Generally known as Old Man Clanton, he was patriarch of the Clanton clan and acknowledged Rustler leader.

Arizona Historical Society

Robert Franklin "Frank" McLaury, date unknown. A short man, he was a vain trouble-maker in Josie's eyes.

Arizona Historical Society

The County Ring men regularly engaged the Rustlers to perform their various touchy little jobs.[13] These "respectable citizens" all associated freely with the unsavory Rustler lot until the gangs' acquisitive habits became a matter of public information. Connections between the two groups are easy to see. For example, someone might make something of the fact that County Ringer Art Fay owned the Texas Claim before it was sold to Galey. This was the Rustler hangout long before Galey developed the Texas Mine that started the town of Galeyville there. The place was ideal for holding, rebranding and moving stolen stock onto the market — and Mr. Fay just let the Rustlers "use it." This is, of course, all speculation — perhaps some would consider it wild speculation.[14]

It was also a known fact that Governor Frémont had planned to acquire for ranching the San Rafael del Valle grant, in the San Pedro valley, on the north perimeter of which were Old Man Clanton's cattle acquisition headquarters.[15] I naturally wonder how much of this may have had a bearing on the surprising appointment of a Democratic sheriff by a noted Republican governor.[16] But again I reiterate — this is all merely the speculation of an old lady who has later learned a lot about the times of her own youth that she never suspected during their passing.

As I said, I did not know Fay, who was probably the brains of the outfit — incidentally, his full name was Artemus Emmett Fay, which somehow I considered hilarious when I first heard it. On appearances alone, in my biased view, I would not have trusted him any further than I could carry a horse, as Wyatt would have put it.

Harry Woods, Fay's lackey as editor of the *Nugget* and Johnny's lackey as under-sheriff, was a clever propagandizer. He was a perfect gentleman toward me, but I sensed that Johnny didn't trust him, perhaps envied him as well, since he was graciously smooth. Apparently Harry's habits were above reproach; at least I never heard of a hint of scandal about him, although most of Johnny's associates, except Billy Breakenridge, were noted as wenchers. Harry's only vice in the eyes of his associates was that

William Milton "Billy" Breaken-
ridge, c. 1880. His latter-day repu-
tation as Tombstone's deputy was
self-generated, according to Josie,
who dubbed him Billy Blab.

N. H. Rose photo,
University of Oklahoma

he didn't drink enough. Behind his back they called him "Old-Three's-My-Limit."

I say without rancor that if anyone finally drove the Earps from Tombstone, Harry Woods did it with the *Nugget*. Wyatt entertained some aspirations after he left in 1882 of returning to face the trumped-up charges against him, then running for sheriff. Harry and the *Nugget* rendered such notions out of the question.[17] Woods' propaganda had raised fatal doubts about the Earps in the fickle public mind. All of the *Epitaph's* efforts to counter him were of little avail.

John Dunbar, the county treasurer, was in my opinion the nicest of the County Ring. I liked him. I think he was sometimes taken aback at the shenanigans of the others. But he had to make a living. He kept his mouth shut and went along.

This leaves only Billy Breakenridge. I hesitate to say much, since I was deeply embittered when he proved himself such an ingrate toward Wyatt and me. When he was old and down and out, we spent a great deal of time and money helping him earn an investigator's fee in the Lotta Crabtree estate settlement.[18] Yet shortly afterward he boasted to Albert Behan (who then told us) how he intended to burn up the Earps in his book *Helldorado.* Anyone who has read it may judge whether this was done. I know he burned me up.

So I may be accused of spite in observing that Billy Breakenridge was not the law officer he claimed to be. The notion of him as "Tombstone's deputy" grew out of his own stories in later years. He was a tax collector and jailer.[19] The one thing I can say in his favor is that he avoided the liaisons with the dance-hall women who so enamored his associates.[20] I know for a fact that he peddled secrets from the sheriff's office and much worse.

This briefly rounds out what I knew of the contending parties — the Earps with their allies (which included most of the decent, honest citizens of Tombstone), the Rustlers and the County Ring. I'll describe a fourth faction — the Townlot Company — in my next chapter.

All of these groups were anxious to exploit the opportunities of a boomtown in one way or another — both legally and illegally. When their purposes crossed, the famous shootout was the result. These killings were not a matter of good versus bad, as so many writers have tried to portray, but, as I realize now, the tragic outcome of some very complicated struggles for political and economic power.

HISTORICAL NOTES AND EDITORIAL COMMENTS

1. For example, the Behan collection in the University of Arizona Library Special Collections contains the romantic notes penned to Johnny by a lady named "Bert" Dunbar.

2. Here Josie refers to Doc's conviction that Johnny was responsible for Morgan Earp's murder. The dentist said, "It is almost certain he [Behan] instigated the assassination of Morgan Earp." (*Denver Republican*, May 22, 1882.) As Josie later testified, "If Doc had found Johnny on the night Morgan was murdered, he'd have shot him on sight."

3. Here Josie refers to Doc's penchant for getting into trouble when drunk. As time went by, however, Wyatt apparently learned how to handle the unruly dentist. Judd Riley, a police officer at Gunnison, Colorado, where Wyatt and his supporters went after the Tombstone vendetta, said in a late 1920s interview, "Doc Holliday was the only one ... that seemed to drink much, and the minute he got hilarious the others promptly took him in charge, and he just disappeared." (Interview with Judd Riley, September 1929, quoted in a letter from Agnes M. Winters to Stuart Lake, Lake collection, Huntington Library.)

4. The Dodge City papers record no such event. The mention of this incident first appears in the testimony of Wyatt Earp at the hearing before Judge Wells Spicer, November 1881, regarding the killing of the McLaurys and Billy Clanton in Tombstone. Apparently Wyatt told Lake the same story, and Josie confirms it, probably passing on what Wyatt told her.

5. Doc was born in Griffin, Georgia, in 1852. His family moved to Valdosta during the Civil War, probably to get out of the path of General Sherman's army advancing on Atlanta. Although the details vary depending on the account, young Holliday got in some trouble after the war and, probably as a result, was sent away to dental school. (See Chapter 2, note 29.) Doc seems to have been in and out of a series of difficulties thereafter, all attributed to a touchy sense of honor associated with Southern notions of chivalry. Bat Masterson, who knew and disliked Doc, said, "Holliday had a mean disposition and an ungovernable temper and *under the influence of liquor was a most dangerous man.*" (Bat Masterson, *Famous Gunfighters of the Western Frontier*, p. 35.)

6. The obvious implication here is that Wyatt normally stayed with Josephine at her house, even though his wife Mattie was still living in Tombstone at his house at First and Fremont.

7. The lot was located on the northeast corner of Seventh and Safford streets (lot ten, block forty-nine), just a half block north of the Harry Jones residence. Josie apparently never gained title to the lot herself; however, she does say she was able to sell the house, which may have been moved to another location. (Cason notes.)

8. She probably moved shortly after the ambush of Virgil Earp on December 28, 1881, an event that alerted the Earps to the grim sincerity of the threats being made on their lives. Shortly before Virgil was shot, the families of the three married Earps (Virgil, Wyatt and Jim) had moved into the Cosmopolitan Hotel. The immediate cause was the appearance one night at Virgil Earp's house of a mysterious veiled visitor, whom they later figured to have been a man impersonating a woman. When Jim Earp answered the door, the visitor mumbled something about wrong house and left. Wyatt felt that if one of the three brothers involved at the O.K. Corral had answered the door, he would have been shot. Wyatt's fears for Josie's

safety undoubtedly prompted her move to Mrs. Young's boardinghouse. (Cason notes.)

9. Clanton's death is treated by Josie in Chapter 5.

10. I am satisfied that John Ringo was related to the Youngers, infamous as members of the Jesse James gang. Ringo probably attended William Jewell College at Liberty, Missouri, hometown of the James boys. He is listed on the 1882 Cochise County Great Register as thirty-nine years of age, registered on May 16, 1882, suggesting a date of birth of 1842 or 1843. He moved to Texas and was a respectable school official until he became embroiled in a local feud. (Letters in the Turner/Oster collection.) Beyond this, there is little dependable information regarding Ringo. The literature on him is much like that on Wyatt Earp—either hero worship or denigration. Breakenridge, who knew him personally, probably provides the most reliable character sketch: sober, a gentleman; drunk, a dangerous man.

11. R. J. Campbell, in his testimony after the so-called shootout at the O.K. Corral (Document 94, Clerk of the Superior Court, Cochise County, 1881) stated: "The reputation of Frank McLowrey [sic] was a brave and courageous man and that he was an expert in the use of firearms." At the same hearing on November 17, E. F. Boyle testified regarding the McLaurys' ability to use guns: "The hearsay is that they are the finest in the country." In modern times, after every rain it is possible to find scores of old expended pistol and rifle cartridge cases at the former site of the McLaury ranch, making it obvious that someone once assiduously practiced shooting there.

12. The County Ring consisted of the group of Democratic politicians holding county offices and allegedly growing fat by siphoning off taxes for personal gain. John Clum frequently referred to the County Ring in the pages of the *Tombstone Epitaph*, and, as John Myers Myers observed, "It was probably Clum who coined the phrase, 'the ten percent ring.'" (*The Last Chance*, p. 221.) With the latter appellation, Clum was implying that the Ring added a ten percent collection fee to all taxes due.

George Parsons also refers to the County Ring, but it must be recalled that he was a close Republican political associate of Clum, having managed the newspaperman's successful campaign for mayor. On March 25, 1882, Parsons wrote in his Tombstone journal, "Feeling is growing here against the ring. Sheriff, etc., and it would not surprise me to know of a necktie party some fine morning."

Beyond the references of individuals such as Clum, Parsons, and Josie Earp, the only documented evidence of possible wrong-doing by Ring members is found in the office of the Clerk of the Superior Court, Cochise County, in the Criminal Register of Actions, recording three felony counts and two misdemeanor counts against Johnny Behan after he left office. (Action 102, misdemeanor indictment, May 19, 1883, and felony indictments, Action numbers 174, 175, 176 for 1883 and another misdemeanor indictment action number 177, February 21, 1884.) Unfortunately, the full text of the indictments and testimony are not on file, or at least they have not been found. Regardless of what the charges or evidence may have been, all counts were designated nolle prosequi. Case 177 is the only one outlined in the minute book; the specific charge against Johnny was collecting taxes after his term of office had expired. The case was dismissed when Behan showed by affidavit that he had done so based on a legal opinion. In this regard it should also be noted that county treasurer's warrants show that Johnny Behan collected at least four times the fees of any of his next three successors.

In addition to the charges against Johnny, felony indictments for forgery were brought against another alleged County Ring leader, county treasurer John Dunbar, Behan's partner in the Dexter Livery. In May 1883, Actions 140, 141 and 142 were brought; again neither the full indictment nor the testimony has been found, and all the actions died due to lack of pursuit by the plaintiff.

Despite the paucity of conclusive historical documentation, it is my opinion that there was indeed a County Ring, the members of which did all or at least most of the things alleged by Clum, Parsons and the Earps. For the earliest and by far the best speculation regarding such Ring activities, see John Myers Myers' book, *The Last Chance*, Chapters 9 through 19.

13. Jobs Mrs. Earp alleges were hired by the County Ring ranged from such fairly innocuous things as employing Curly Bill as deputy tax collector upward through contracting for the assassinations of Doc Holliday, John Clum and Virgil and Morgan Earp.

14. Someone more in-the-know than Josie very likely provided her with this well-thought-out speculation — probably John Clum.

15. See Bert M. Fireman, "Frémont's Arizona Adventure," for confirmation of Frémont's ranching plans.

16. The Lake notes in the Huntington Library indicate that Frémont had an additional opening in mind for Johnny. His proposal for an Arizona lottery envisioned Behan as the prospective administrator, according to Lake. This does not seem to be entirely confirmed by other sources which identify Tom Fitch (later Wyatt Earp's attorney) as the guiding spirit of the lottery. (Jay J. Wagoner, *Arizona Territory*, p. 122.)

17. The first item in the *Tombstone Weekly Nugget's* anti-Earp campaign was an article regarding Holliday as an accomplice of Leonard, Head and Crane. (See Chapter 2, note 30.) Another was the article in the January 27, 1882, issue entitled "A Pestiferous Posse" which concluded with a telegram describing the "state of complete terrorism" being imposed on the nearby hamlet of Charleston by "Doc Holliday, the Earps, and about forty or fifty more of the filth of Tombstone." In my opinion the product of the *Nugget's* editorial staff, this so-called telegram went on to state that these well-armed culprits were "stopping good, peaceable citizens on all the roads

leading to our town, nearly paralyzing the business of the place." The sender then enjoined Sheriff Johnny Behan to "please come here and take them where they belong."

What this obvious satire refers to is the Earp posse, which, under the funding and authority of the U.S. marshal, was at that time out looking for the ambushers of Virgil. Significantly, the guilty parties, Ike and Phin Clanton, came in and surrendered, escorted by Peter Spencer, who was at that time the territory's leading suspected stage robber. (*Nugget,* January 31, 1882.)

A final example of the *Nugget's* distortion was a story to the effect that the Earps on the eve of their final departure from Tombstone pulled their weapons on the sheriff when he attempted to detain them. The *Epitaph* took the *Nugget* to task for this lie by commenting: "The mission of a journal is to give news...devoid of distortion and misrepresentation. The *Nugget* this morning was guilty of a gross mis-statement...." (*Epitaph,* March 22, 1882.)

18. The Earps assisted Breakenridge by helping him locate old-timers who may have had knowledge of Jack Crabtree's alleged marriage to Anne Leopold. Mrs. Carlotta Crabtree Cockburn of San Gabriel, California, alleging herself the daughter of that marriage, through Tucson lawyer John B. Wright, had brought suit in the Suffolk, Massachusetts, Probate Court in 1925 for a share of the four-million-dollar estate of actress Lotta Crabtree, which had been left to charity due to a lack of known heirs. Breakenridge was hired by Wright to obtain depositions supporting his client's claim. The Earps spent days with Breakenridge at their Los Angeles home, trying to recall pertinent names and providing him the use of their phone in contacting possible deponents. (See Breakenridge, *Helldorado,* p. 253, and Walter Noble Burns, *Tombstone,* p. 270 ff, regarding the estate; the time devoted by the Earps is indicated in the Cason ms. and notes.)

19. See Chapter 2, note 27, for further commentary on Breakenridge's career.

20. As mentioned in Chapter 3, note 16, subtle suggestions have been made that Breakenridge, who never married, was a homosexual. (Conversations of the editor with old-time Tombstoner Mrs. Burton Devere, who knew Breakenridge well.) Mrs. Earp also implied this in the Cason manuscript, amplifying her remarks here by adding, "When I grew older it dawned on me that Billy had nothing to do with women at all."

5

Stormy Times

I had been infatuated with Johnny Behan. He was a skillful manipulator of people. Young as I was, the difference between him and Wyatt was clear to me as soon as I got to know my future husband. Wyatt was a man, a fact that made me see that Johnny had been something less. I soon forgot all about Johnny.

Wyatt trusted and confided in me. Despite our age difference of thirteen years, he treated me as an adult. From our conversations, the intrigue to which I had been totally blind was soon clear to see. I could now look back with wiser insight on the little things that I'd innocently observed going on around Johnny. The constant traffic of his questionable associates at the house, the veiled remarks they made, the secretive private conversations in the backyard — all these took on a new and sinister meaning.

The scheming and conniving had all been there before, the political choosing-up of sides and maneuvering for advantage. Johnny was surely aware of every aspect of it, and up to his eyebrows in most of it behind the scenes, yet he gave me no inkling at all. He was never an open fighter. On the few occasions when my curiosity was piqued to question him, he was evasive. For example, my inquiry regarding what he saw in such rare specimens as the Clantons brought the noncommittal response, "They can be useful."

"How?" I'd pressed him, since I really hoped he wouldn't bring any of them around any more.

"They get around the country a lot and see things," he'd said. "A lawman has to know what's going on — have sources of information."

I'd accepted that at the time, but Wyatt's confidences let me in on what was really happening even before I left Tombstone. The periodic poker games were occasions for innocent appearing pay-offs. Johnny never failed to win something substantial. It was the Rustlers' means of assuring that he looked the other way regarding their smuggling, rustling and highway robbery. I suppose after his associates became entirely too notorious they had to slip him *his* some other way. I have always since thought Stilwell, who was Johnny's deputy until he was caught robbing stages, was Johnny's and the Ring's collection agent with the outlaws. The gangsters in the 1930s, from what I read in the Sunday supplements, would have called him a bag man.

After I began to see Wyatt steadily, I learned something of his career in Tombstone up till then. And he let me in on the grim realities of the brief, intriguing history of the town. What I found out frightened me. Tombstone no longer seemed like an innocent, entertaining village filled with fascinating characters. It soon dawned on me that perhaps the life of my new-found love, and those of his friends, could be forfeited in a very deadly competition with some of those fascinating characters, who were beginning to assume in my eyes their true aspects as murderous rivals. I learned about the prior attempts to get Wyatt and his brothers out of the way of the ambitions of the County Ring and their underworld gang of supporters.

It was during this period that Wyatt told me that the Earps didn't have any significant trouble with the other contending factions for almost a year, although Wyatt must have become deputy sheriff about April of 1880,[1] as nearly as I can figure now. Wyatt told me he suspected that Johnny Behan's maneuvering may have been one reason that good party Democrat Shibell reoffered him the job after he'd turned it down once. Johnny's motive would have been to get Wyatt off his Wells Fargo job — his Rustler friends didn't cotton to tangling with a shotgun guard like Wyatt. However, they were disappointed to discover that Morgan Earp, who was equally game for a fight, replaced Wyatt. Soon they were circulating veiled threats to try to scare Morg off the job. Knowing perfectly well that the threats came from Stilwell, Curly Bill and Ringo, Wyatt made it a point to tell them they all would be wearing pine overcoats if they ever managed to carry out those threats. Some two years later, these Rustlers discovered that Wyatt's words were no idle talk; they were solemn promises. He killed all three personally.

Aside from that, Wyatt had little excitement as deputy sheriff till the summer of 1880. Then he took in a hard character, Frank Leslie, for the killing of Mike Killeen, over the latter's wife. I learned something about the so-called "Code-of-the-West" from Wyatt's account of that shooting. He told me, "Leslie got off scot-free, since Killeen was armed and had threatened him." I had heard Leslie was seeing Killeen's wife and naturally thought that put Leslie in the wrong. "The woman in those circumstances didn't figure in the right or wrong of it as the community saw it," Wyatt told me. "It was a square fight. On the other hand if Killeen had got Leslie, the woman would have been the major consideration in Killeen getting off under the 'unwritten law,' whether it was a square fight or not." That's the way the Westerner of those days thought.

We used to see Leslie years later as an old derelict in Oakland as late as the 1920s. He had had quite a checkered career, typical of the frontier. He married Mrs. Killeen a few months after he was acquitted of her husband's killing. They must have split up, since in the late 1880s Frank went to the Yuma Pen for life for killing a woman named Edwards, with whom he had been living then. Still later another woman was instrumental in securing Frank's pardon from Yuma, and I believe he married her too.[2] We never knew what finally happened to him.

Among the local political shenanigans I learned of from Wyatt was the Townlot conspiracy. The townsite had been platted, and many homes and substantial businesses were located on various lots. However, lot titles were not clear.[3] I couldn't believe the situation was so lawless without my having realized it. Almost every day attempts had been made to occupy lots by force. This had been going on right under my nose. Of course by this time Virge Earp was acting as chief of police and put a stop to that sort of thing. It was the main reason his predecessor, Marshal Ben Sippy, had been fired and replaced.

The trouble was made possible because an official election of a city government did not take place until December 1880. By then the camp was two years old. Alder Randall had been acting as temporary mayor, on what legal basis I don't recall.[4] I tried to digest all this, since Wyatt was vitally concerned with it, but I'm afraid, in girlish fashion, I was more amazed than really interested.

It seems that rather than try to solve the townlot confusion in an open and fair manner, Randall had conveyed title to all the city lots to the firm of Clark and Gray, otherwise known as the Townlot Company.[5] The city charter permitted temporary transfer so long as it was for administration of titling. Randall however, transferred the titles outright, an action which was clearly not intended by the city constitution.[6]

Clark and Gray, whom I had known by sight and assumed were respected businessmen like my father, had leaped onto this flimsy pretext of legality to attempt to obtain large purchase fees from existing occupants, threatening to evict them and sell their lots to others.[7] I suppose Wyatt told me at the time and I'd forgotten, but recently John Clum told me how he and others obtained an injunction in December 1880 to stay Clark and Gray from such action.[8] This vigorous move propelled John into public favor and resulted in his replacing Robert Eccleston as Republican candidate for mayor. Clum was elected by a landslide. He was already mayor the first time I recall having seen him in Tombstone.

But before this came the Marshal Fred White killing, which I have already described as my first exposure to Tombstone violence. Now I heard from Wyatt that for his year in office Fred had directed his efforts toward thwarting the strong-arm tactics of Mayor Alder Randall and his close associates Clark and Gray. These endeavors to prevent unlawful use of political power, in the mature opinions of Wyatt and his friend Wells Fargo detective Fred Dodge,[9] were directly responsible for the city marshal's death. The extortionists wanted White out of the way before they tried their big coup with the title transfer. However, Wyatt had come around to that view long after Fred White was killed. His opinion was soundly based on discovery of the extent of cooperation between the County Ring, the Townlot Company and the Rustlers, the latter of whom were always available, at the right price, to do the dirty work of either of the former two.

Recently I paid a visit to Wyatt's old friend of Tombstone days, Fred Dodge. He showed me how a good circumstantial case can be made to show that the Townlot parties actually engineered the White shooting. Fred told me first of all that Curly Bill and some of the Clantons were neighbors and friends of Mike Gray at his Animas valley ranch. And it was the Rustlers who were directly responsible for the White killing. However, the *Epitaph* article of October 28 reporting the event clearly shows that little or no local suspicion of conspiracy existed at the time: "A lot of Texas Cowboys, as they were called, began firing at the moon and stars on Allen Street, near Sixth. City Marshal White, who happened to be in the immediate neighborhood, interferred to prevent violation of the city ordinance, and was ruthlessly shot by one of the number."

The subsequent inquiry tended to show the shooting of White was an accident. Fred Dodge, who was there that night, told it to me another way. I'll try to boil down Fred's words as I took notes of them when I visited him in 1932:

"The thing fooled us all at the time. We didn't know how well that crowd was already organized. As I see it now it was no accident that the shooting started where it did. It was practically on Fred White's doorstep. That Rustler crowd was clever enough to know that Fred would come out and head for the first Cowboy he saw. So they planted Curly Bill right outside — the rest were down in Tombstone Gulch maybe a hundred feet below.

"Well, Fred came out and headed for Curly, just like they planned. When he got close he could see a pistol in Curly's hand held down along his leg. Fred told him to hand it over. Billy

Breakenridge, who ought to know, said Curly later told him that he raised the pistol, pulled the border roll[10] on Fred, then plugged him. Fred couldn't see in the dark that the pistol was cocked; he probably grabbed it just as Curly fired. He thought he'd set it off himself and said so before he died. That's the only reason Curly went free.

"But I've thought a lot about it since. That shot was no accident! If Curly wasn't planning to use his pistol it wouldn't have been cocked, and being an old single-action equalizer it couldn't have gone off. But the clincher in my mind is that we found only one cartridge exploded in Curly's pistol. At the time a lot of ignorant people said that the single empty chamber proved that Curly was innocent, that he hadn't even been in on the earlier shooting. Instead it shows that Old Curly was saving his ammunition because he meant business.

"Curly was a gunman. Normally he would carry only five cartridges in his gun for safety's sake.[11] But he had six! He loaded up all around and was ready for a fight! Two empty cartridges would have made that accident story 'wash' all right, but that single empty chamber is mighty suspicious.

"And it's clear to me whose dirty work he was doing. Who had the motive? Clark and Gray!

"Undoubtedly Curly planned to run as soon as he shot Fred. But before he could Wyatt came up and knocked him cold with the barrel of his six-shooter. Wyatt had been about a block down the street at Vogan's with Morg and me when the shooting started. He ran up there just in time to nail Curly Bill. Morg and I were almost right behind. Then Virge, Doc Holliday and Jack Johnson[12] showed up. We had quite a little posse!

"The Rustlers were still shooting from down in Tombstone Gulch; some of the slugs hit the adobe wall above us. That shows that they thought old Curly had got away by then; if they'd known their pal was lying there 'laid out cold' they wouldn't have taken a chance on hitting him. As it was, they could have shot any one of us. Another thing, if we hadn't had to put out a fire in Fred's pants started by a powder burn from Curly's pistol we might have thought a stray slug from anyone over in the gulch had got the marshal. Only Curly had been close enough to powder-burn him. The whole thing was a pat setup to get Fred, and Curly was the trigger man."

That, in substance, was what Fred Dodge said. It makes sense to me. Incidentally, it also shows Wyatt's methods very well. Almost anyone else would have shot Curly Bill in his tracks rather than risk the chance of trying to take him alive. It was ironic that Mike Gray of the Townlot Company was the justice of the peace to whom Wyatt took Curly Bill to have him bound over for White's shooting. It probably graveled Mike to do it, but he couldn't drop his "respectable" cover by seeming overly concerned for his hired killer. He must have sweated out Curly "talking" and spilling the whole story.

Shortly after the White shooting the new county, Cochise, was partitioned from Pima County. That was in early 1881. Wyatt was therefore no longer deputy sheriff for Shibell, and, of course double-crossing Johnny Behan didn't make him under-sheriff like he had been promised either. However, at Wells Fargo instigation he did get a U.S. deputy marshal's appointment. So he and Virge were both U.S. officers by the time of the fatal stage robbery attempt in March 1881. I've already gone into the details of that, back in Chapter 2. More important than the attempted robbery were the things that came in its aftermath — Wyatt's falling out with Sheriff Johnny Behan over the engineered escape of Luther King and the County Ring's effort to frame Doc Holliday for the holdup.

One of the first things Wyatt told me when our courtship started was that the Earps had decided to stay in Tombstone with part of their long-range plan being to capture the lucrative steady income from the sheriff's office. Since this was the case, it had been necessary to clear their friend Doc of suspected complicity in the attempted stage robbery and the two murders it had entailed. Obviously the only sure way to do this was to catch the real robbers — Harry Head, Billy Leonard and Jim Crane. These, of course, were the three Rustlers implicated by King when he squealed because he was tricked into believing Doc's woman Kate had been killed on the stagecoach. Recall that Wyatt and Bob Paul had almost scared poor King out of his wits with their cooked up story about how he and his pals had killed Kate in all that shooting in the dark. Of course King had squealed to lie his way in the clear.

Now Wyatt, as a detective for Wells Fargo, and of course as deputy U.S. marshal, resorted to another accepted bit of routine police procedure — he located an informant, or as they call them today a "stool pigeon." To do this he first got in touch with Billy Breakenridge, since this small-time sheriff's "stooge" was already getting to be known as a handy contact with the Rustlers. Wyatt asked Billy to get him a likely stool pigeon. Who should Billy provide but Ike Clanton? Knowing what I know today, I must say this figures. Wyatt had a confab with Ike on the business. By this time he had thousands of dollars of Wells Fargo reward money for the three highwaymen to offer as a carrot.

Ike soon showed he had no scruples about double-crossing his buddies for a price. He probably only regretted having to get some help to pull it off. His help turned out to be Frank McLaury and Joe Hill. Wyatt later had a meeting with all three at which Ike insisted on knowing if the reward still went *dead* or alive. He may have preferred them dead, to make sure they didn't suspect how they'd been arrested. Ike, Frank McLaury and Joe Hill were taking a heavy risk — they knew what their lives would be worth if killers such as Curly Bill and Ringo ever suspected they were squealers on the gang. But the reward split three ways came to better than a thousand dollars apiece — a lot of money in those days.

The deal was queered by the fact that two of the wanted men — Bill Leonard and Harry Head — were killed in an ostensible robbery attempt at the store of the Haslett Brothers in Hachita, New Mexico. The general suspicion was that rather than attempting robbery, Leonard and Head had actually been hired by Townlot Company leader Mike Gray to rub out the Hasletts, since he was contending with them over a piece of property.[13] Before long Jim Crane was also killed. With him at the time were Old Man Clanton and Mike Gray's son Dixie.[14] All three were engaged in the innocent practice of trading cattle when they were shot by the owners of the animals. It seems these ranchers had tracked the Rustlers up from Mexico a little more quickly than usual and caught them still on the run.

Of course Wyatt didn't know me well enough then to let me in on all of this. After all, I'd been his enemy's girl just a short time before. You can bet that when I did find out I was amazed. And that wasn't the end of it. Like murder, betrayal eventually will out. Regardless of how the three betrayers became suspect, the fact remains that they did. I personally think Billy B. made a shrewd guess from what he knew and blabbed to his outlaw chum Curly Bill. After all, Billy admits in his book that he and Curly were practically sidekicks. But John Clum thought the cat got out of the bag another way — because Wells Fargo agent Marsh Williams, who had figured out what Wyatt was up to, had a few too many and foolishly, but typically like a drunk, told Ike he'd never squeal on him about the double-cross. Ike had a fit in any case and as usual exercised his mouth instead of his brain. Whatever the first tip-off may have been, it was Ike's stupid public denials of guilt and nothing else that alerted the general public to what he'd been doing. This fact ultimately caused all the killing.

An old friendship of mine undoubtedly put the Earps on guard against being murdered over this affair. Recall that Marietta Spencer had come to Tombstone on the same train and stage with me and Kitty. We frequently got together thereafter. In addition, she did housework for my good friend Addie Bourland, so I often saw her there as well. She, of course, knew I was seeing Wyatt after I broke off with Johnny. One day she ran into my house very excited and out of breath. In a mixture of English and Spanish she blurted out the news that the Rustlers were going to wipe out the Earps. She had heard this from her husband Pete. This was about mid-October 1881.

I assume that her husband's personal hatred for the Earps dated from the previous month. In September Wyatt and Morg had been part of a posse that arrested Spencer and Frank Stilwell for robbery of the Tombstone-Bisbee stage.[15] Laughably, Stilwell was one of Johnny's deputies, as I mentioned earlier. I recall that at the time I had fretted and worried over Wyatt's safety, knowing he was trailing some probably dangerous outlaws. I was on pins and needles until I saw him back safe. You can imagine how I felt when you hear what Marietta had to tell me.

Marietta had an excellent picture of what the Rustler confederacy had in mind. They planned to force Ike Clanton and Frank McLaury to kill the Earps in what would appear to be a fair fight man for man but promised Ike and Frank that the whole crew would be there to back them for the showdown at the last minute. The reason those two were singled out, she said, was that they had been unsuccessfully trying to explain away their double-cross of Leonard and company as an Earp lie cleverly cooked up to get them in trouble with the gang. (I have no idea how Joe Hill escaped the gang's suspicions, if he did.) The characteristic Rustler twist to the scheme was that the others had no intention of being on hand for a showdown with law officers.

In his usual fashion, Ike had to get in a lot of blow, like Mark Twain's two raftsmen in *Huckleberry Finn,* before rolling up his sleeves to fight. His blowing shortly led to his getting in trouble with Doc Holliday. Doc told Ike he heard he had been lying about Doc and the Earps and cussed him out. The Rustler denied it. Doc invited him to jerk his pistol. Ike claimed to be unarmed. Doc told him he was a liar, that he was armed and too yellow to draw, or if he really wasn't armed to get a pistol and come back. Wyatt and his brothers who were nearby at the time separated the two, but Ike had some more blow later that night about how he'd have his friends and be "fixed right" for a showdown in the A.M. This had happened the night of October 25, 1881. Wyatt and his brothers, now forewarned, suspected what was coming. It came the next day. Having an inkling of what was in the wind I was terrified. After warning Wyatt, there was nothing I could do but wait and pray.

How can I explain my feelings as a teenaged girl in a town I'd discovered to be a haven of thieves and murderers, all by myself in my little house waiting for the worst as the minutes ticked by? Kitty was home in San Francisco visiting, so I didn't even have her comforting presence. I thought of going uptown to see Addie Bourland, not knowing of the grim events shaping up at that very time downtown. If I had gone to Addie's I'd have been right in the midst of the trouble, since she was a witness to the shooting from her shop directly across the street. Mercifully I knew only of the impending trouble and hoped it would somehow blow over. I didn't know the day and hour had come till the shots went off.

Only later did I discover what actually had been happening on that terrible day. Ike was on the street early, armed with a rifle and six-shooter, drunkenly bragging about what he and his friends were going to do to the Earps and Holliday. After awhile Virge, as chief of police, and Morg, as city policeman,[16] came on the scene and arrested Ike. John Clum witnessed this arrest. When Ike tried to shoot Virgil, the police chief knocked him down with his pistol barrel. They hauled Ike off to court with a sore head.

At the court Ike and Wyatt had words. Wyatt told the blustering outlaw that he was tired of his threats, that he'd fight him anywhere he pleased. Ike boasted that fight was his racket. He'd have come closer to the truth in my opinion if he'd said "racket was his fight." Meanwhile, the judge fined Ike twenty-five dollars and released him.

The Earps were then certain that the threatened showdown was on the way and that Ike's friends would soon show up. Therefore, when Wyatt bumped into Tom McLaury outside the courtroom, he took him to be looking for trouble. In later years I heard Wyatt say of that encounter: "I figured I'd take all the fight out of Tom then and there, so I buffaloed him. If he'd jerked his pistol I intended to have it out with him right quick, before his crowd could get together and try any tricks." Wyatt left Tom laying sprawled in the road, stunned.

In the next hour or so Frank McLaury and Billy Clanton also showed up in town. The stage was set now for real trouble. All four moved around town, checking several corrals, obviously looking for the arrival of their promised reinforcements. No one showed up; the double-crossers were getting a taste of their own medicine.

Their presence in town was getting on the nerves of the residents, who knew what was brewing. Substantial citizens demanded that Virgil arrest the outlaws immediately.[17] Virge said he preferred to let them have their "mouth" and then leave town. It appears that this quite likely would have occurred if the four braggarts had been left alone awhile longer with no help on hand. Both Ike and Tom had sore heads and may have had the fight fast leaking out of them.

However, Johnny Behan butted into the affair, probably to get a little publicity, since he knew he had nothing to fear from his friends. Sadly for him, he found them stubborn. Frank McLaury unreasonably demanded of Johnny that he go disarm the Earps (two of whom were city police on duty at the time), because Frank wanted to conduct some business in town yet. Otherwise, he said, he intended to remain armed himself. He refused to submit to arrest. Johnny should have pulled a pistol and arrested Frank, but, as usual, talked instead.

At last Virgil decided to see what had happened to Johnny, who had bragged that he could arrest the Rustlers with no trouble. Virge took along Wyatt, Morg and Doc, the latter carrying Virge's sawed-off shotgun under his long coat. Virge was carrying Doc's cane in his pistol hand, a significant fact showing he hardly expected to do any quick shooting.

What happened in the next few minutes is not public knowledge, and is not told by the court record, yet I have heard the story in the Earp family circle often enough to make no mistake about it.

The confusing, conflicting testimony that later surrounded the shooting was due to the vast amount of lying that took place on both sides. For the Earps it was a matter of countering the lies of others in order to survive under the circumstances. For Johnny and his friends it was a case of trying to railroad the Earps to the penitentiary or, better yet, get them hung. If a similar shootout had occurred elsewhere in the West, where the sheriff wasn't violently prejudiced, the matter wouldn't have gone beyond a brief preliminary hearing.

One added fact not mentioned in any testimony is worth establishing. Addie Bourland, whose business was directly across the street from the fight, saw the Clanton party passing the well-known frontier bottle around pretty actively in the time they were loitering there. She said someone tossed away the empty just as Johnny came up to talk to them. In addition, by that time of day Doc would have a good load of whiskey in him, and perhaps Morg as well. Whiskey caused a lot of shootings.

The fight that followed has been covered so often I'm not going to go into it extensively. The Earps approached the site going west down the south side of Fremont. Johnny tried to stop them, but, like the Rustlers, the Earps simply ignored him. Johnny told them he had disarmed the four trouble-makers, but it was plain that at least Frank and Billy were still armed.

A woman in a butcher shop testified that as the Earps approached she overheard one say to the other: "Let 'em have it!" She said the other replied, "All right!" This is probably discounted by some as not likely, after reading all the Earp-heroizing fiction in recent years. Nonetheless, these truly are the words that passed between Doc and Morg, unheard by either Wyatt or Virge, who were both walking ahead, still hoping to simply make an arrest. If they had heard that exchange, they would have tried to calm the two hotheads, and there may have been a different outcome.[18] But that's now only a might-have-been. Within a few seconds the Earps confronted the Rustlers man for man.

Virge still held the cane in his shooting hand, an obvious indication he was really expecting no serious resistance. Frank and Billy placed their hands on their holstered six-shooters. I think this may have been a bluff even then. Without their trigger-happy friends to help them, this crowd may have hoped to get off and save face with a public mouth battle. Even in the so-called Wild West, shooting members of the police force was not lightly accepted. It could lead to a necktie party in a town like Tombstone, which had a vigilante organization, even though it was a pretty tame excuse for one.

Virge testified in court that he heard these two cocking their pistols. What he had really heard, as he well knew, was Morg and Doc cocking theirs. Virge threw up his right hand with the cane and yelled, "Hold on, I don't mean *that!*" Everyone since erroneously has assumed he was addressing the Rustlers rather than his brother and Doc.

Johnny Behan and the adherents of those killed have testified that Doc fired first and Morg second. This, of course, is absolutely true. They were tired of the threats and mouth they'd been receiving for months and decided to bring the business to a head.

I jumped up as I heard the firing start. I knew in my heart it could be only one thing. A picture flashed through my mind of Wyatt falling before the gunfire of Johnny's horrible poker-playing cronies. What if Ringo, Curly, Spencer and Stilwell did show up after all and with the others ambush Wyatt or his brothers? I didn't imagine them all together and prepared as it really happened. I could scarcely breathe. Without stopping for a bonnet I rushed outside and toward the sound of the firing before it died down. It seemed to me in my panic that there must have been a hundred shots. Breathlessly I reached Fremont Street a block away and looked toward downtown. Numerous people were gathering in the street in front of the *Epitaph* office. I started to run that way. A man in a wagon, whom I'd never seen before yelled, "Hop in, lady — I'll run you up to the excitement!"

Without a second thought I clambered over the wheel as soon as he stopped. We went at a trot. Later I discovered exactly what had happened.

After Doc shot Frank McLaury in the belly, Billy Clanton jerked his pistol and aimed at Virge just as Morg shot him in the chest. This shot probably saved Virge's life. Billy's shot went wild.

Even though I was in a panic, I remember the distinct lull that occurred during the shooting. The fight might have ended with the first exchange. Ike Clanton ran. Tom McLaury had ducked behind a horse and hadn't fired yet. But unfortunately either Ike, Johnny or Ike's friend Will Allen[19] fired a sneak shot from the passageway between Fly's house and photo studio. All of the Earps turned in that direction, and at this time Tom sneaked a shot at Morg, who was closest to him. It hit Morg in the back. Tom had fired it by aiming across the saddle of the horse he was hiding behind. That shot was his sad mistake. Doc had backed a short way into the street out of the smoke. He had reholstered his pistol and held the shotgun ready. Tom got both barrels at short range right after he had fired and turned to run.

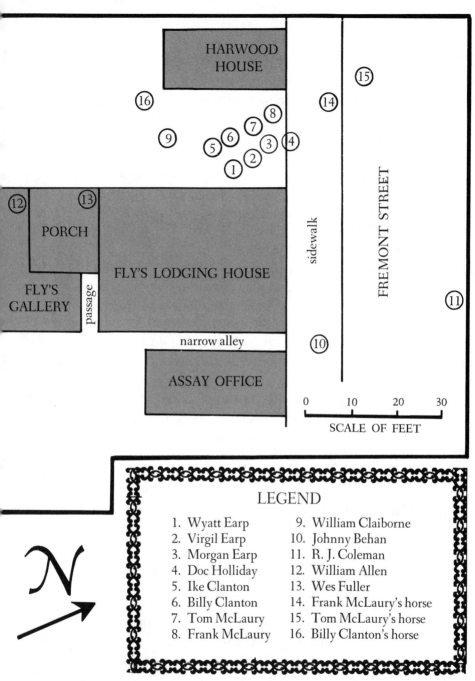

HARWOOD
HOUSE

16

9 5 6 7 8
1 2 3 4
14

15

sidewalk

FREMONT STREET

12 13

PORCH

FLY'S LODGING HOUSE

FLY'S
GALLERY

passage

narrow alley

10

11

ASSAY OFFICE

0 10 20 30

SCALE OF FEET

N

LEGEND

1. Wyatt Earp
2. Virgil Earp
3. Morgan Earp
4. Doc Holliday
5. Ike Clanton
6. Billy Clanton
7. Tom McLaury
8. Frank McLaury

9. William Claiborne
10. Johnny Behan
11. R. J. Coleman
12. William Allen
13. Wes Fuller
14. Frank McLaury's horse
15. Tom McLaury's horse
16. Billy Clanton's horse

Note: Map is drawn to scale from Sanborn map of Tombstone, 1882.

TOMBSTONE GUNFIGHT
October 26, 1881

These are the positions of the principal actors and witnesses at the start of the gunfight. Virgil Earp had just called on the Rustlers to give up their arms.

Billy and Frank, both mortally wounded, still showed grit, but couldn't shoot straight anymore. One of them fired a shot that went through the calf of Virgil's leg. After that Virge finished off Billy. Morg, who had been knocked down but risen right up to continue the fight, or perhaps Wyatt or Doc, put the finishing shot into Frank, who was still on his feet, faced off in the road with Doc. Frank's last shot hit Doc in the left hip, but his pistol holster deflected it; he got only a bruise. Morg thought his shot finished Frank. Doc thought his did. Wyatt fired also, but was noncommital on the subject.

Wyatt had fired his first shot, contrary to his later testimony, to suppress the fire of the hidden ambusher who tried to get them in the back from Fly's place. Then he snapped a shot at Tom just before Doc got him, but missed Tom and probably grazed the horse, which leaped away, exposing Tom to Doc's fire. (Don't ask me why the horse hadn't run before. I wondered myself. I assume the Rustlers had trained it not to be gun-shy.)

It is clear that at the hearing in court Wyatt and Virge both said what was necessary to protect Morg and Doc, as well as themselves. Anyone would have. They had no choice. By the time Johnny and the Rustlers' friends had given their grossly dishonest testimony to the effect that the deceased were shot with their hands in the air and that Tom was unarmed, and by the time Harry Woods had likewise distorted the events in the pages of the *Nugget* — the uninformed might have supposed that cherubic choir boys were gunned down on their way to singing practice.

On the contrary, the first two men shot had pistols in plain sight and showed every evidence of intent to draw them. Ike made no attempt to draw a pistol if he had one and was not shot at. Tom was killed only after he had shot Morg in the back.

The victims got just what they asked for. It was a fair fight even by today's standards, much less by the so-called "Code of the West." In so many words, Frank and Billy were simply beat to the draw. How it must have surprised them!

You can bet though that Wyatt and Virge were hot under the collar, especially at Doc, but almost equally at Morg. I can imagine the priceless conversations the first couple of days afterward down at Virge's house where he and Morg were convalescing in the same bed. Virge could cuss some, as I can vouch from later observation. I'll bet he did plenty of it back then, despite Morg's condition.

After time had passed, Wyatt himself admitted that he really couldn't blame either Doc or Morg. It obviously didn't break up his friendship with Doc or unduly strain the family tie. Since Wyatt and Doc were uninjured, they bore the brunt of going to jail and of the long trial that followed.

As one added point, I must say I can't imagine why anyone called it the gunfight at the O.K. Corral, the name by which the tragedy lives today. It could more accurately be called the gunfight west of Fly's house. The O.K. Corral was several doors up the street, and at that only the rear alleyway was on Fremont Street.[20]

By the time my impromptu ride ended on the corner of Fourth and Fremont, they were already putting the wounded Virge and Morg into a wagon. The jubilant vigilantes, who approved of the fight's outcome, didn't even wait for a horse, but took the shafts in their hands and ran the wagon with Virge and Morg in it the few blocks to Virge's house. I didn't know at the time who was wounded and was too frightened to get closer. I almost swooned when I saw Wyatt's tall figure very much alive, starting up Fremont with Doc and Fred Dodge on the opposite side of the street.

He spotted me, and all three came across the street. Like a feather-brained girl my only thought was, "My God, I haven't got a bonnet on. What will they think?" But you can imagine my real relief at seeing my love alive. I was simply a little hysterical. Can you blame me?

HISTORICAL NOTES AND EDITORIAL COMMENTS

1. See Chapter 3, note 10.

2. This woman was living at Yucaipa, California, in the mid-1920s, remarried as Mrs. Alec Derwood. (Lake notes; and Walter Noble Burns, *Tombstone*, p. 271.)

3. Probably the most extensive mention of the Tombstone townlot problems appears in George Parsons' journal. For example, the May 10, 1880, entry reads: "Bad state of feeling in town tonight and throughout the day. Shooting and rows of various kinds. Lots being jumped. . . ." Numerous other townlot comments are scattered throughout the journal.

4. I have not been able to find a clear account of the means by which Randall became mayor, though it is said Fred White became town marshal by the authority of a miners' meeting — perhaps Randall acquired the mayor's post in the same manner. Both Lake and Burns agree this was the case but do not cite their sources.

5. Organizers of the Townlot Company were James S. Clark, John J. Anderson, M. E. Clark, John D. Rouse and Mike Gray. Parson's journal entry for November 7, 1880, clearly reveals that Mayor Randall and these parties were out to feather their nests.

6. In his journal entry for November 12, 1880, George Parsons comments on this transaction: "We know the Mayor who received the patent [of the town] in trust for the people cannot deed in bulk to speculators as he has done — for the U.S. and Territorial statutes provide against that." See also note 5 above.

7. The boomers of Tombstone, of course, did not passively accept this extortion. One morning's sample search of Index to Civil Action for 1881, Cochise County, unearthed more than one hundred townsite suits against Clark or Gray. When these cases came to trial, almost without exception the courts judged against the Townlot Company. (Minute Book, Civil Actions, Superior Court for the First Judicial District, Cochise County, Book 1.)

8. The injunction was dated December 4, 1880. It was not dissolved until February 12, 1882. On February 17, 1882, the officers of the Townlot Company entered a $50,000 damage suit against Clum and the coauthors of the injunction, A. Bauer and J. V. Vickers. The plaintiffs were James S. Clark, John J. Anderson, M. E. Clark, John D. Rouse and M. Gray. The civil action number is 389, for the year 1882.

9. Fred Dodge was an undercover man for Wells Fargo in Tombstone and worked for them in the capacity of a detective all his life. (Fred Dodge, *Under Cover For Wells Fargo.*)

10. The "border roll" consists of holding a pistol upside down, butt forward, with the trigger finger in the trigger guard, then quickly spinning the pistol on the trigger finger to bring it upright aimed forward, quickly cocking it as it comes to bear on the target. It might succeed on an inexperienced opponent in the dark, but I think it has an over-rated, storybook reputation as a serious maneuver against a professional.

11. The single-action Colt pistol of those days had no half-cock safety mechanism; a blow on the hammer could accidentally discharge a cartridge

if the gun were loaded in all chambers. As a safety precaution, experienced gunmen normally carried these pistols with the hammer resting on an empty cartridge.

12. For a brief biographical outline of "Turkey Creek Jack" Johnson, see Dodge, *Under Cover For Wells Fargo*, p. 32. Johnson was on Wyatt's side in his Tombstone troubles and was a gunfighter with a reputation throughout the West.

13. The fate of the Haslett brothers is a good example of the Rustler-style justice risked by Ike Clanton and his informer friends. After the Hasletts killed Leonard and Head, Crane organized a party of Rustlers and killed the brothers in a running fight. (*Arizona Daily Star* [Tucson], June 23, 1881.)

14. In his journal entry for August 17, 1881, Parsons reports this killing: "Dick Gray the lame one — was killed by some Mexicans along with several others, among them the notorious Crane — Am glad they killed him — as for the others — if not guilty of cattle-stealing — they had no business to be found in such company."

15. This event is reported in the *Tombstone Epitaph,* September 10, 1881.

16. On November 19, 1881, Virgil Earp testified before Justice Wells Spicer that his brother Morgan Earp, on October 25 and 26, had been "sworn in as a Special Policeman and wore a badge with 'Special Police' engraved on it, and he had been sworn and acted as a 'Special' for about a month." (Document 94, Clerk of the Superior Court, Cochise County, 1881.)

17. See testimony of Reuben Franklin Coleman at Coroner's Inquest, Document 48, Clerk of the Superior Court, Cochise County, 1881. Coleman also demanded that Behan arrest the Cowboys.

18. There are compelling reasons for accepting Josie's story of the fight. Foremost is the fact that most of the witnesses, including the hostile ones, said it happened in that manner. Her reason for, in effect, "blowing the whistle" on Doc and Morgan is simple: she recognized that they made Wyatt appear as a cold-blooded killer in many people's eyes. Jeanne Devere of Tombstone, whose family has lived there since 1880, told me in 1974 that all the old-timers who dated their residence back to the time of the fight claimed it was a simple case of Doc Holliday starting the trouble. Since Doc shot first, it shielded Morgan Earp from similar blame on the part of eye witnesses who were not aware, as Josie was, of Morgan's equally deadly intent in the matter.

Nonetheless, the result can hardly be considered murder. The deceased had repeatedly threatened the Earps and Doc and had their hands on their pistols, probably ready to draw them at the first evidence of an advantage. Doc was simply not one to tamely permit that sort of threat to his face.

No doubt the two older Earp brothers would have been equally ready to settle the issue in gunsmoke if it hadn't meant their bread and butter in the bargain.

19. Doc Holliday later shot Will Allen in Leadville, Colorado, but didn't kill him, although he undoubtedly was trying to. (*Leadville Daily Herald*, August 20, 1884.)

20. It is likely that some writer, perhaps misinformed as to the fight's location by a typically self-styled "Tombstone old-timer," misnamed the affair. The name came to use in print in the 1920s and 30s, and, despite its inaccuracy, the catchy title "Gunfight at the O.K. Corral" took hold and became ineradicable. The fight actually started on the vacant east fifteen feet of lot two, block seventeen, at a spot just west of Camillus Fly's house. The back entrance of the O.K. Corral was on the west fifteen feet of lot six, block seventeen, which is some ninety feet east of the start of the fight. The spot indicated by tourist signs in 1976 as the location of the shootout is roughly correct. However, the life-sized manikins of the participants are inaccurately positioned, since too many feet separate them from each other. The eight men had only fifteen feet of fighting space from side to side, between Fly's house and the Harwood house just fifteen feet to the west of it. (Tombstone Tax Rolls designating locations in 1881; official city plat map, 1881; Sanborn 1882 map.) Virgil Earp testified: "...I saw the parties [McLaurys and Clantons] before we got there, in a vacant lot between the photo gallery and the house west of it." (Superior Court Document 94.)

It is obvious that many who testified, such as Virgil, were referring to the whole Fly establishment as the photo gallery. However, Fly's house was immediately adjoining the sidewalk on the extremely detailed Sanborn map, which shows the gallery as located in back of the house. Perhaps Fly did his picture-taking in a front room of the home, then developed the prints in the rear building, an arrangement which would resolve these contradictions. To settle another point of confusion, there were definitely two small houses west of Fly's then, though in 1976 there is only one in the restored area. Wesley Fuller testified to the carrying of Tom McLaury into "the second house below Fly's, the one directly on the corner." (Superior Court Document 94.)

6

Tombstone Finale

When I was down to see Fred Dodge in 1932, we were reminiscing on the front porch of his ranch house. He and I agreed that the funeral for the McLaury boys and Billy Clanton may have "laid it over" Buck Fanshaw's in Mark Twain's classic short story "Buck Fanshaw's Funeral." "The band, firecrackers and the works!" was how Fred put it. "It was the only good thing those boys ever did for Tombstone!" I don't mention this with disrespect for the dead, but because some writers, such as Billy B., have pointed to the size of the funeral as evidence of the popularity of the Rustlers. This wasn't so. A funeral in those times was like a circus; the people weren't primarily mourners but spectators.

Johnny and his friends made sure after the shooting that a major attempt was undertaken to vilify the Earps. Someone — I bet Johnny himself — made off with Tom McLaury's pistol after he dropped it, so they were able to make a big thing of how Doc shot poor unarmed Tom. Somehow poor unarmed Tom had managed to shoot Morg in the back with that pistol he didn't have!

I am going to tell this chapter from my point of view today, since my attitude back then was simply incoherent through terror and dread. Besides, I have learned most of what I have to relate since that time, as far as objective facts are concerned.

The hearing before Justice Wells Spicer lasted a month. Wyatt, his brothers and Doc were completely exonerated and released. Several excerpts from Spicer's decision are worth repeating. Before I do however, I want to make clear that the claims that the judge was partisan[1] are true in one sense only. He was partisan in the same way that all the good, honest people of Tombstone were partisan. They recognized the "Cowboy Curse," as John Clum dubbed it. They saw that the Earps' action was a blessing to the community. And they recognized that what was required, in view of the hostile testimony designed to make a public service appear like murder, was a legal exculpation that at least made a bow in the direction of the ideals of justice. With this preamble, here are some of the pertinent excerpts from Judge Wells Spicer's decision:

". . . I am of the opinion that the weight of evidence sustains and corroborates the testimony of Wyatt and Virgil Earp that their demand for surrender was met by Wm. Clanton and Frank

From left to right in their elaborate coffins lie Tom and Frank McLaury and Billy Clanton after the so-called O.K. Corral gunfight.

N. H. Rose photo, University of Oklahoma

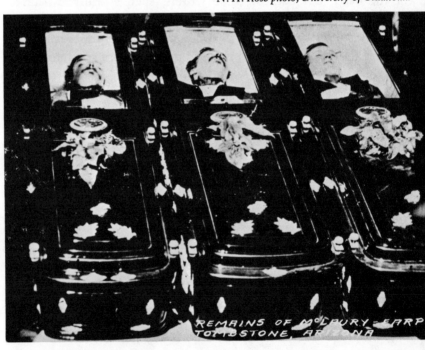

Wells Spicer, date unknown. This rumpled and deceptively mild-appearing justice knowingly made a fearless decision that jeopardized his life.

McLowry [sic] drawing, or making motions to draw, their pistols. . . .

"The defendants were officers charged with the duty of arresting and disarming brave and determined men who were experts in the use of firearms . . . and who had previously declared their intention not to be arrested or disarmed. . . ."[2]

". . . The testimony of Isaac Clanton that this tragedy was the result of a scheme on the part of the Earps to assassinate him, and thereby bury in oblivion the confessions the Earps had made to him about 'piping' away the shipment of coin by Wells Fargo & Co.,[3] falls short of being a sound theory, because of the great fact, most prominent in the matter, to wit, that Isaac Clanton was not injured at all, and could have been killed first and easiest. . . ."[4]

"In view of the past history of the country and the generally believed existence at this time of desperate, reckless and lawless men in our midst, banded together for mutual support, and living by felonious and predatory pursuits, regarding neither lives nor property in their career, and at this time for men to parade the streets armed with repeating rifles and six shooters and demand that the chief of police and his assistants should be disarmed is a proposition both monstrous and startling. . . .

"I . . . cannot resist firm conviction that the Earps acted wisely, discreetly and prudentially to secure their own self-preservation — they saw at once the dire necessity of giving the first shot[5] to save themselves from certain death . . . ; it was a necessary act done in the discharge of official duty."

The long trial was finally over, and the Earps and Doc had been publicly vindicated. But their troubles had only begun. Spicer's decision was published on December 1.

Almost at once threats by mail began to reach the Earps, Doc Holliday, Judge Spicer, John Clum and Wyatt's lawyer, Tom Fitch. Then on December 15 the night stage for Benson on which John Clum was a passenger was attacked. It was a sham robbery; the object of the attackers became fairly obvious when someone yelled, "Get the old bald-head s.o.b.!" John had been bald since his youth.

Of course, they didn't get John Clum. In the darkness and confusion Tombstone's mayor dropped off the stage into the desert and walked away undetected. Later he was able to borrow a horse at one of the mills on the San Pedro, ride to Benson and catch his train.

At about the same time Judge Wells Spicer received a letter pointedly suggesting he leave the country before he got a hole in his coat. After adding several crude insults, the writer signed himself "A Miner."[6] Spicer responded to the threat in the pages of the *Epitaph*:[7]

". . . I am well aware that all this hostility to me is on account of my decision in the Earp case . . . that every vile epithet that a foul mouth could utter has been spoken of me, principal among which has been that of corruption and bribery. . . .

"It is but just to myself that I should here assert that neither directly or indirectly was I ever approached in the interest of the defendants by them or for them. Not so the prosecution — in the interest of that side even my friends have been interviewed. . . ."[8]

Spicer made it clear he was not referring to the Clantons as the bribers, but to the pro-Rustler rabble in the city, a league that had formed with the purpose of breaking the power of the Earps. This consisted of Johnny Behan; a McLaury brother named Will who had come from Fort Worth, where he had been an attorney; and Clark and Gray of our old friendly Townlot Company. Necessity had made bedfellows of them. Money provided by this group undoubtedly purchased the murderous services of the usual crowd of Rustlers.

As Spicer said elsewhere in his letter in the *Epitaph*, "The attempt to assassinate Mr. Clum has been made — who will come next?" We didn't have a long wait to find out. The next blow fell on December 28. George Parsons, who was close by the place where it all happened, recorded his impressions in his journal:

"Tonight about 11:30 . . . four shots were fired in quick succession from very heavily charged guns. . . . Virgil Earp [had] crossed to the West side of 5th and was fired upon . . . by 2 or 3 men concealed in the new 2 story adobe going up for the Huachuca Water Co.[9] He did not fall, but recrossed to the Oriental and was taken from there to the Cosmopolitan, being hit with buckshot and badly wounded in left arm with flesh wound above the left thigh. Cries of 'There they go, Head them off!' were heard but the cowardly, apathetic guardians of the peace were not inclined to risk themselves . . . [I] went to hospital for Doc [Goodfellow] and got various things. Hotel well guarded, so much so that I had hard trouble to get to Earp's room. He was easy. Told him I was sorry for him. 'It's hell, isn't it?' said he. His wife was troubled. 'Never mind, I've got one arm left to hug you with,' he said."

After this the Earps moved only in pairs or groups. Investigation after Virge was shot turned up a hat with Ike Clanton's initials in it at the site from which Virge's ambushers ran. Wyatt took a posse out after Ike. Perhaps with visions of how his arrest by Wyatt was apt to work out, Ike came in and gave up as soon as he heard Wyatt was on his trail.[10] Not surprisingly, a convenient number of friends provided him an alibi. The hat? It was a plant by his enemies! Perhaps it was. Aside from Ike, Wyatt's guess on who might have done the shooting was Will McLaury and, according to the grapevine, his hired accomplices, Ringo, Spencer and Stilwell. They were always available for a price, especially for jobs that appealed to them.

It was now obvious, Wyatt told me, that his choices boiled down to three: break the back of the Rustler organization, leave the country or be assassinated. He still sought to proceed legally. Judge Stillwell provided him a handful of warrants for Rustler rank and file. Wyatt was determined to harass the Indians in the gang, as he said, till they deserted the country, leaving the chiefs high and dry. His tactics started to pay off so well that the opposing faction had to strike back. Their plot this time was to try to have the Earps re-jailed on the same old charges resulting from the October gunfight. Ike Clanton pressed the charges again this time with a Contention justice of the peace. Johnny Behan rearrested them and took them to the little town. Due to well-founded suspicions that they might not reach there alive in charge of Johnny, some well-armed Earp friends went along. George Parsons covered the incident in his Feb. 15, 1882, entry:

"Yesterday Earps were taken to Contention to be tried for killing of Clanton. Quite a posse went out. Many of Earps' friends accompanied, armed to teeth. . . ."

As could be expected, there wasn't a shred of new evidence. Judge Lucas released them on a writ of habeas corpus, and Wyatt continued his harassment campaign. The opposition struck back again in desperation, once more in darkness and from ambush. The *Epitaph* of March 20, 1882, carried the story of this attack:

"At 10:30 Saturday night [March 18], while engaged in playing a game of billiards in Campbell and Hatch's Billiard Parlor . . . Morgan Earp was shot through the body by an unknown assassin. . . . [He] was standing with his back to the glass door in the rear of the room. . . . The assassin . . . took aim for about the middle of his person, shooting through the upper portion of the whitened glass. The bullet entered the right side of the abdomen, passing through the spinal column, completely shattering it, emerging on the left side, passing the length of the room and lodging in the thigh of Geo. A. B. Berry, who was standing by the stove, inflicting a painful flesh wound. Instantly after the first shot a second was fired . . . which passed across the room and lodged in the wall near the ceiling over the head of Wyatt Earp, who was sitting a spectator of the game. . . ."[11]

Following the shots, some of the men in the billiard parlor ran out into the alley, but of course it was useless. The murderers had already fled.

I cried my eyes out when they told me what had happened. Poor quick tempered, good-hearted Morg. I'll never forget how he was willing to sit on my porch all night freezing, with the notion he was somehow protecting me.

Wyatt's last moments with his favorite brother had been heart-rending. Near the end Morg had told him, "They got me, Wyatt. Don't let them get you!" Then he said, "Tell ma and pa goodbye." After that he drew a deep, ragged breath and never breathed again.

When Doc got the news shortly after Morg died, he went berserk. With a couple of others he kicked in the doors of several private homes where he expected to find Will McLaury or Johnny Behan, entering with a cocked pistol in hand and murder in his eyes and heart. With all of his other trouble, Wyatt had to go get Doc in hand, not that he felt much different himself.

Will McLaury was not seen in town again. Whether he was guilty, or fearful, or both is hard to say. At any rate, my old friend Marietta Spencer again turned up to help. Marietta's husband Pete had stupidly beaten her and threatened both her and her mother with death if they told about his part in Morg's murder. She, being fiery-tempered, was determined after that to tell, whether it cost her life or not. She revealed what she knew to the coroner's jury on Monday morning. The substance of her speech comes through in the following exerpt:

"On Sunday morning 'Spence' told me to get breakfast about 6 o'clock, which I did — after that we had a quarrel, during which he struck me and my mother, and during which he threatened to shoot me; my mother told him he would have to shoot her too. His expression was, that if I said a word about something I knew, he would kill me; that he was going to Sonora and would leave my dead body behind him. Spence didn't tell me so, but I know he killed Morgan Earp; I think he did it because he arrived at the house all atremble, and both the others who came with him. Spence's teeth were chattering when he came in. I asked if he wanted something to eat and he said he did not. Myself and mother heard the shots, and it was a little after when Spence came in with Indian Charlie." [12]

Marietta told enough more to establish that Indian Charlie, or Florentino Cruz the half-breed,[13] had been the finger man who kept others informed of Morg's whereabouts that night.

This was the final straw. Wyatt persuaded Virge that he must leave town, since he couldn't protect him any longer and still be free to go after Morg's murderers. Virgil's wife Allie sided with Wyatt in this. They finally got Virge to agree. Till then he wanted to stay in Tombstone and get even with his ambushers.

Virge's shooting is one case in which I can clearly recall my attitude. I was furious. Although I hardly knew Virge at the time, I knew there was a strong bond of affection between him and Wyatt. I felt that I knew Virge from what Wyatt had told me about his good-natured older brother. But along with that another thing almost immediately came to mind. Would Wyatt be next? I had begged him before this time to run away somewhere with me. I tried again. He was absolutely deaf to my pleading. I began to understand the side of the Earps that made it possible for them to stand up to men reputed to be the toughest in the country and exchange shot for shot with them, not knowing if their enemies might be reinforced by more of their kind at any moment. Wyatt was simply immovable. He was not a runner. He was the bravest man I ever knew.

Another trouble was the attitude of my parents. Tombstone was in the nation's headlines as the scene of daily violence. Every letter from home entreated me to return. I can't imagine what their attitude would have been if they had known I was keeping steady company with one of the Earps, who were making those headlines. Fortunately, time would take care of even that problem.

Meanwhile, I imagined danger lurking in every doorway or window. I jumped at loud noises. The sound of a shot sent me into an agony of anticipation until I found out the cause, and Tombstoners heard a lot of shooting. I was completely miserable.

Wyatt figured his first responsibility was to get Virge safely to their parent's home in Colton, California. Morg's body was to go on the same train. As a precaution my sweetheart took a posse along: his brother Warren and his friends Doc, Jack Johnson and Sherm McMasters.[14] Wyatt planned to go all the way to Colton for the funeral then return. Something happened in Tucson that changed his mind.

When the train stopped at the Tucson depot, Wyatt and his friends spotted Stilwell and Ike Clanton. Even Billy B. in his prejudiced account, *Helldorado,* admitted that it looked like Stilwell was there to make a try for another one of the Earps. This time it worked out the other way. Stilwell's body was found beside the tracks the next morning. Wyatt had loaded him with buckshot; Doc had emptied his pistol in him for good measure.

This act put Wyatt outside the law. Realizing that his time for further revenge was short, he decided to return to Tombstone, quickly wind up his affairs in town, attend to some unfinished business out in the chaparral and leave the territory. I knew that killing was wrong and contrary to my upbringing, but as a woman in love I gloated that Wyatt had destroyed an enemy, especially the one who had probably murdered Morg, whom I had loved like a brother. I probably rationalized my attitude with the thought that Stilwell had been trying to kill Wyatt when he got his.

Good old dependable Ike Clanton had a warrant sworn out for Wyatt and Doc for the Stilwell killing. Johnny tried to arrest Wyatt before he could get out of town. Always a timid hare, Johnny approached him with a six-man group of reserves, saying politely, "I'd like to see you, Wyatt."

Wyatt retorted, "If you're not careful, Johnny, you're going to see me once too often!" Wyatt and his friends then rode out of town unmolested.

First they visited Pete Spencer's wood camp in the Dragoons on the chance he was hiding out there. They couldn't find him, but Indian Charlie had the bad luck to be there. They adjusted his case so he would be finger man for no more murders. His riddled body was left for the coyotes and ravens.

After that they returned to the outskirts of Tombstone and by prearrangement met a messenger with the latest news on Johnny Behan's activities. What they heard suggested they should go into the Whetstone Mountains. Knowing that the rank and file of the Rustler gang stayed in the hinterlands, camping around the water-holes, the Earp party was making the rounds to see who they could find. Incredible luck came their way.

The next afternoon, as they were approaching Mescal Spring on the eastern escarpment of the Whetstones, they stumbled onto none other than Curly Bill. In the exchange of shots that followed, Wyatt downed Curly with a double load of buckshot from his favorite ten-gauge shotgun, a formidable weapon. The range was close enough for Wyatt to be sure of the identity of his victim. Still, members of the pro-Rustler faction have insistently asserted that this body was not in fact Curly Bill's. One of the most ridiculous of these arguments can found in Billy B.'s *Helldorado*. The fact remains that no one ever saw Curly Bill Brocius after late March 1882.

Wyatt's cleanup sweep netted no one else of importance, though word of what he was doing rid the country of far more Rustlers than his shotgun did.[15]

Johnny, when he finally found out the whereabouts of Wyatt's posse, seemed strangely unable to get within a long rifle shot, even with a posse full of such stalwarts as John Ringo and Phin Clanton. Those two, as well as a lot of others, had heard all about the Earps' *daylight* shooting; they didn't care to experience any of it firsthand. In fact, the redoubtable Billy B. had been so impressed that he didn't even ride with the posse; he conveniently got mad at Johnny for giving the horse he wanted to Ringo (so he said) and remained in Tombstone sulking like Mighty Achilles. His staying behind resulted in his stumbling into the only gunplay I ever heard of him being involved in. As the sole county lawman left in town, he was forced to take a posse out after two members of the Rustler gang who had murdered Judge Peel's son. If I read his story right, Billy B. himself was behind a tree when the shooting took place. Two of the posse and one of the Rustlers were killed.[16]

With the deck stacked against him, Wyatt had little choice but to leave Arizona. He realized he'd probably sooner or later be murdered, probably in Johnny's jail if he ever landed there again. Doc felt the same.[17] On the advice of excellent legal talent[18] they decided to have their case heard in an extradition proceeding in a more friendly clime.

Colorado was their chosen refuge. As it happened, only Doc, who holed up in Denver, had to have an extradition hearing. When Governor Pitkin of Colorado refused extradition on grounds that Doc couldn't get a fair trial in Arizona, that he in fact would probably be killed instead,[19] no one even tried to apprehend Wyatt, Warren, Jack or Sherm, who all had gone to Gunnison.

But this was not quite the end of the Arizona affair. There still were unsettled scores there. I would like to set at rest one thing in relation to them. That is this: Wyatt was a bulldog. He conceived it as his responsibility to put an end to the organized activities of the Rustler gang. This meant getting the leadership. The only remaining leader with the talent to keep the organization running was John Ringo. Without going into details I can assure you that I am mortally certain that Wyatt and Doc returned to get him, and that they achieved their purpose.

I know this fact not only from family discussions, but from Fred Dodge and one of Fred's old friends, who made me promise I would never give his secret away. I'll say only this about him: he was a friend of Doc's, and he was there when Ringo got his. A respectable old age and a set of country-club descendants who were ashamed of his past — even though he was the author of their affluence — prevented his openly admitting his part in the killing and thus solving that half-century-old mystery.[20] Fred Dodge's own reluctance to talk of Ringo's fate was based on an equally sympathetic motive; for years he thought he was shielding Wyatt, to say nothing of himself and Wells Fargo. After all, the latter had paid blood money for Ringo's death, even though he'd never so much as been indicted for a crime.[21]

I won't treat this killing in depth here. This chapter has already told enough of death. Suffice it to say that Wyatt and his friends had intended to string Ringo up where he could be readily found so that it could not be claimed he had simply left the country, as was done in the case of Curly Bill. But the Earp posse was unable to get the drop on the wary killer. Ringo was smart. In the end Wyatt caught him on the run and dispatched him with a fast rifle shot, admittedly a lucky one, since it hit the last of the Rustler leaders square in the head.[22]

HISTORICAL NOTES AND EDITORIAL COMMENTS

1. An example is an undated article from Tucson's *Arizona Weekly Star* quoted by Miller in *Arizona: The Last Frontier*, p. 154, "...the magistrate [Spicer] in releasing the slayers was guilty of culpable ignorance of his duty or was afraid to perform the same, or acted corruptly...." The article goes on to include the grand jury in its criticism, observing: "...the Grand Jury was either intimidated from taking action on the case, or were in full harmony with the murderers...." In weighing these comments, it must be remembered that the *Star* was politically aligned with the *Tombstone Nugget*.

Information available on Wells Spicer is, for the most part, sketchy and uncertain. The 1882 Great Register of Cochise County lists him as a fifty-year-old lawyer living in Tombstone. His oath of office as one of Cochise County's justices of the peace is on file at Bisbee with the county clerk. It is not questioned that he came to Tombstone from Utah, where in 1875 he defended John D. Lee, a man who was subsequently executed for his part in the immigrant killings known as the Mountain Meadows Massacre. A good source for additional speculation regarding Spicer's background is Gary Roberts, "The Wells Spicer Decision: 1881," listed in the reference section of this book.

2. It is questionable that Johnny Behan seriously attempted to disarm the four Rustlers; he probably hoped they would kill the Earps if allowed to remain armed. The fact that he did not join Police Chief Virgil's posse sheds yet more doubt on Johnny's sincerity in this matter.

3. Space does not permit reciting all that Josie had to say about this "piping away." She thought the unique terminology was delightful, in fact too original for Ike Clanton to have dreamed up; she felt the Rustler had been fed the words by Harry Woods. Specifically, Ike claimed that the Earps and Marshal Williams had "piped away" the Wells Fargo shipment of bullion before the strongbox was put on the March 15, 1881, stage to Benson and that the robbery itself was a sham cover-up. Unfortunately, logic suggests that if this were so someone would have missed the gold when the already empty strongbox reached its destination, since the robbery was unsuccessful. Despite this obvious fallacy, anti-Earp writers have embroidered Ike's vengeful fabrication into a whole series of Earp/Williams "pipings away." Fred Dodge indicates that Williams, *and only Williams* actually may have been involved in some tip-off shenanigans at Wells Fargo's expense. (Fred Dodge, *Under Cover for Wells Fargo*, p. 246.) Dodge has nothing but praise for Wyatt Earp and his brothers.

4. Furthermore, if the idea had been to dispose of Ike, it could have been done more simply, surely and with greater justification that morning when Virgil and Morgan arrested this Clanton brother.

5. This may reveal that Spicer knew what really happened — that Morgan and Doc had in fact fired the first shots.

6. This note appears to be the work of an educated man who is not too successfully appearing to be crude. My guess is that the author was Will McLaury.

7. *Tombstone Epitaph*, December 13, 1881.

8. The finger points to Johnny Behan as the would-be briber. The full transcript of the testimony at the Spicer hearing shows that the defense asked Behan if he hadn't offered money to secure a conviction.

9. This building was on the southeast corner of Fifth and Allen streets. Virgil had walked from the Oriental on the northeast corner of this inter-

section and reached a point in front of the Crystal Palace (then the Eagle Brewery Saloon) on the northwest corner of Fifth and Allen, was shot there, then walked back to the Oriental, probably in shock, to tell Wyatt he'd been hit.

10. This was not quite the case. The Clantons didn't surrender till late January, nor did Wyatt's posse go after them before then. (*Nugget*, January 27, 31, 1882.)

11. Morgan was coldly murdered, as this newspaper account indicates. Typical of the misinformation that surrounds the Tombstone killings is the description of Morg's death which appeared in an official Arizona guidebook compiled in the late 1930s by the Works Projects Administration: "The *Morgan Earp Marker* . . . is in front of what was Bob Hatch's saloon. Here Morgan Earp is said to have picked a fight with one of the Clanton gang. His opponent beat him to the draw." (WPA, *Arizona, A State Guide*, p. 249.) Stuart Lake alleged that this palpable inaccuracy was probably due to the hand of one Pat Hayhurst, who was the last of a long line of politicians in Johnny Behan's clique. Lake also believed that Hayhurst had purloined the original transcript of the O.K. Corral hearing. (Introduction to Lake's copy of Document 94, Clerk of the Superior Court, Cochise County, 1881, in editor's collection.)

12. Coroner's inquest into the death of Morgan Earp, March 19, 1882, filed with Clerk of the Superior Court, Cochise County.

13. Cruz was apparently of Mexican and Indian descent and was known as Indian Charlie. (Stuart Lake, *Wyatt Earp, Frontier Marshal*, p. 337.) However, there seems to be some confusion about this, since the coroner's inquest identified him as a Mexican, Judah Florentine. There is no question about the fact that whoever he was, he was known as Indian Charlie to Marietta Spencer. (Coroner's inquest, note 12 above.)

14. Information on McMasters is sketchy, and as usual in the Earp area, contradictory. Mrs. Earp in the Clum manuscript identified him as a Wells Fargo undercover man, such as Dodge. Lake in his notes comments that McMasters; after separating from the Earps as told in *Frontier Marshal*, eventually died in the Philippines during the Spanish American War, or its sequel. On the other hand, a letter from Will McLaury to his father dated April 13, 1884, indicates that McLaury had somehow disposed of both McMasters and Morg Earp. (Copy in editor's collection.)

15. Evidently even minor figures of the Rustler contingent were fleeing the territory. One former Idahoan told me of meeting a Cochise County fugitive in Idaho many years later. The fellow told him, "I wasn't taking any chances. The Earps were riding up to the waterholes and shooting the Clantons' friends on sight. I hauled my freight for Mexico, took a boat for the Northwest and I've been up here ever since. Those boys meant business." (Interview with Harry Stewart, Tombstone, June 1970.)

16. The killers were Zwing Hunt and Billy Grounds. (Billy Breaken-ridge, *Helldorado,* p. 180ff.) Significantly, Breakenridge admits on p. 185, "Hunt told me that they thought it was the Earp party after them, and if he had known who it was, he would not have made a fight." This says a lot, both about the chumminess of Breakenridge and the outlaws, and about the effectiveness of Wyatt's throwing the fear of God into them with his cleanup. Contrary to Josie's assertion, only one posseman was killed.

17. In the *Denver Republican,* May 22, 1882, Doc was quoted as saying, "If I am taken back to Arizona, that is the last of Holliday."

18. Josie does not identify the legal talent. Probably Tom Fitch, Wyatt's lawyer, was among the advisers; perhaps they also included acting Governor John Gosper.

19. Although Josie represents this ruling as an act based on justice and kindness, partisan politics was probably the key factor. Governor Pitkin of Colorado was a Republican, as was Wyatt. Johnny Behan and his crowd were, of course, Democrats.

20. Lake, based on letters from Fred Dodge, attributes the killing of Ringo to Johnny-Behind-the-Deuce. (Lake, *Frontier Marshal,* p. 357; and Dodge, *Under Cover,* in section containing Dodge letters to Lake, letter of September 30, 1929, p. 240.) In the foregoing letter Dodge wrote, signifi-cantly, "I was riding in that part of the country quite a little bit right at that particular time." So was Breakenridge. (*Helldorado,* p. 187.) If one assumes, as I do, that Dodge was covering up for Wyatt and Breakenridge for himself, it can readily be seen that there was a lot of smoke even before Josie pointed to the precise location and nature of the fire.

21. This is to say that companies such as Wells Fargo offered rewards, as in the case of Leonard, Head and Crane, for mere suspects who had not been indicted by any proper authority, or for whom no warrants were currently issued, and offered the rewards dead or alive. They did the same in Ringo's case, and apparently paid off. This fact was sufficient, as Josie implies, to assure Fred Dodge's silence in this matter.

22. Ringo's body was found, according to Breakenridge (*Helldorado,* p. 188) across Turkey Creek from the mouth of Morse Canyon, with a bullet hole in the head, sitting in a clump of black oaks. The Rustler's grave is just a short distance from this spot. A teamster hauling lumber for the sawmill found the body. Josie's very detailed story of the Ringo killing can be found in the *Epitaph,* December 20, 1974.

7

Travels Together

I left Tombstone with a sense of relief, glad that Wyatt had got safely away, and relieved to be away from the dreadful place myself. It had come to mean nothing but suppressed terror to me.[1]

Following the killing of Ringo, Wyatt picked me up in San Francisco and we traveled back to Gunnison by way of Salt Lake City and Denver.[2] Bat Masterson[3] was one of the first people we saw on our stop-over in Denver.[4] I had never before met him. He was a handsome, happy-go-lucky sort of person. One wouldn't expect him to hold a reputation as one of the deadliest gunfighters in the West. When I got to know him better he confided to me, "Most of that is hot air. If you ever have the bad luck to have to kill someone, the tall tales will grow about you. Even the tough ones hesitate to go up against you if they think you've knocked off a couple of dozen hard cases just like them. Wyatt would tell you the same thing. It's all part of the game."

In addition to Bat we soon ran into Doc Holliday, who looked us up as soon as he heard Wyatt was in town. As I've already mentioned, the trouble in Arizona had made national headlines, so the news got around that Wyatt Earp and Doc were in Denver. He and Doc were both plagued by a great deal of hero-worshipping curiosity on the part of the crowd who hung around the gambling halls.

Through Bat Masterson I came to realize that I had married a very unusual man, one who bore a reputation for fearless law enforcement as a deputy marshal in Dodge City when it was considered the toughest town in the West. Later I was to see

William Barclay "Bat" Masterson, c. 1882. This staunch friend of Wyatt's appears personable and debonair, confirming Josie's first impression of him when they met in 1882.

Beeson photo

Dodge City and meet many of Wyatt's old friends there, who bore out in almost every particular what Bat had told me.

Meanwhile Colorado was an idyll. Wyatt prospected considerably, as did his brother Warren. Sometimes he took me with him on trips to the hills. Other times I was left behind to amuse myself as best I could. Very often it was the mining magnate H. A. Tabor and his wife Baby Doe[5] who helped keep me occupied during Wyatt's absences. We partied, went riding, had sumptuous dinners, played genteel card games, gossiped, did the shops and generally had a very good time together.

Wyatt never struck it rich or even made a promising find; however, he always managed to make a good enough living through investments or gambling. He often financially backed games of chance run for him by others.

Wyatt also worked for Wells Fargo on occasions, just as he had in Arizona. He continued to investigate for the company off and on until the turn of the century. Jim Hume, the chief investigator for Wells Fargo, was a life-long friend of Wyatt. I might point out that this is a strong refutation of the lies alleging that the Earps were stage-robbers in Tombstone.

Gradually my prospecting jaunts with Wyatt taught me to enjoy the outdoor life. We also went on hunting and fishing trips. I remember one campout with John O'Toole,[6] his wife and Bat Masterson. We hired a big covered wagon and set out for the Laramie River. The wagon carried our bed rolls and camping supplies, and I made sure personally that it was amply supplied with good things to eat.

"What are you going for?" Wyatt teased me. "You can't shoot a gun. I'll bet you don't even know which end the bullet comes out of. Furthermore you can't bait a fishhook."

I told him, "I'm going along to see that you great hunters and fishermen don't have to depend on your own kills for something to eat!"

Wyatt decided he'd better make a rifle-shooter of me anyhow, just to justify my presence. He showed me how to hold and shoot the gun and explained the fine points of aiming to me. He then encouraged me to put the rifle to my shoulder and aim at a knot on a tree. Standing by ready to laugh was Bat Masterson, who didn't do a thing for my self-possession.

"Don't get in a hurry to shoot," Wyatt explained. "Concentrate on holding the gun on the target and squeeze the trigger easy till she lets go."

"And get ready to pull leather when she bucks!" Bat added. That did it. I'd seen guns kick up when the men shot them. The thought of the kick from the gun was too much for me. I'd heard men use such expressions as "She kicks like a mule!" I dropped the gun and ran for our tent. Mrs. O'Toole was sympathetic, but the men just roared. Wyatt never tried to teach me to shoot again, although I learned to get by passably in an emergency.

I'm sure many will be disappointed to find my story of our life filled with so many of these commonplace incidents, but this was largely the way it was. After leaving Tombstone, Wyatt desired nothing more than to renounce completely the life of a lawman. Therefore the reader will have to content himself with the fairly mild diet of our everyday life. For me, it held just the right amount of excitement.

For example, one day we were trying to get from Ouray, Colorado, to Silverton.[7] These are mining camps high in the Rocky Mountains. It was early spring, and the snow was still deep. We left Ouray in a buckboard but had not gone far when we found the snow too heavy to proceed and returned to the hotel at Ouray. But Wyatt was determined to reach Silverton; he got a mule for me to ride while he walked.

"You'd better put on overalls," he told me. "Those skirts will be wet before we get halfway to Silverton." But I was ashamed to wear men's clothes. Wyatt finally convinced me they were the only sensible things to wear.

The mule was frisky, and I was so bundled up I could hardly manage him. As a matter of fact, I was afraid of him. When we reached a little camp called Iron Mine we got a burro for me to ride in place of the mule.

The snow was deep, but we were able to get along on the rocky ridges where it was thinner. As we topped the summit we met three men coming up from Silverton. Two were reporters from a Chicago paper and the third a Denver newspaper man.

"We can't believe our eyes!" said one. "Here we've been trudging through this upended wilderness of snow all day without seeing a soul!" Obviously they were surprised to find a woman way up there.

We talked for awhile and they took our name and address. They were interested when they heard Wyatt's name, and one of them said, "I never realized before that Wyatt Earp was a real flesh-and-blood man."[8] This reporter had read some of the lurid hogwash written concerning my husband, Bat Masterson, Wild Bill Hickock and their type.

Some time later we received in the mail a copy of the Chicago newspaper with a glowing account of our chance meeting on a remote mountain summit. The article went something to the effect of: "The prettiest sight we have ever seen — the snowy mountain wilderness, the brown-eyed goddess, the blond Apollo who turned out to be none other than the famous Wyatt Earp, tamer of wild western desperados" and several other such flowery phrases. Some more hogwash, in other words.

Sometime after we got to Colorado I recall Wyatt saying, "In her heyday there was probably never any place like Dodge!" The first time I saw the town in 1883 I would have been hard put to see why there was never any place like it. It looked like all the other rundown prairie towns.

Wyatt must have been attracted to it by memories. I could tell by his reminiscing that he was considering a visit back to his old stamping grounds. But in the end it was circumstances that called us back to Dodge. The event was a testimonial to the stature of my husband in the eyes of the people of that city.

It seems that Luke Short,[9] an old friend of Wyatt and Doc, was in trouble with the city fathers. Bat, who had been sheriff at Dodge when Wyatt was deputy marshal, had gone back to see if he could help Luke. Bat was highly regarded by most of the people of Dodge, but he also had made enemies. These were strong in the city government of which Luke had run afoul.

The best face that can be put on the affair is to admit that both Bat and Luke were run out of Dodge at gunpoint. As Bat later said, "Those old boys were downright serious. I looked down a double barrel that was about right for a narrow-gauge railroad tunnel and decided to keep right on going while I still had a whole skin. All around I was damn glad to see that iron hoss pull out of the station."

Bat wrote Wyatt regarding the situation. Reading the letter, Wyatt observed to me, "We may have to take a little trip to Dodge. How would that suit you?"

"Fine," I told him. I was always ready to see new scenery. Besides I recalled stories Bat had told me of Wyatt's lawing days in Dodge City. I had sometimes wondered though if Bat were not over enthusiastic in his estimate of Wyatt. On this trip I became satisfied that perhaps he was not. People in Dodge whose integrity was above question told me eyewitness stories that verified what Bat said.

If they all told the truth, then Wyatt certainly must have possessed, as Bat put it, "a strange power over men." He had again and again without touching a weapon walked up to men known to be dangerous outlaws, some of whom had their six-shooters in their hands, and cooly requested them to hand their weapons to him. Whatever the reason may have been, these bad men tamely handed over their arms and were placed under arrest. Bat said, "It takes more guts to arrest a desperate man peaceably than to shoot him and discuss the case later. No *other* man I ever heard of did such things day after day as Wyatt did and lived. It often seemed to me he led a charmed life."

Luke's trouble was not of his own making, but he hadn't realized the extent of the forces allied against him and had played into their hands. A policeman by the name of Hartman had arrested some of Luke's employees. When Luke sought to obtain bail, he ran into Hartman, and they ended up shooting at each other. Luckily neither was hit. I suppose Luke was pretty hot under the collar over being pushed around. At any rate, he put himself in deep with the law by firing on an officer.

He used his shotgun to stand off the policemen who came to arrest him, sitting in his locked saloon till the next morning, but he had to come out sometime. When he finally negotiated with the officers, they promised a trip to justice court and said that the matter would end there.

Unbeknownst to Luke, the city administration had other plans in mind for him. When he was finally disarmed and helpless they escorted him to the jail, where he was given either of two choices — the eastbound or westbound train. He went east to Kansas City and promptly contacted Bat Masterson, with the final result being our trip to Dodge.

The upshot of our coming was that the city in-crowd, having a healthy respect for Wyatt and his friends, allowed Luke to return to Dodge. Wyatt arranged this through a meeting with the city council. Luke arrived, accompanied by Bat, a few days after our arrival.

Now that the odds were more in Luke's favor, the city's shotgun posse was not in evidence. Still he decided that it wouldn't be healthy for him to remain in Dodge after Wyatt and his friends pulled out again, so he sold out his interest. He moved to Fort Worth, where he was living when next we saw him.

While Luke was winding up his affairs, a group known as the Dodge City Peace Commission was formed to maintain peace in the city. Mr. Moonlight,[10] the adjutant general of Kansas, was the chairman, and the members consisted of Wyatt and several trusted friends of his and Luke's.

The trouble all blew over as quickly as it started, no one was injured and I'm glad I got to see Dodge City before it became a small farmers' market type of commercial village. It was still wild enough for anyone's taste in those days, though by no means as bad as it had been.

We returned from Dodge to Colorado, soon to embark on several years of wandering in the West. We made a trip to Texas later that same year. In our travels it turned out that Wyatt knew someone in almost every town we came to.

HISTORICAL NOTES AND EDITORIAL COMMENTS

1. The exact date of Josie's departure is uncertain, but it is likely that she stayed in Tombstone until at least March 25, 1882. On that date a money order number 5664 was recorded at Tombstone payable to Josie's mother, Mrs. H. Marcus of San Francisco. It was purchased in the name of Annie Lewellen. At first I assumed this might be a pseudonym of Josie's. However, the 1880 U.S. census for Tombstone shows an Annie Lewellen. Interestingly, in the 1920–1944 time frame, Josie often stayed with Sarah Lewellen in Los Angeles. Sarah was Annie's daughter and was about the right age to have gone to school in Tombstone with Albert Behan when Josie was his foster mother. Perhaps this is how Josie came to know Annie Lewellen well enough to have her purchase such a money order for her. Either Sarah Lewellen, or Josie using that name, corresponded with Albert Behan at Ajo, Arizona, as late as 1942. (Copy of money order in editor's collection; original in collection of Jeanne Devere, Tombstone, Arizona; letter from Sarah Lewellen to Albert Behan in Special Collections, University of Arizona Library, Tucson.)

2. It is quite understandable why Josephine at this point does not dwell on her marriage to Wyatt or on his meeting of and acceptance by her parents, since in all probability neither event occurred at this time. She had

a great deal to conceal in telling her story and did so by being noncommital. Her rejoining of Wyatt at San Francisco must have been simply another running away from home. Regarding a marriage to Wyatt, all Josie would say was that they were married by the captain of Lucky Baldwin's yacht beyond the three mile limit. (Letter from Mrs. Cason to Mrs. Irvine, February 13, 1959. See Boyer, *The Suppressed Murder of Wyatt Earp*, p. 83, for full text of this letter.)

3. William Barclay "Bat" Masterson was born November 24, 1853. His birthplace is not definitely established, but it was either eastern Canada or Illinois. His death certificate lists his place of birth as the U.S. His family came to Kansas from Illinois about 1870, settling in Sedgwick County near Wichita.

Bat and Wyatt met in Kansas, where both were Dodge City lawmen during the same period, roughly 1876–80. Bat became sheriff of Ford County in the election of 1877. He appears to have been an unusually enterprising and effective sheriff, popular locally but not without some enemies. His last official duty as sheriff was performed January 10, 1880, since he failed to gain reelection.

Bat drifted from Dodge City to Tombstone and back to Dodge, then went on to the boom towns of Colorado, gambling for his living in places such as Trinidad, Leadville, and Creede, and finally settling in Denver. Eventually he became a professional newspaper sports writer in New York, where he died at his desk at the *Morning Telegraph* on October 25, 1921. (Nyle H. Miller and Joseph Snell, *Why The West Was Wild*, pp. 314–449.)

4. This stop-over occurred on the way to Gunnison, where the Earps spent the better part of a year before they moved to Denver. Wyatt operated the faro games in Charlie Biebel's saloon. For some reason Josie slides over this Gunnison period. A brief description of Wyatt by Judd Riley, a Gunnison police officer of the early 1880s, serves to partially fill us in: "Earp was a fine looking man, tall with drooping moustaches that curled at the ends. He was quiet in manner and never created a bit of trouble here, in fact, he told us boys on the police force we could call on him if we needed help at any time. He was a dead shot, I guess; always wore two guns high up under his arms, but he never used them here." (Lake collection.)

5. Horace Austin Tabor (born November 26, 1830) and his first wife, Augusta, came to the Colorado "diggings" in the first "Pikes Peak or Bust" gold rush in 1859. Horace Austin, or Haw as everyone called him, drifted from camp to camp and had become a store-keeper at the site of Leadville when it was first incorporated in 1878. He was elected its first mayor. Rather reluctantly he provided a sixty-four-dollar grubstake to two prospectors that eventually led to a half-million dollars in silver as his share, plus another million netted from selling his one-third interest. From this point onward, everything Tabor became involved in panned out. When he invested five

hundred dollars for Marshall Field of Chicago, it netted the latter seven hundred thousand. By the time the Earps knew him in 1882, he had deserted his first wife for a young woman — Baby Doe — and was a multimillionaire. Characteristically, he died broke. (Amanda M. Ellis, *Bonanza Towns.*)

6. I have been unable to identify John O'Toole or find out anything more about him than what Josie relates here, which is from the Cason ms.

7. This little jaunt of more than twenty miles in the raw spring weather over Red Mountain Pass at eleven thousand feet, under the threat of unpredictable late blizzards, indicates Josie's devotion to Wyatt. It also illustrates Wyatt's hardiness and determination, qualities that existed quite apart from violence. Josie makes very little of these quite challenging expeditions, unless it is to overplay her timidity, as she does here. It is obvious that she was a spunky character in her own right.

8. Of interest is this evidence of Wyatt's nationwide fame *in his own day,* a fact which modern debunkers have tried to deny.

9. Luke Short was a Mississippi boy by way of Texas, who became a typical Western sporting man. Wyatt first met him when he was part owner of the Long Branch Saloon in Dodge City with Chalkley Beeson and Bill Harris, around 1876. Like most of his kind, Luke was a gunfighter when the occasion demanded, killing two rather well-known pistoleers in his time —Charlie Storms in Tombstone and Long-Haired Jim Courtright in Fort Worth. He died at Geuda Springs, Kansas, of dropsy on September 8, 1893. He is buried in the Oakwood cemetery at Fort Worth. (William R. Cox, *Luke Short and His Era.*) For the best coverage ever done on the Dodge City troubles of Luke Short, see the foregoing reference.

10. Thomas Moonlight later became territorial governor of Wyoming, appointed in 1887 by Grover Cleveland. Mrs. Earp's principal recollection of him was that his stomach seemed to growl a lot. Wyatt laconically suggested to her that the adjutant general simply might not be up to Dodge City cooking. (Cason notes.)

⚓ 8 ⚓

More Wandering With Wyatt

Wyatt and I were discovering new things about each other each day, just as all new couples do. One of the first things we realized we had in common was an insatiable desire to travel — to see new people and places.

Naturally it wasn't long before we left Colorado. We set out excitedly for Idaho in the late winter of 1883–84, after hearing the news of the silver-mining boom in the Coeur d'Alene.[1] Wyatt's older brother Jim had preceeded us there, coming over from Montana where he had been for some time the previous year.[2]

On the road to the Coeur d'Alene I got some real insight into Wyatt's gentle character through Dickie, my yellow canary. Bat Masterson's wife had given Dickie to me, knowing my great fondness for pets of all kinds. I insisted against Wyatt's wishes that we must take the bird along. He told me, "The poor little thing will freeze!" But my husband's words made no great impression on me. I was not going to leave my beloved Dickie behind, no matter what the risks were.

However, it wasn't me that fussed and fidgeted over Dickie throughout the trip. The bird's safe arrival was mainly due to Wyatt's seeing that I didn't neglect the feeding and watering containers. And it was Wyatt who saw to wrapping an extra overcoat around the cage after I'd covered it for the night. Due to Wyatt's thoughtful care, Dickie arrived in fine feather and voice. The cheerful little thing's flitting and warbling did much to cheer us up in the lonely surroundings of new mining camps, such as Eagle City.[3]

Dickie was not our only pet. Someone gave Wyatt a tame bear cub who kept us in stitches with his clown-like ways. More unusual yet were the two young beavers that someone or other gave to Jim, who promptly presented them to me. We provided a tub of water for a playground so they'd feel at home. They were interesting to watch but too wild to really make pets of. One morning we arose to find them gone. They never returned. I hope they found a happy life somewhere in the wilderness.

Wyatt and Jim located and developed several claims. In addition they operated the White Elephant Saloon for several months. But the mining prospect didn't really pay off. We left Idaho that fall headed for Texas, where the winter was bound to be warmer. We'd had our fill of cold weather for a while.[4]

Wyatt was in the employ of Wells Fargo on this Texas trip. I don't recall much about the case, except that we later met Bat Masterson in Texas engaged on the same investigation, which led to Mexico where the trail was lost. They were probably tracing some fugitives.

In El Paso we met Lou Rickabaugh,[5] one of Wyatt's former partners from the Oriental Clubrooms in Tombstone. He now had a clubroom in El Paso. (Clubroom, of course, was a polite term for a gambling parlor.) He wanted Wyatt to stay, but my husband said he "had some other fish to fry" just then. While we were in El Paso a smart aleck drunken trouble-maker tried to pick a fight with Wyatt. His name was Raynor. Before he got into serious trouble with Wyatt someone else obligingly shot him to death.[6]

On this trip, which was in the spring of 1884, we went across Texas on the train. As we traveled through the farmlands in the eastern part of the state, now and then we would pass a plain, unpainted cabin looking pretty set in green fields and shaded by large trees. Some of these little dwellings were built of logs. The country was rolling and covered with flowers, oak thickets and nice little creeks.

Passing one of these cabins, I was impressed by its peaceful appearance. The sight of wood-smoke coming from its stone chimney made me feel that I'd love to call it my home. "How happy the people who live there must be!" I remarked to Wyatt.

My husband had been gazing from the window at the scene too. "Yes," he agreed. "But you wouldn't be happy living that way." It was as much a question as a statement of conviction.

"Oh, but I would, Wyatt!" I assured him. "I'd be happy living with *you* in a quiet, out-of-the-way place like that."

And that's all there was to the incident. More than a desire for stability, which in our hearts neither of us really wanted, it expressed a certain dissatisfaction with town life. But it was to be years before we could finally escape from the towns.

We made a stop in Fort Worth for several days to see Luke Short, who by now had an interest in a restaurant and clubrooms there, also, by coincidence, called the White Elephant. He mainly concerned himself with the gambling, which took place in the upstairs clubrooms. Wyatt and I had our evening meals in the restaurant below, which offered a menu as good as that in any large-city eatery. I suppose Fort Worth must have had twenty-five or thirty thousand population at that time. Wyatt would escort me back to our room at the Mansion House just a few doors up the street, then return to gamble. He struck a winning streak, and we were several thousand dollars richer when we left Fort Worth than when we came.

It may seem like a strange, lonely life for a woman, but I saw more of my husband than most women ever do. When alone there was always plenty to occupy me. Reading has always been one of my vices, and I read voraciously. There were always new people to meet too, and new things to see. Even the small things in life served to amuse me. At the Mansion House in the evenings when the street lights were lit, I used to watch the city urchins playing around the street, perhaps following the ice wagon returning from its daily route and leaping on the rear step to snitch a small sliver of ice to suck on.

Wyatt always returned by 1:00 or 2:00 A.M., and I usually waited up for him, since our days consisted of the same hours, rising around 10:00 or 11:00 A.M. In this way we took the mid-day and evenings meals together and spent our afternoons care-free as honeymooners, gadding about seeing the sights and doing the shops. Our third meal, if we had one, was a snack before bed, sometimes in an all-night restaurant if the town we were in had one. We did this every place we went, so, contrary to what one may think, it was actually a happy life for me.

Our next stop after Fort Worth was Austin. All this time Wyatt was still working on a case, and gambling was an ideal cover, since gamblers moved around on a regular circuit.[7] But Wyatt would tell me, jokingly, "You're my cover. Who would expect a man-hunter to take along his wife?"

We found it hard in those days, as it is in these, to find a good place to eat in a new and strange town. In Austin the year before we'd been lucky enough to find a place where they served fine steaks. We immediately looked it up to see if it was still operating. It was. As we were waiting for our food we talked of an encounter we'd had there on our first trip to Austin, the year before. One day as we had seated ourselves a man called out to my husband, "Well I'll be jiggered if it isn't Wyatt Earp!" I could see as he came over to our table that he was short, heavy set and slightly bald. I took him to be some sort of drummer or other. Wyatt introduced him as Mr. Thompson, but called him Ben.

"Ben and I knew each other in the Kansas days," Wyatt explained for my benefit. I was a little surprised to hear that he was the town marshal. Later someone told me he was a famous gunman and killer. I found that hard to believe. He'd impressed me as a gentleman and good company. Ben Thompson didn't look like he'd harm a fly, regardless of what they say about him. They probably made most of it up anyhow just as they have about Wyatt.[8]

We next went to San Antonio, where we were joined by Bat Masterson and two of his associates. From there we went to Laredo, Texas, on the Rio Grande. It lies across the river from the Mexican town of Nuevo Laredo. Whether we went over to the Mexican town for sightseeing or in the interest of Wells Fargo business, I cannot remember, but I went along as usual. I had never been in Mexico before and was anxious to see how the Mexicans lived in their own land.

It was fiesta time. The men of our party found plenty of games of chance in progress, for the Mexicans love gambling.

Monte was the game of chief interest as I recall. You'll laugh when I tell you what happened to Wyatt. He was wearing the expensive watch that had been given him by Senator George Hearst in Tombstone.[9] One evening when he was playing monte he got so interested in the play he forgot to keep his eye on the watch. When he left the table Bat glanced at him. "Your chain's hanging, Wyatt!" he exclaimed. "Where's your watch?"

Wyatt clapped his hand to his watch pocket. "My God!" he said, "They've touched me!"

He never got the watch back. Reporting it to the Mexican police was a waste of time.

HISTORICAL NOTES AND EDITORIAL COMMENTS

1. Unlike most Western mining excitements, the Coeur d'Alene District has been lucratively mined since the boom started in 1884, touched off by discovery of gold on Prichard Creek. This resulted in the development of the short-lived boomtown of Eagle, where the Earps spent their time in the Coeur d'Alene. Andrew Prichard is given credit for having led the first successful party into the district in search of gold. Eagle was soon supplanted by the town of Murray, then Wallace. The Coeur d'Alene District produced some two and one-quarter billion in ore from 1884 through 1967, including gold, silver, lead, zinc and copper, yielding fifty-seven million dollars in 1967 alone. (Richard G. Magnuson, *Coeur d'Alene Diary*.)

2. Family recollections are that Jim Earp settled in California and seldom left after Tombstone, the Coeur d'Alene being one exception; also the 1900 census showed him at Nome, though Josie didn't mention this. The family remembers him principally as a hack driver in and around San Bernardino for years. His wife died in that city in 1887. His income was supplemented by a pension for his Civil War disability. He apparently was close to Wyatt until his death in 1926. As Josephine later relates, he was on the desert with her and Wyatt after the turn of the century, when he was a man over sixty.

3. Richard G. Magnuson writes: "I am satisfied that Wyatt Earp was a deputy sheriff of Kootenai County in 1884.... At that time there was jurisdictional dispute between the sheriffs of Shoshone and Kootenai Counties regarding the gold fields around Eagle and Murray, Idaho." (Richard G. Magnuson, prosecuting attorney, Shoshone County, Idaho, to the editor, May 2, 1975.)

4. In her light summary of their period at Eagle City, which included the winter and spring of 1884, Josie consciously underplays the violence and gambling in Wyatt's career, as she does throughout her narrative. Undoubtedly she would have done the same regarding the Tombstone incidents had they not been so well known already.

At least three areas of controversy regarding the Earps' short Idaho sojourn deserve clarification. First, they were not guilty of widespread claim-jumping, as various debunkers have asserted. The Earps merely tested in court the validity of several claims previously filed by proxy. (Turner/Oster collection.)

Second, as deputy sheriff of Kootenai County, Wyatt entered the so-called "Battle of the Snowdrifts" as a peace-maker. This involved a gun-fight over lot-jumping, which pitted Wyatt's friend, gambler Dan Ferguson, and two other gamblers against the Buzzard brothers. Respectively forted up behind a log pile and a snowdrift, the two sides exchanged volleys until Ferguson eventually shot one of the Buzzards. The remaining brothers ran into a nearby cabin, at which point Wyatt walked out between the two groups and persuaded them to end the shooting. No one was arrested. (Lake collection.)

Later, the same Dan Ferguson killed a gunman named Tom Steele while trying to stop him from choking a prostitute. Ferguson was discharged after the coroner's inquest, but friends of the deceased gunman put the grand jury up to indicting the gambler. They even had the telegraph operator "fixed" so no one could warn Ferguson, who was out of town at the time. Wyatt persuaded the operator to send his friend a message by threatening to "beat him to death" if he didn't. (Lake collection.)

Wyatt's embroilments in Eagle City were similar to his adventures in other boomtowns. Clearly he was not the dove his wife would like us to believe he became immediately after Tombstone.

5. I have been unable to obtain reliable background material on Ricka-baugh beyond what Lake says Wyatt provided him (*Frontier Marshal*) and what little Josephine wrote of him in the Cason ms.

6. In his book *Wyatt Earp, Frontier Marshal*, Stuart Lake magnified this event into a classic showdown. A letter to Lake from one of Raynor's old friends who had been on the scene at the time makes it clear that Lake knew that Wyatt had had no encounter with Raynor personally, but that the writer used artistic license to add drama to his story. (Frank D. Scotten, Jr., to Stuart N. Lake, October 10, 1928, Lake collection.)

7. It is obvious that Wyatt's traveling the gambling circuit was more than just a cover; it was his major means of livelihood at the time. In the 1880s, the Southwest gambling circuit included all the mining boomtowns, whichever ones were in bonanza at the time, and such cities as Denver, Albuquerque, Fort Worth, Dallas, El Paso, Kansas City, Austin and New Orleans.

8. Lake asserted in *Frontier Marshal*, pp. 91–92, that Wyatt Earp arrested Ben Thompson in Ellsworth, Kansas, August 15, 1873, after Ben had stood off the whole town with a shotgun following the killing of Sheriff C. B. Whitney by Ben's brother Bill. It is perfectly obvious from the account in the *Ellsworth Reporter* (August 21, 1873) that the arrest of Ben Thompson was actually made by Deputy Sheriff Ed Hogue. (See Nyle H. Miller and Joseph W. Snell, *Why The West Was Wild*, p. 635, for a reprint of this news article.) Further, Lake must have been aware of this, since a copy of the same article is in his papers in the Huntington Library. Since Thompson had a reputation as a gunfighter on the order of Wild Bill Hickok, the allegation that Wyatt arrested him, particularly in the dramatic fashion described by Lake, would significantly build Wyatt's reputation as a gunslinger. This appears to be more of Lake's artistic license, and two random notes confirm that Josie thought so. Significantly, Wyatt never mentioned to her the highly dramatic alleged arrest of Ben Thompson. A letter to Lake appears in the Lake collection bearing the signature "Wyatt Earp," which acknowledges that Wyatt, contrary to the foregoing, did arrest Ben; however the signature is conclusively not Wyatt's.

9. Senator George Hearst, father of newspaper magnate William Randolph Hearst came to Tombstone early in 1882 to size up the town for investment purposes. He engaged Wyatt Earp as a bodyguard at that time, since there were rumors of an attempted kidnapping. Hearst fell sick while in Tombstone and was nursed by Josie. Apparently the Senator was quite taken by Wyatt and presented him with the gold watch mentioned here. With respect to the credibility of the kidnapping rumors, Hearst and Wyatt were sufficiently convinced of their reality to plant a phony newspaper story regarding the senator's departure time and route, then leave secretly at night ahead of time by a different route. (Cason notes.)

9

Home Again

Despite all our trotting around it seems to me that Wyatt and I always intended to make California our real home, even though we also loved Colorado. Our favorite towns among those we were to know on our travels were Denver, San Francisco[1] and Los Angeles. Since our families both lived there, we chose California for a home base.[2]

After Mexico, we returned to Colorado to pack some of the things we'd left behind and said goodbye to friends, then headed west. Wyatt wanted to see his parents, who were growing old, and I was pretty homesick myself.

We went by the southern route, stopping at Globe, Arizona, where Wyatt wanted to take in the gambling. This was our first time back to Arizona since leaving Tombstone. I didn't draw a relaxed breath during our entire time there. "Won't they arrest you if they find out you're in Arizona?" I asked.

"No, Sadie,"[3] he reassured me, "not with Johnny Behan and his crowd out of office."[4] We looked over the prospects at Globe. Wyatt gambled a little, but we decided not to stay.

Something happened just before we left that gave me much satisfaction at the time. I still get tickled thinking of the poetic justice of it. Wyatt ran into Johnny Behan in town.[5] If it had occurred a couple of years previously, Wyatt may have shot him. As it was he got back to our room grinning and whistling. He then did a thing very uncharacteristic of him, the nearest I ever saw him come to bragging. He blew on his knuckles and smiled at me.

"Whatever has you so tickled?" I wanted to know.

He chuckled. "I just met Johnny Behan down on the street. We almost bumped into each other. It reminded me I owed him something, so I put a real head on him."

"You what?" I asked, the term not being familiar to me then.

"I knocked him cold," Wyatt stated with satisfaction. He then poured some water in the washbowl and rinsed his hand.

If Wyatt said he knocked Johnny cold, he probably did a good job of it. I had heard, from Bat and others, of Wyatt's skill as a boxer. In the cowtowns he had whipped several bruisers a lot larger than he was and had done it quickly and thoroughly. I expected some repercussions from the law after Wyatt's impromptu bout with Johnny, but there were none.

Once on our way again, I felt relieved. We had a hot train trip to Colton, California, which was then a little desert town about five miles from San Bernardino. We were both pleased with the area we observed along the Colorado River, but never dreamed we'd some day spend many years in that country.

As we neared Colton I got pretty nervous. I had never met Pa and Ma Earp, as all the boys called them, but I'd heard enough of them to want them to like me. They were the kind of sturdy pioneer stock that had settled and civilized the country.

When I first met him Wyatt's father[6] was in his seventies, but he looked and acted twenty years younger. He was one of the peppiest people I ever knew, moving around like he was on springs and always interested in some project or other. The project when we arrived was growing oranges on the desert around Colton. He had set out several young trees, and they seemed to be thriving. He must have been one of the first to try it. Colton later became one of the big citrus-growing areas in the state.

Wyatt's married sister Adelia, who lived near there, had children who called Pa Earp "Grandpa," as Adelia did herself. Soon I started calling him Grandpa too; the old man loved it.

Wyatt's mother[7] was the quiet type, but always at the center of things, looking out for everyone. I never knew a better cook. And she was one of the sweetest people that ever lived. Wyatt's devotion to her was obvious. When she died in 1893 Wyatt never got over it. I could tell he was thinking of her loss for months afterward, and his eyes would grow misty right up to his death whenever we talked of her.

Wyatt and Virgil had purchased for their parents the house they were living in when we visited them. Virgil and his wife, Alvira, were also visiting in Colton, though they made their home in San Diego just then. Somewhat later, when Colton was first incorporated, Virge became the first marshal and Grandpa Earp became city clerk, recorder and justice of the peace.

Grandpa Earp loved all his girls, as he called us. When we first met he grabbed me and squeezed me like a long-lost daughter and rubbed his beard against my cheek. I remember he smelled pleasantly of soap, talcum, tobacco and leather. The soap was from his beard, of which he was inordinately fond. He washed it every day.

He was always kidding us girls. The first thing he said to me in a great booming voice was, "My goodness you're a little mite! I'll bet Wyatt has to shake the covers to find you in bed!"

I know I turned red as a beet, but this didn't stop him. It only tickled him and egged him on. "How about that, Wyatt?" he asked. Wyatt smiled, but didn't say anything to rescue me from my confusion.

Later Grandpa looked me over carefully again and observed to the world at large, "That's some filly you got there, Wyatt!"

I was more pleased than anything, since a body couldn't help but like Grandpa. He lived in a black-and-white world. I was family; this was clear from the first. Grandpa knew only two kinds of people — friends and enemies. His friends could do no wrong, and his enemies could do no right; I was sure glad to be family.

Wyatt's mother was a Southern woman with a soft Southern voice; hospitality and love radiated from every part of her. What Wyatt loved, she loved, and a whole world besides. Her life was full of kittens, puppies, birds, little wild animals that came to be fed, ragamuffins, the livestock on the place that all came to her like pets, her menfolks and their women and children, plus anyone and anything in need of help or encouragement. If they were

Nicholas Porter Earp and Virginia Ann Cooksey Earp, parents of the Earp boys, pose for a photographer on their golden wedding anniversary in San Bernardino, 1890. Nicholas is sporting the gold-headed cane Josie said he once broke over an enemy's head. It is clear that the boys all closely resemble their mother.

hurt or sick, all the more reason to love and tend them. I could see why Wyatt loved her so much. With her passing the world grew poorer indeed.

Will you believe me when I say they were a great family to be a member of? I am proud of it. I think it will be awhile before the sun shines on their like again.

The Earps all mixed upright pride with fierce family loyalty and spunk. One story about Grandpa Earp shows that last quality to a "T." It seems it was traditional to pass an honorary gold-headed cane to the oldest living member of the San Bernardino Pioneers' Society. Grandpa Earp got it in his turn. He hadn't had it long when someone said something to him to which he took exception (no doubt on his usual grounds of right, honor and justice). He broke the honorary cane over that unfortunate person's head! This was the patriarch of the Earps of San Bernardino County!

We stayed in Colton for a couple of weeks, then I decided to take the train home while Wyatt investigated Virgil's story of a real-estate boom which was starting in San Diego as a result of the arrival of the Santa Fe Railroad. Wyatt went home to San Diego with Virgil and his wife Allie.

The stories about San Diego proved true. Wyatt wrote telling me to join him there when my visit was over. This was our first real separation. The old saying that absence makes the heart grow fonder was certainly true in this case. He met me at the train and hugged and kissed me right in front of everyone, much to my surprise. He was usually quite shy about such things.[8]

I was innocently happy as only a young person can be. San Diego was a wonderful new place to find out all about. Wyatt and I had some of our most wonderful times together there.

Shortly after we settled in San Diego, who should turn up but Bat Masterson? In those days he frequently worked as a U.S. deputy marshal or sometimes as a private investigator for various express companies. Wyatt did the same. On such assignments, Bat kept crossing our path during the 1880s.

"What brings you down here, Bat?" Wyatt wanted to know.

"I'm going to Enseñada in the A.M. to pick up an army deserter. They tell me he's a pretty tough bird. When I heard you were in town I thought I'd ask you to come along, just to make darn sure this hombre doesn't get any ideas."

That made sense to Wyatt. There was no thought in his mind that Bat had any real fears about his ability to take care of himself, I'm sure. But this careful approach, so characteristic of both these men, may account for their survival to a ripe old age despite years in a dangerous business that claimed the lives of many. Neither of them took unnecessary chances.

Wyatt asked me "How about it, honey, you mind staying alone? Virge and Allie will put you up if you'd like."

I couldn't bear to be separated again so soon, even for a night. I wanted to go along and plainly said so.

"Why not, Wyatt?" Bat agreed. "I don't really expect any trouble. She might as well have an outing too."

"Suits me," my husband agreed. "Pack your grip."

The next morning we boarded a little coastwise steamer for Ensenada. I was a little nervous. The Ensenada of that day was a far cry from the tourist town it later became. I was pleasantly surprised when we found a clean little hotel operated by a "Norte Americano."

After Bat visited the justice court to make arrangements to pick up his prisoner, the three of us had a pleasant day together waiting for sailing time. Best of all we found a little posada that served delicious Mexican food. All three of us had picked up a taste for it on the border.

The little packet we were going back to San Diego on made the trip at night. Wyatt put me aboard in our cabin, then went to help Bat with the prisoner. I knew it was not five minutes' walk from the court to the pier. I got scared and nervous when the men didn't get right back. In a short time I heard a couple of gunshots somewhere. It brought back Tombstone. I was sure that the worst had happened to Wyatt and Bat.

When they finally did get back I almost fainted with relief. "What took you so long?" I asked Wyatt shakily. "I'm glad you're still alive! I heard shots!"

Wyatt regarded me in genuine surprise. My teeth were still chattering. "It's all right, honey, we had to wait for some sort of big wig on the night squad to show up. Like all of 'em, he had his hand out. It cost Bat a double eagle."

Bat took his prisoner to a cabin and shackled him to a steel berth riveted to the wall. "What if the boat sinks?" I asked. The prisoner, who didn't look tough but merely frightened, gave me a grateful look. I imagine when you're in such circumstances you're grateful for even the smallest kindness.

"We'll get him loose," Bat said. "But I don't see any lifeboats. Unless he can walk on water, he'll be in the same shape as all of us — loose or not."

A little later we got under way. I was almost asleep when someone knocked loudly on our door. We both thought it must be Bat. "Who is it?" Wyatt called out.

"The purser," a brusque voice answered in border patois, which we both understood.

"You'll have to vacate this cabin at once!" the purser informed us.

"Why?" Wyatt called in Spanish, still not opening the door.

"Because his excellency General Carlos Sancho Diego Morelos Morelos[9] such-and-such and his staff just came on board, and we must let the general have this cabin."

"The hell you say!" Wyatt said in English. "We paid for this cabin and we're staying right here!"

We were still in Mexican waters at this time, and I was scared out of my wits at the thought of defiance. I didn't know these people as well as Wyatt.

"Let them have the cabin, Wyatt; I don't mind moving!" I whispered in terror.

"Let me handle this," my husband told me. "Just keep quiet and stay where you are. We paid for this cabin, and I intend to keep it!"

"Open up!" the purser shouted, this time in English. "I tell you that you must give this cabin up for the general!"

"You'd better go away!" Wyatt suggested, and an edge of steel crept into the quiet voice. "Put the general in the cabin you want us to move into."

"You must get out! Captain's orders!" the purser argued.

Wyatt said no more. In a while we could hear the purser move off. Neither of us really expected it to end there. We were not disappointed. Voices could be heard, then footsteps. A loud knock on our door followed.

"Open up!" a commanding voice ordered. "I am the captain!" I earlier had noted the captain's small stature. Now it became apparent that he had the pompous self-importance that so often accompanies the sawed-off individual.

"I'm not opening the door tonight," Wyatt stated flatly. "I'll open it in San Diego and not before!"

"Open the door at once!" the captain blustered.

Wyatt's reply was quiet and controlled, but his voice had a quality to it I had never heard before and would only hear a few times after.

"If you don't go away and leave us alone," he said in slow, clear, measured words, "I'll throw you overboard."

The captain went away, blustering some more to someone with him.

That spoiled my night. I tossed and turned until dawn. I awoke in the A.M. with Wyatt shaking me. "What is it?" I asked, still half asleep and afraid something else terrible was happening.

Wyatt grinned. "We're in San Diego!"

"Oh thank heaven!" was all I could say, dressing in a hurry so we could escape that dreadful little tub. I heaved a tremendous sigh of relief when my feet touched solid ground.

Bat's prisoner awkwardly removed his hat when he saw me. Bat had unshackled him on his promise not to make a break. "Goodbye, ma'am," the prisoner said, somewhat to my surprise.

"Goodbye," I replied. "Vaya con Dios!"

It was Wyatt's and Bat's turn to look surprised. Wyatt grinned slightly. When Bat and his prisoner had moved beyond earshot, Wyatt leaned over near my ear. "Softie!" he said.

"So what if I am? He looks like a scared boy!"

"I've seen scared boys just like him kill some good men as quick as you can blink your eyes," Wyatt told me.

We heard the sequel to our shipboard showdown from Pedro Manriquez,[10] the steamship company's agent and a friend of

Wyatt's. The captain had stalked in and informed Pedro he was demanding the arrest of a passenger who had threatened and defied him.

"And who might that be?" Pedro inquired. The captain gave him our cabin number, and Pedro checked the passenger list. "Hmmm!" he observed. "Wyatt Earp! And you say he threatened to throw you overboard?"

"Yes!" snorted the captain indignantly.

"Then you're lucky to be here," Pedro said. "Do you know who Wyatt Earp is?"

"Who cares?" the captain shouted.

Pedro decided to lay it on thick, since he had never liked the pompous little pipsqueak. "Have you heard of the terrible American town of Tombstone, Arizona? It is said that Wyatt Earp killed at least half of the population there in a single afternoon!"

Pedro had never before lied to the captain, who wasn't smart enough to suspect a company official of pulling his leg. The visibly impressed man inquired, "Was this a very big town?"

"The largest in the territory," Pedro assured him, without knowing he was actually telling the truth. "Of course his brothers are said to have helped him."

"Madre de Dios!" the captain muttered, crossing himself. "A terrible family! I could tell from his voice." He rushed to the window to catch a glimpse of Wyatt's retreating form, then shook his head in wonder.

When I asked Wyatt why he had been so sure the captain would back down he said, "The little such and so wasn't a big enough man for his job — it stuck out all over him."

⌒⌒⌒

HISTORICAL NOTES AND EDITORIAL COMMENTS

1. Wyatt called San Francisco his favorite town. (Wyatt Earp to George Earp, February 13, 1928, editor's collection.)

2. Although Wyatt and Josephine called California home from 1885 onward, I have been unable to ascertain whether they ever actually owned a house there, other than their cottage at Vidal, pictured in Chapter 18. When living in Los Angeles they rented various small houses and apart-

ments, and in San Francisco they either rented or stayed with relatives. This is revealed by their correspondence in the editor's collection and by city directories; for example, in 1893 their San Francisco residence was at the address of Josephine's mother, whose husband had recently died.

3. The entire Earp family, including Wyatt, called Josephine by her middle name, Sarah, and shortened it to Sadie. To outsiders she was Josephine by her preference; this is the name by which the Casons knew her. (Cason notes and conversations of the editor with Mrs. William Miller, San Bernardino, 1965; Mrs. Miller was Wyatt's niece and had been named Estelle Josephine after Mrs. Wyatt Earp.)

4. Behan and his political cohorts left office at the close of the year 1882, when their official terms expired. Both Johnny and his partner in the livery stable, County Treasurer John Dunbar, left office under a cloud. (See Chapter 4, note 12.)

5. I have found no other documentation regarding this encounter, but do not question its having occurred. Behan, a ubiquitous small-time office holder, popped up in many locations during his career; he was probably looking over the prospects for landing some political job at this time.

6. Nicholas Porter Earp, son of Walter and Martha Early Earp, was born in North Carolina on September 6, 1813. Wyatt's mother, Virginia, was his second wife, the first having been Abigail Storm, mother of Newton Earp, the half brother of the more famous Earp boys. Nicholas married Virginia Ann Cooksey July 30, 1840, at Hartford, Kentucky. She bore him five sons and three daughters; of the latter Martha and Virginia Ann died young, and only Adelia, born in 1861, survived to adulthood. Nicholas died on November 12, 1907, in the Soldiers' Home at Sawtelle, California. (Colyn collection; Earp genealogy in the editor's collection.)

7. Virginia Ann Cooksey Earp was born in Kentucky on February 2, 1821, and died in San Bernardino, California, on January 14, 1893. (Colyn collection; Earp genealogy.)

8. Undoubtedly Wyatt was publicly undemonstrative, although far from as bashful with ladies as Josie sometimes suggests. See Chapter 10, note 1, for Wyatt's extramarital interests.

9. This appears to have been an attempt at humor on Josie's part, mocking the Latin tendency to have lengthy names, perhaps coupled with deliberate omission of the real name, since no such officer appears in the Mexican army register of that time. If this was the actual name of the dignitary, perhaps the title was honorary.

10. It is my suspicion that Pedro Manriquez's relationship with Wyatt had more to do with business than friendship and that Pedro was an informer. It is probable that Wyatt was moonlighting then and for many years afterward as a detective, or less politely, as a bounty-hunter. This is, of course, only speculation based on unconnected information regarding Wyatt's otherwise rather odd occasional excursions.

10

San Diego and
Our Horse-Racing Days

Wyatt was a handsome man. He was tall with a trim, erect figure, and he was unusually muscular and powerful for his build. He was also quick and graceful as a cat. His dress was always neat but inconspicuous. His habits of grooming and personal cleanliness were all any woman could hope for in her ideal.

Wyatt's personal exploits and those of his brothers had been widely publicized in the papers. All this adds up to the fact that women were attracted to my husband. And he admired good-looking women as well.[1] This posed a problem for me early in our marriage. I didn't quite know how to handle it.

Fortunately Wyatt was soon greatly absorbed in real-estate transactions. He made a great deal of money during this period of our lives and owned many saloons and much real estate. Later he let most of this slip through his fingers due primarily to his generosity in financing friends in unwise mining ventures. I would guess that at the peak of our prosperity Wyatt may have been worth a half-million dollars.[2]

It was during this period of our lives that we started a custom that smoothed out some rough spots in our marital relations. Our friends who knew of it laughed, but it worked so well I merely recommended it to them. Like any couple, we had our differences.[3] Wyatt seldom found fault with me, probably far less than is the case with the average husband. I had little to complain of as a result. But it's inevitable that a couple living together will have disagreements. How easily these little flareups can develop into complete domestic dissolution if one or the other won't back off or listen to reason.

I sometimes flew off the handle over little things. Other times I thought I was justified. Like most women, I fell back at such times on my handiest weapon, words. If what I said did not rile my husband too much, he simply grinned and took it. But when I got him mad he would fill and light his pipe, put on his hat and walk out. Any wife who has had this happen knows that it is the most exasperating thing a husband can do to her. Tears do no good with no one to see them.

I was determined to find a means of getting even with Wyatt, and one day when he walked out I had an inspiration. I simply sat down and finished my speech to him on paper. By then I was beginning to think it was funny and must have conveyed that in my note, without leaving unsaid anything that I had wanted to say in the first place.

Leaving the note in a conspicuous place, I went to a friend's home nearby. I watched until, in an hour or two, I saw my husband come back. Then I hurried home.

There was Wyatt, hands in his pockets, reading my note, a broad grin on his face. We looked at each other and laughed. So we started the custom that prescribed good humor as the medicine for most of our domestic difficulties thereafter. Wyatt always called the notes my "love letters" and told our friends how they always allowed me the "last word."

To add to the harmony of our marriage, I studied Wyatt's tastes in food and learned to cook well. I botched a lot at first, but my husband understood. His taste was for simple food, and one of the first things I learned to make was cornbread. Wyatt, being of Southern extraction, had learned to love it. As the years passed, I got to be an excellent cornbread-baker.

Wyatt also loved hot biscuits, especially with butter, strawberry preserves, and coffee. They were the last meal that he ate, a day or two before he died. He could be entirely happy as well with only plain bread and milk. But I learned to cook more complicated dishes because Wyatt enjoyed inviting his friends to our home and was proud of my meals.[4]

It may surprise you to know that Wyatt was fond of the theater and was especially partial to Shakespearean plays. When he heard that the famous Lily Langtry was to appear in "As You Like It," he bought tickets.

We made lots of friends in San Diego, who continued to see us for years afterward. One of these was Eliza Burns, whom I continued to visit long after Wyatt died. Our first rooms in San Diego were in the home of her mother.[5]

Those were the days when San Diego was coming out of its Mexican serape and putting on an American suit. The tourists hadn't got there yet, thank goodness. We were visiting Coronado Island across the bay when it was subdivided into the lots they built all those old mansions on. The lots were sold from a big tent, and it seemed like a circus to me. This was my first experience with a real-estate boom. We saw the foundations laid for the old Hotel del Coronado. It became the ritzy spot.

I mentioned that Wyatt was practically a teetotaler. It was there in San Diego that I saw my husband under the influence of liquor for the first time since I had known him. Several fiction writers have represented Wyatt standing at a bar drinking hard liquor. As a matter of fact, he drank very little at any time in his life and, until this period in San Diego, would refuse even to take a drink. He simply had never cared for liquor.

Mr. Fortlouis[6] opened a wholesale liquor house in San Diego, and all the businessmen of the city and many others attended his opening. Wyatt, of course, was there and drank enough of the champagne that was served in honor of the occasion to upset his equilibrium. When he came home he was laughing.

"What *is* the matter with you, Wyatt?" I asked.

He smiled at me in an absent-minded sort of way and without answering hurried with his undressing. He hung up his clothes with less care than usual and went on chuckling to himself as though he had a secret joke. He flopped into bed, heaved a great sigh, waved agreement toward some shadowy companion of his mental haze, and said, "I'm wise to the proposition!" Then he fell immediately asleep.

One night Wyatt returned from one of his absences at what he described as a "friendly little game" at the place of Mr. E. B.

Gifford. "How would you like a fine trotting racehorse?" he asked.

I thought he'd been on champagne again. "Whatever for?" I queried. "Why would you ask a question like that at a time like this?"

"Well," Wyatt said, yawning and stretching as he sat on the bed to take off his shoes, "we've got one whether we like it or not."

"What did you buy a racehorse for? Where will we keep him?"

"I didn't exactly buy him. A fellow named Jim Leach sorta donated him to me in a poker game."

So this was how Wyatt got his first racehorse. His name was Otto Rex. I fell in love with him the first time I laid eyes on him. How could anyone who has ever been around truly fine horses fail to love them? I even love the poor dear plugs that pull the junkmen's wagons. I never fail to pat one when they are hitched at the curb.

Later we bought other racehorses. These beautiful, intelligent animals were a source of great joy to me and Wyatt. I got acquainted with each one individually. Each had a personality, just like humans. Mr. Gifford⁷ became Wyatt's racing partner. It was the beginning of a new era for us.

My ignorance of horses in those days made me the butt of a family joke. Wyatt and I were returning from the turf club at Pacific Beach where they had been exercising the horses. He was driving two dark bay thoroughbreds pulling a light rubber-tired buggy, and we were stepping some. Gifford, driving his finest horse, a trotter called Logan, came up behind us with a light rubber-tired buggy like ours. When Wyatt saw that his partner was trying to pass us, he whipped up the bays, and the race was on.

I did my best to hang on. "Don't go so fast, Wyatt!" I yelled. "You can beat him anyway. Two horses can surely outrun one!"

Even in the midst of the excitement of the race Wyatt had to laugh. He didn't let me forget it. Whenever I talked through my hat he would say, "Two horses can surely beat one!"

Mr. Gifford and Wyatt took their trotters, with several other horses they had bought, around the California circuit — San Francisco, Santa Rosa, Napa, Exposition Park in Los Angeles, and

Santa Ana. Of course I went with Wyatt. I sat in the grandstands and watched him. My handsome husband fairly flew over the track in his rubber-tired sulky behind a sleek trotter. As in games of chance, he wore a poker face.

Back in our racing days we made a lot of friends. Among these were Lucky Baldwin[8] and his daughter, Clara Baldwin Stocker.[9] Lucky bred fine horses on his great Santa Anita Rancho. Wyatt often worked his horses out there. I saw a different side of Lucky than we heard about in the papers. He was an unusual character. He never placed bets on his own horses, but he was as delighted as those who had when any of them came in first. He never drank, and he neither smoked nor swore. His strongest language was, "By gaddies!" which he accompanied by an irritated motion of the right hand pulling his left lapel across his chest.

A lot of gossip has been written condemning Lucky, which may or may not be true, but he had many friends who seemed to care sincerely for him. He was an entertaining companion, and because of many mutual interests,[10] Wyatt and I saw a lot of him in those days.

I'll never forget the first race that Wyatt won. It was in Santa Rosa. Our horse Jim Leach came in first, with Wyatt driving. Charlie Durfee was driving another of our trotters called McKenny, a thoroughbred we all considered a favorite. We felt quite certain that McKenny would far outrun Jim Leach. When I saw Jim Leach leading and Wyatt sailing along guiding him I forgot all about McKenny and rooted for Jim Leach.

"Well, honey, what do you think of the racing game now?" Wyatt asked me that night when we returned home.

I said something like "Oh, it's fine, Wyatt! I never was so excited in my life as I was when I saw Jim Leach winning over all those other horses!"

"Even McKenny?" he asked me slyly.

"Yes, even McKenny. All I could see was you and Jim Leach, and I forgot everything else. I yelled myself hoarse!"

Wyatt sat for a moment regarding me thoughtfully. "Are you game enough to take the losses too?"

Elias Jackson "Lucky" Baldwin, his daughter Clara, his granddaughter Rosebudd and his great-grandson Joseph. The Earps were social intimates of this elegant-living multi-millionaire and his family.

"Well," I answered with a laugh, "I suppose I'll have to be, but I'm so excited now over our winning that I don't feel as though we could ever lose!"

But we did. Sometimes our fortunes were up, sometimes they were down,[11] but there was always Wyatt with me, and nothing mattered a great deal to me so long as I had him.

Later my husband had racing stables in the old Bay District in San Francisco. This suited me well, for San Francisco was home to me, and many of my relatives lived there and in Oakland.

Our colors were navy blue polka dots on a white field. By far the most famous jockey to wear them was Tod Sloan, who added to his distinction by riding two of our horses to victory in one day. Our stable was, of course, much too small to keep on the payroll such a highly paid jockey as Tod Sloan. He was one of a number who were "loaned" to our stables for certain races by some of the owners of bigger "strings" than ours.

In our stable Wyatt had two maiden two-year-olds, Don Aguirre and Cardwell, which Tod Sloan was to ride for us one day. In the first race he rode Don Aguirre to a win. We were elated over the winning of that race and felt that the day was a complete success whether our second entry made a showing or not.

When Tod mounted Cardwell we hoped, of course, for a win, but with one already we didn't expect too much. Cardwell was fast though. We watched him with as much suspense as if he had been our only hope for the day. Tod put his best efforts into his management. He came in first! With two victories in one day, considering the size of our "string" we felt we were doing all right.

Wyatt had formed the habit of celebrating our winnings by buying me a piece of jewelry, and I believe it was then that he bought me a beautiful bracelet all set with rubies. I never dared ask the price, for I knew I would feel that we could not afford as much and that would spoil my pleasure in the gift. At another time he brought me a brooch in the form of a peacock that was encrusted with diamonds.

Of all Wyatt's horses, the one I liked best was called Lottie Mills. She was a thoroughbred he had bought in San Francisco, and one of the most affectionate and intelligent animals I have ever known. She would nuzzle my husband's shoulder whenever he went to the stable. Usually he carried sugar lumps for her. He returned this horse's devotion with a warmth that only a true lover of animals can appreciate.

Lucky Baldwin and a judge from New Orleans and several other men wanted to buy Lottie Mills, but Wyatt didn't want to part with her. After winning several races in San Francisco, he shipped her with some others to the World's Columbian Exposition in Chicago in 1893.

Lucky, who was in Chicago with some of his horses, often sat with me in the grandstand. Wyatt, of course, was engaged most of the day with his animals. He went to the stables early every morning, and I would go later from the hotel directly to the stables to be with him for a little while before going up to the grandstand for the races.

One day I passed a spot where some stable boys were shooting craps four or five stables from ours. As I passed I overheard one of them say, "I'm going to bet this on Lottie Mills; she going to run in the seven-furlong race. She's a bottled-up cinch!" Then he added, "She belongs to that big Missourian over yonder."

My husband was pleased when I told him what I heard. And she was a favorite that day and won her race. We finally sold our Lottie Mills to Barney Schrieber for breeding purposes after she had served her day on the track.

Buffalo Bill[12] had his Wild West Show at the fair in Chicago. My husband had known him slightly in the early days of buffalo hunting and introduced me to him. He was a pink-cheeked man with mustache, goatee, and flowing hair. He always rode a beautiful pony and was as straight and agile as a boy.

One race that Wyatt and I watched in company with Lucky Baldwin stands out in my memory. It was at the derby in Chicago. The stakes were very high, a hundred thousand dollars. There were many notable entries. An immense crowd was in attendance. One of the entries was a little-known horse named Boundless owned by a poor man who was also little known to the racing world. The horse, it was said, had never so much as possessed a blanket, and his coat lacked the sleek, groomed look which could only be maintained by the attention of tireless and expensive grooms. We all hoped he would at least come in the money. The crowd went wild when the unknown Boundless won. It meant riches to the owner.

Lucky Baldwin was tickled pink that an almost penniless man should make such a sudden leap to wealth. It took him back to his own surprising rise from poverty. In those days there were no income taxes to diminish the purse. Consider also that a working wage might be only three hundred and fifty dollars annually.

The years that Wyatt spent in racing saw us in many places during the track season — Santa Rosa, Chicago, Tanforan, Latona, Cincinnati, Saint Louis, Kansas City, Santa Anita and many another track in many a town. I can still see it all, the jockeys, both black and white, in blue-and-white polka dot satin, in crimson, rose, gold, purple, and green satin; horses, bay and brown, sorrel and black, legs flying, jockeys crouched low on their withers, or sulkies flying like birds behind them; crowds with people screaming, yelling, roaring; bright banners, trumpets, gay parties, lovely women, handsome men, special trains, horsey smells, music, brave laughter — and Wyatt coming home to me. If he had won, the light of triumph was in his eyes; if he had lost, there was the gleam of hope for a better showing next time.

Wyatt often remarked, "Someone must lose every race, and a fellow who wants to stay with racing might as well make up his mind to take his turn at losing along with the rest and be cheerful about it." *Cheerful* was one of Wyatt's favorite words.

HISTORICAL NOTES AND EDITORIAL COMMENTS

1. This is a case of understatement. As Josephine was well aware, Wyatt was what could be termed a "skirt-chaser." That she knew of her husband's philandering has been confirmed in the Cason notes as well as by Jeanne Cason Laing. In addition, Wyatt's nephew by marriage, Bill Miller, the husband of Wyatt's sister Adelia's daughter Estelle, offered the following comment: "Why, Wyatt was a good-looking fellow! He probably had a gal in every port, just like a sailor." (Cason notes; Jeanne Cason Laing tape, 1975, in editor's collection; conversation of editor with Bill Miller, San Bernardino, 1965.)

2. Octogenarian Carmelita Mayhew, who knew the Earps since their Harqua Hala days, said that Wyatt was quick to grubstake a friend; in her opinion, money meant very little to him. She believed that Wyatt had sunk much of his San Diego stake into Harqua Hala and lost it. (Conversation of editor with Carmelita Mayhew, Yuma, Arizona, 1957.) It is likely that Josephine's estimate of her husband's net worth in the late 1880s is grossly exaggerated. A study of Wyatt's San Diego real-estate transactions by Al Turner and Bill Oster indicates that his probable gains were nominal from that source. However, Agent G. W. Caldwell, representing the Bancroft book sales agency in 1888, sold a Bancroft history set to Wyatt, who represented his worth as $30,000, to include $6,000 cash. This seems reasonable, and it should be recalled that by modern standards this would amount to at least $180,000. (Turner/Oster collection and G. W. Caldwell's records of sales, Bancroft Library, University of California, Berkeley.)

3. This is another understatement by Josie. Long-time Earp family friend John Flood observed that the main reason he never married was the example set by Josie as a domestic partner. As indicated in the introductory section of this book, Wyatt's wife could be peevish and domineering and was well known for her quick temper. (Conversation of editor with John Flood, Jr., Yuma, Arizona, 1956, and Laing tape.)

4. She became a gourmet cook in regard to Wyatt's favorite dishes. (Laing tape.)

5. Mrs. Burns was a respectable boardinghouse keeper in San Diego. The Lake/Earp letters mention plans of the Earps to stay with Eliza during a projected trip to San Diego in 1928. Apparently the excursion was called off due to Wyatt's terminal illness.

6. Albert T. Fortlouis was a German immigrant about Wyatt's age who had served a hitch in the U.S. army. He became a wine and cigar merchant in Tombstone when the Earps were there and a liquor merchant in San Diego, apparently being primarily a businessman rather than a member of the sporting crowd. (Cochise County Great Register, 1882; Cason notes; Lake collection.)

7. The obituary of Eli Bruce Gifford in the *San Diego Union* of July 6, 1908, is typically discreet regarding this pioneer's activities. In part it specifies: "Deceased was a native of New York, 77 years of age.... [He] came to San Diego in 1868 and returned to the mines at Mokalmune Hill, Calaveras County, and disposed of his interest and returned to San Diego to make this city his home in 1869.... For several years he took an active interest in owning and developing good horses. He was a member of the San Diego lodge No. 153, I.O.O.F., also the Veteran Odd Fellow and Masonic lodge."

The inaccuracies of this obituary, whether due to tact or error, are not unusual when the subject involved is a frontier figure such as Gifford. The 1869 date for his San Diego residence is particularly questionable, since the directories of that city do not list him before 1889. (Rhoda E. Kruse, San Diego Library, to the editor June 6, 1975.) Furthermore, other sources make it clear that E. B. Gifford was living in Tucson in 1886, when the Thirteenth Legislature granted that city the state university if it could come up with the land within the year. E. B. Gifford and Ben C. Parker, owners of the "biggest gambling layouts" in town, and Billy Reid, proprietor of the "finest saloon," donated the desert acres upon which the University of Arizona was built. (*Arizona Daily Star* [Tucson], June 9, 1975, "Beer and Poker Chips To Honor Founders.")

Of additional interest is the fact that Gifford was in the Arizona House of Representatives, Eleventh Session, in 1881, the session that created Cochise County, and hence must have known County Ring members Thomas Dunbar and Harry Woods. One wonders what reminiscences Gifford and Wyatt shared regarding them. (Jay J. Wagoner, *Arizona Territory*, p. 213.)

8. Elias Jackson "Lucky" Baldwin (1828–1909) was one of the most colorful and infamous characters of California's early days. He made a fortune trading in stock of the mines on the famous Comstock Lode of Nevada. His wenching kept readers of the daily scandal sheets titillated for years. Two of his conquests managed to get him shot; Verona Baldwin, a young cousin who accused him of "ruining" her "mind and body" did the job personally; Lillian Ashley's sister shot him while in the courtroom where he was being tried for seducing Lillian. Beyond this he ran through five wives and in his later years was seldom mentioned by the papers except in the company of a "dizzy" blond or "vivacious" brunette. His more substantial accomplishments included developing Lake Tahoe real estate, building San Francisco's palatial Baldwin Hotel and building the Santa Anita racetrack on his Santa Anita Ranch. He kept a substantial stable of racehorses from about 1870 until his death. The Baldwin Hills and Baldwin Park are named for him. (Carl B. Glasscock, *Lucky Baldwin*.)

9. Lucky Baldwin's oldest child, Clara Baldwin Stocker, was born in Valparaiso, Indiana, May 14, 1847, making her fourteen years Josephine's senior, though they seemed to hit it off as lifelong friends. (Cason notes.) Clara's mother was Sarah Ann Unrah of Crawfordsville, Indiana. Clara took after her father in matrimonial affairs; she married J. Van Pelt Mathis when she was sixteen in 1863. In 1869 she divorced Mathis and married Albert Snyder, with whom she lived for three years. In 1873 she married a famous harness-racing driver, Budd Doble. She divorced him because "he wanted me to keep house and I wanted to live at a hotel." Clara's fourth and last husband of record was an opera singer, Harold Stocker, whom she married in 1882. She inherited about ten million dollars from her father. On her death in 1929, at age eighty-two, she endowed the Clara Baldwin Stocker Home for Women. (Glasscock, *Lucky Baldwin*, pp. 220 & 308.)

10. We may judge from the Cason notes that these interests included horse-racing, the theater, yachting (recall that Josephine once told Mrs. Cason she and Wyatt were married at sea by the captain of Lucky Baldwin's yacht) and the good life to be enjoyed both at the Baldwin Hotel in San Francisco and Lucky's Santa Anita Ranch near Los Angeles. It is natural to wonder if Baldwin restrained his well-proved tendencies where Josephine was concerned, or whether she also was one of those mutual interests. My judgment is that Josephine's youthful and mercenary nature does not definitely rule out this possibility.

11. Since racing was an expensive sport, the Earp stable was always small, probably never containing more than a half-dozen horses at one time. The Earps' racing years as owners were from 1885–97; however, they followed the turf for years thereafter. (Cason notes.)

12. At this time Cody was forty-seven years old. It is possible that Wyatt met him somewhere on the Great Plains, since the old marshal allegedly stated to Stuart Lake that he hunted buffalo for several seasons in the early 1870s before the southern herd was decimated. (Stuart Lake, *Wyatt Earp, Frontier Marshal*, Chapter 5.) However, Lake has Wyatt hunting in 1871, perhaps a year before he actually started. Also, in view of his other known activities, it is doubtful that Wyatt hunted as extensively as Lake states.

11

Our Goodbye to the Sporting Game

The unfortunate Fitzsimmons-Sharkey[1] fight took place in Mechanics Pavilion in San Francisco. The date was December 2, 1896.

The facts are extremely simple. Wyatt was chosen to referee the fight,[2] although he tried to avoid it. He preferred to watch the event as a spectator. However, at the time it did not seem possible to find another referee who was suitable to both fighters and their managers. It turned out that Wyatt was not appropriate either, but it was too late then. He reluctantly agreed to act as referee about noon the day of the fight. The choice was considered a good one then.

Immediately before the event, however, there was a squabble at ringside. Fitzsimmons' manager loudly stated he had heard the referee had been "fixed." Wyatt again tried to sidestep the job on these grounds, asking to be let out. The promoter, influenced by the impatient mood of the crowd, finally insisted that the referee they had selected be accepted. The unfortunate turn of fate lay in the fact that Fitzsimmons accidently fouled Sharkey. The blow crippled Sharkey, so far as continuing the fight was concerned. Wyatt had no choice but to give the decision to underdog Sharkey, which he did. Since Fitzsimmons was the heavy favorite and most bettors had given odds on him, there was naturally a great hullabaloo. Many claimed there had been no foul.

Others in a position to see claimed there had been. Wyatt was accused of having been fixed.[3] This was predictable in view of the large sums bet.

You would have to have known Wyatt to appreciate the absurdity of the accusation. In the first place, he was chosen because of his reputation for fearless honesty. This was well known to all parties concerned. If there had not been so much pre-fight suspicion on both sides, Wyatt would never have been the referee chosen in the first place. Therefore the very trait for which he was chosen — fearless impartiality — led to the trouble he encountered as an aftermath of his unpopular, but certainly fearless and impartial decision.

Of my personal knowledge I know that Wyatt lost money on his own decision. So did many of his friends, including Bat Masterson. When he was chosen as referee, Wyatt called off as many of the bets he'd made as possible. Those he couldn't he had to pay off, because, being firmly of the belief that Fitzsimmons would win, he had bet accordingly.

The owner of a San Francisco newspaper, who lost a bundle on the fight, led the pack that was baying after Wyatt. He dredged up every incident from my husband's past that could be ambiguously recounted to his discredit. His newspaper rehashed Wyatt's killing of Frank Stilwell, treating the incident as though it were a conviction with no discussion of the extenuating circumstances. With no real knowledge of his financial affairs, it painted him as a pauper, and thus highly vulnerable to bribery. This type of character assassination is familiar to any newspaperman. In modern times they would call it a smear campaign.[4]

I was furious. "Why don't you say something to defend yourself?" I asked Wyatt vehemently.

"What good would it do?" he wanted to know. "My friends know me well enough to know the truth — the others will believe whatever they wish, regardless of what I say. Let it drop!" But for all his patient forebearance and taciturn acceptance of the newspaper's slams, I know he was deeply hurt.

I have read everything I ever saw in print on the matter, and it all boils down to hogwash. Many claimed they saw no foul blow; as many others said they did. It was enough for me that Wyatt said he saw it.

The testimony of the losers always reminds me of Lincoln's placing of a silver dollar over a printed word and asking a man to read the word. He, of course, could not. Picking the coin up, the man read the word *truth.* "You cannot see truth through a dollar," Lincoln said. This was the case with this fight.

To further muddy the water, Wyatt had stepped into the ring armed.[5] When he removed his coat this fact was apparent to the spectators. "My Gawd," he later said to me, "I've gone heeled half my life — I forgot I had the damn thing on!"

The gun was an old six-shooter from his frontier days. He wore it for several reasons: to guard against reprisals from the past, to protect his considerable racing bankroll from the armed robbers who infested the vicinity of race tracks and other large sporting arenas, and I suppose, as he said, he actually did feel undressed without it.

I could name names in connection with this fight incident but consider it all futile. The real explanation of the situation is as I have given it. Wyatt was the victim of an unfortunate set of circumstances. The poor-loser streak in human nature did the rest. To those who may have heard other involved explanations regarding conspiracies, I say — doesn't every such tale depend on some hard-to-believe twist? Compare them with Wyatt's simple explanation and take your choice.

To believe the ready fabrication of the poor losers, all one has to believe is that Wyatt somehow convinced six strangers who hardly knew him before the fight to place their fortunes in his untrustworthy hands. These men were J. J. Groom and J. D. Gibbs of the National Athletic Club, who picked Wyatt as referee; Fitzsimmons and his manager Martin Julian; and Sharkey and his manager Danny Lynch. It was alleged that Wyatt was in cahoots with one, the other or all of them, depending on whose wild tale you heard. Yet, all of them had agreed to his selection in the first place.

Riley Grannon, a professional gambler who had lost heavily to Wyatt before then, apparently spitefully started the pre-fight

Wyatt Earp surrenders his six-shooter before refereeing the highly controversial Fitzsimmons-Sharkey prize fight. This sketch was taken from several pages of similar drawings which accompanied the front-page fight story in the San Francisco Examiner.

rumor that the bout was fixed.[6] He hardly qualified as an unbiased witness. However, not knowing Grannon's motives, Fitzsimmons' manager had raised that ringside howl I referred to earlier. Groom and Gibbs had shouted him down and got the fight started before the impatient crowd tore the house down. As I said, Wyatt tried to withdraw, but refrained only in order to avoid putting the promoters in a spot.

One of these, J. D. Gibbs, said that Wyatt was very highly recommended to him and that he had the reputation of being one of the squarest sports in America. That reputation flew out the window as an aftermath of the unfortunate Fitzsimmons-Sharkey fight. It was one of the major factors in Wyatt's decision to try to quit the life we were living. He longed for peace, quiet and obscurity.[7]

After more than ten years in the sporting game, Wyatt was tired of the contention and greed of the city. He longed more and more for the desert country and talked of going into southwestern Arizona to raise cattle or prospect for metal. His health, too, had begun to show the strain of worry, and he knew that the desert would give him the rest that he needed.

I had never lived in out-of-the-way places, except for my short experience in Colorado. I liked people, but I was willing to follow wherever Wyatt should lead. There was probably also a tinge of selfishness in my motives when I urged him to act upon this impulse, for I knew we could be together a great deal more while living a life of such isolation as he had in mind.

It was some time before he was able to dispose of the last of his interests in the racing business[8] and we were ready to start on our new career. Wyatt bought a Studebaker wagon and four horses. He was like a boy in his eager enjoyment of furnishing our camping outfit. It was complete with every possible comfort and convenience when we started at last for the desert of the Colorado River.

Having never camped out without more experienced outdoorsmen around to take the initiative, I was awkward and slow at first about finding ways to make camp "housekeeping" convenient. My husband, however, was an expert. He had been in cow camps where chuckwagon cooking was a highly developed art and had spent months every year during his buffalo-hunting days with only an assistant in a lonely camp on the buffalo range. Always a neat person, Wyatt had evolved many little ideas for camp management, and now, while we were looking about for a place to locate, he planned to put them into practice. Our hopes were not to be realized at this time, however.

HISTORICAL NOTES AND EDITORIAL COMMENTS

1. Fitzsimmons was an experienced fighter, having fought for some six years previously with a long string of victories. Sharkey was a tyro at the fight racket, although acknowledged a worthy opponent. (*Los Angeles Times,* December 3, 1896.) Fitzsimmons later took the world heavy-weight boxing crown from James J. Corbett on March 17, 1897, at Carson City, Nevada. (*Encyclopedia Britannica,* vol. 6, p. 486.) Wyatt was at the Carson City fight with Bat Masterson as part of a large force of bouncers.

2. James D. Gibbs of the National Club, which staged this fight, explained how Wyatt Earp was picked as referee. He stated that a mutual acquaintance, Mr. Billy Jordan, had recommended Earp to him. Upon Gibbs' questioning Wyatt, the former lawman acknowledged that he had refereed over thirty matches.

Gibbs confirms Josie's assertion that it was necessary to use strong persuasion to overcome Wyatt's reluctance to referee the Sharkey/Fitzsimmons match. When the choice was announced, it initially drew acclaim from all sides, including the managers of the two fighters. Gibbs said that when Wyatt's name was first mentioned he had learned that the former marshal had a reputation as a "cool, courageous sport whose reputation for honesty had never been assailed." (*San Francisco Examiner,* December 4, 1896.)

3. Eye-witness opinions on both sides of the question testified that there was, or was not, a foul. A sample follows from the *San Francisco Examiner* of December 8, 1896:

"*Capt. L. W. Lees,* chief detective: 'The foul was a palpable one. There is no doubt that Fitzsimmons struck Sharkey below the belt.'

"*William Chalmer,* drayman: 'I saw the foul blow struck.'

"*Ed Carrigan,* turfman: 'I was nearer than fifteen feet and there was no foul by Fitzsimmons whatever. Sharkey fouled repeatedly. I did not bet on the fight at all.'

"*Eddie Gaines,* turfman: 'The decision was the worst steal ever perpetrated on the public.'

"*E. J. [Lucky] Baldwin,* capitalist: 'Fitzsimmons fouled Sharkey in as vile a manner as one man ever fouled another....' "

The *Los Angeles Times,* December 4, 1896, summarized the medical opinion: "The three physicians all concurred in the statement, made very positively, that Sharkey had been fouled, the physical evidence they considered being indisputable."

In view of the fact that the sources of the charge that Wyatt was "fixed" were largely backers of Fitzsimmons, who stood to lose on the decision, and in view of the evidence that a foul actually occurred, it is extremely doubtful that Wyatt was indeed "fixed."

4. The *San Francisco Chronicle,* December 9, 1896, commented: "...Earp is filled with joy over the notoriety that has come upon him in the last few days. He enjoys hugely the curiosity of the people whenever he appears in a public place and gratifies himself by parading in localities where the bigger crowds congregate." This newspaper referred to him slightingly as the "Arizona Terror."

The *Chronicle,* therefore, was probably not happy when, on December 18, Sharkey was awarded the purse at the conclusion of futile legal attempts by Fitzsimmons' manager to block his receiving it. However, the decision was not based on the case's merits, but on a determination of lack of jurisdiction, since the fight itself was ruled an illegal proceeding. (*Los Angeles Times,* December 18, 1896, by AP wire.)

5. The *Los Angeles Times* of December 11, 1896, by AP wire reported the outcome of that issue:

"San Francisco, Dec. 10—The case of Wyatt Earp, charged with carrying a concealed weapon, was heard in Police Court today. Earp said that he was employed at the race track and had to be abroad at late hours. Moreover, a number of Arizona Criminals whom he had been instrumental in sending to prison, had vowed to kill him on sight. He carried a gun for self protection.

"Police Captain Wittman told how he had disarmed Earp on the night of the fight between Fitzsimmons and Sharkey. Earp was fined $50.00, the minimum penalty."

6. The rumor which Josie attributes to Grannon stated that Wyatt had telegraphed all his friends to put their money on Sharkey. The truth of this allegation, if it was made, seems dubious in view of the fact that neither newspaper reporters nor bitter losers of big bets uncovered a single telegraph operator who would admit to having sent such a message. On the other hand, aside from Josie's claim, no public record survives of Grannon having made such a charge. What Grannon did admit to saying was: "Yes, I did advise Fitzsimmons to be on his guard. The betting operations

assumed such proportions yesterday afternoon that I felt something was wrong." The problem, Grannon stated, was the sudden appearance of big-monied men who were willing to bet on the underdog. He smelled a rat. (*Los Angeles Times,* December 4, 1896.)

7. As a pertinent aside, the *Los Angeles Times of* December 5, 1896, printed a little testimonial that came from far down Wyatt's back trail:

"Wichita, (Kan.), Dec. 4 — In 1875 Wyatt Earp, the referee of the Fitzsimmons-Sharkey fight, was a policeman in Wichita under the notorious Chief of Police, Mike Meagher.

"Dick Cogwell, who succeeded Meagher as chief says, "Earp is a man who never smiled or laughed. He was the most fearless man I ever saw. He was Marshal at Ellsworth, Kansas, when that was a cattle shipping point, and he was a success. He is an honest man.

"All officers here who were associated with him declare that he is honest, and would have decided according to his belief in the face of an arsenal."

8. Wyatt's liquidation must have realized a substantial amount, since it enabled him to live very well for the years 1897 and 1898 and to finance his Alaskan adventure in high style without other employment until the late spring of 1899.

12

We Catch Gold Fever:
The Klondike Gold Rush

For the next few years we were to become acquainted with places and people soon to become American household words. In 1897, these were still little-known names: the Klondike, Dawson, Fortymile, the Yukon River, Bonanza Creek, Lake Laberge; the southern Alaskan towns of Wrangell,. Juneau, and Skagway; the northern Alaskan towns of Circle City, Rampart, Saint Michael, and Nome. The people were McQuesten; Mayo; Harper; Ladue; Henderson; Cormack; Steele; Big Alex McDonald, King of the Klondike; the Mizner brothers — Edgar, Addison and Wilson; Tex Rickard; Rex Beach; Jack London; Swiftwater Bill; and many more.

What wonderful memories those exotic places and people evoke! Wyatt and I met, at one time or another, almost every sourdough whose name figures large in the Klondike strikes, and saw many of those far places, though we ourselves never got any closer to Dawson than Rampart, several hundred miles down the Yukon River.

Curiously, the original strikes in 1896, due to the isolation of the Klondike, were totally unknown to the outside world until July of 1897. On July 15, 1897, the S.S. *Excelsior* reached San Francisco from Saint Michael, Alaska, and the newspapers quickly headlined the fact that she brought over a ton of gold. Two days later, when the S.S. *Portland* reached Seattle from the same Alaskan port, the news had already swept the country, which was then locked in the grip of a depression. The papers said the *Portland* brought over two tons of gold. The rush was on! We were in Yuma, Arizona, when the news reached us. It was hot as Hades, and we were fondly remembering cool San Francisco. Letters from friends aware of Wyatt's interest in prospecting urged us to join the rush. Many were closing their businesses and leaving for the gold fields. It was rumored that nuggets were almost growing on bushes. The call of the wild, coupled with the rumors of the strikes' richness, was too much for us to resist. We sold our wagon, team and carefully put together outfit in Yuma and set out for San Francisco.

On the train all we could hear was GOLD and the KLONDIKE. Alaska was a remote, frozen country few of us had heard much of before. By the time we reached the beautiful Bay City we were as feverish as any.

During our outfitting period in San Francisco, my husband suffered an accident that put off our proposed departure three weeks. Ultimately it resulted in delaying our arrival in the actual gold country till 1898, after first reaching Alaska in 1897. Wyatt slipped while running for a trolley car and badly dislocated his hip. He lay in bed for three weeks, chafing and fidgeting, burning up with "gold fever."

Few people at that time had any idea of the obstacles in the path of those setting out to reach the Klondike. I know we didn't. Wyatt was planning to take the short route over the White Pass from Skagway. A couple of years later, after talking with those who went that way, or over Chilkoot, we thanked God we had not made the attempt. Neither of us doubted we'd have made it sooner or later, but the hardships would have been staggering. At one place, known thereafter as Dead Horse Canyon, it is said that six thousand pack horses were sacrificed to man's greed.

None starting as late as we would have could have possibly made it to Dawson by *any* route in 1897. But if by some miracle a person did get there, he'd have arrived to suffer through a winter of hardships and near-famine. Those who got over the passes spent a deadly numbing winter camped near lakes at the Yukon River's headwaters, waiting for spring in order to be able to make boats from whipsawed green lumber and thus to float down the river to the Klondike. I was not sorry we had missed such an adventure, though if Wyatt had tried it I'd have been at his side.

We finally got our outfit together and left on the S.S. *City of Seattle,* a well-regulated ship. We reached Wrangell without event. Here the U.S. marshal for Alaska, who was in town on an inspection trip, approached Wyatt with a request to take the deputy marshal's job in that town. Wrangell was another Tombstone. Wyatt politely declined, but accepted the job for a week or ten days to help out till a permanent man could be obtained. He was still gimping around with his hip, which was the reason we stopped off in the first place — the ship hadn't a single doctor on board.

Wrangell, at the mouth of the Stikine River, was, as Wyatt put it, "just like a Hell-on-Wheels," which was the name given in the old days to camps at the end of the newly laid Union Pacific track. It was full of boomers, con men, gamblers, ladies of the night, gunmen, pickpockets and all sorts of flotsam from every corner of the earth. I don't recall any incidents in which Wyatt encountered unusual difficulty in enforcing the law. His name, in this respect, was a big help.

One funny thing did occur. A large, noisy man was creating a disturbance, waving a pistol in a saloon. Wyatt was shortly sent for. He walked up and said, "I'm the marshal. I'll take that pistol!"

The large rowdy looked a little surprised, then perplexed. He did not offer to use the pistol, however, so Wyatt let him take his time. Finally the man seemed to put his finger on what was bothering him; he blurted out, "By Gawd, y'all're Wyatt Earp, ain't you?"

"I am," Wyatt told him, "and I don't allow pistols to be carried in town."

The man meekly surrendered the pistol. "By damn!" he said, "if this don't beat all! Here I go to the end of the earth, and the first man I run into when I let off a little steam is Wyatt Earp. Y'all threw me and a bunch of the boys in the pokey in Dodge City for the same thing twenty years ago!"

It turned out the man was an ex-cowboy. Contrary to show-ing resentment, he was elated to meet someone from the old days and invited Wyatt to take a drink. As was his custom, Wyatt had a cigar instead, and they talked over old times for a long while.

Shortly after this incident Wyatt's hip improved consider-ably, so we moved on to Juneau, where we had to stop to arrange passage through the Lynn Canal to Skagway. I had already begun to hear tales of the hardships associated with the trail from Skag-way to the interior. My coward's heart quailed at the prospect of unknown dangers, but I was equally concerned over how Wyatt would hold up with his only partially healed injury. I had already started to hatch schemes whereby I could prevent him from going through with his plan to cross White Pass before winter.

Then fate came to my rescue. I had suspected but was not sure that I was pregnant. Now there was no doubt of it. We had already prematurely lost one child in San Diego. Wyatt had been heartbroken, since he had already named it, after positively decid-ing it would be a girl. No argument was necessary when he learned of my condition. At thirty-six I was already fairly old to be a mother for the first time — and there might be no other chance if another accident occurred. We booked passage back to the outside, as we had started to call the states, after the manner of the sourdoughs. As it happened, we lost this baby prematurely as well. Appar-ently God didn't make me right for having children, though we both loved them and longed for some of our own.

At any rate, for that reason we never saw Soapy Smith's[1] town of Skagway. In a way I wish we had. We remembered Soapy Smith from our visits to Denver and Creede, which Wyatt and I had visited at the urging of Bat Masterson. Soapy was not the kind of gambler Wyatt and Bat were. He played the sure things, rather than gambling in the true sense of the word. However, he fancied himself a true gambler and had once sat in a card game with Wyatt and Bat at Creede.

"Soapy knows all the tricks," Wyatt stated, "but he also knows what's good for him and doesn't try any of that nonsense on peo-ple like Bat and me, who are onto him." Besides I judge that he was afraid of both Wyatt and Bat — justifiably so. From what I gathered after Soapy's death, he was no fighter, certainly not a gunfighter.

When the facts of Soapy's death got around,[2] Wyatt explained to me what he considered his old acquaintance's downfall to have been. "He shouldn't have gone down there with a gun in his hand if he didn't intend to use it. He was a bluffer. As soon as he saw that Reid meant business, Soapy yelled for Reid not to shoot him. Instead he should have gone to shooting. If Reid's pistol hadn't misfired on the first round, Soapy wouldn't have got off a shot. As it was, the shot he did fire may have been a lucky accident." It was not lucky for Reid. It hit him in the pelvic region, and he died from the effect a few days later.

But all in all I'm glad we didn't go to Skagway. It was the kind of town where someone who knew Wyatt's reputation would have asked him to take a hand. I'd have worried every minute, not that anyone of Soapy's caliber would have got him.[3]

By the next July Soapy was dead and we were on our way back to Alaska, after having returned to San Francisco. We were both deeply mourning the loss of our second child. Probably if the baby had lived, we never would have gone back to Alaska. Instead Wyatt may have started the ranch he always wanted. That was what I prayed for — a healthy outdoor life of invigorating physical exercise for him and a husband at home every day for me. But that was not to be for a long while yet. We had to try Alaska again.

The second time we decided to try the all-water route, around Alaska, up its west coast, then up the Yukon River. The ship we picked this time was a far cry from our first. By now the rush was on full tilt, and they were using any old tub that could be got to float. The S.S. *Brixom* on which we took passage was certainly in the old tub category. It provided poor food, ultimately getting almost down to none. The passengers grew sullen and angry. Finally the crew itself mutinied.

Due to his wide reputation Wyatt was finally called upon to arbitrate the dispute. My husband, along with some others, considered buying the ship. Finally Wyatt determined that he simply would loan the captain the money to buy adequate supplies when we put into port at Unalaska, which we were scheduled to reach shortly. This worked out fine and immediately improved the spirit of both crew and passengers.

We reached Saint Michael near the mouth of the Yukon when the summer was well along. Many riverboats were in various stages of construction. The *Brixom's* passengers were scheduled to sail on a not-yet-finished boat. The people dumped down at Saint Michael by a fleet of steamers from the states far exceeded the carrying capacity of the former river fleet. We were lucky to receive the promise of a passage even on a boat not yet afloat.

The best description of the frustrated group at Saint Michael, thwarted in their expectations of a quick passage upriver to Dawson, is to call them a mob. They begged and threatened, bribed and connived in every conceivable manner in trying to secure passage to Dawson. Not all were successful. We were.[4]

During the two-week delay the men worked day and night on our boat. The season was getting well along. Already we had missed one year in getting onto the ground where the bonanza was. I had "gold fever" as badly as Wyatt. We were told that winter could very well settle down early in that country. We would be icebound.

Finally our boat was finished. It was christened the *Governor Pingree* after the governor of Michigan, whose brother was one of our fellow passengers. We set out, overloaded as was usual for all boats in that time and place. It's a wonder they didn't lose half of those tubs.

The first leg of the journey south to the Yukon River was another cause for tension; it was open sea. With our small, overloaded and top-heavy shallow-draft riverboat, the thought of what an arctic storm could do to us was not a pleasant reflection. I worried over that until we were safely inside the river's mouth, moving through the delta country.

This worry was just behind when something else happened, giving me a new cause for fretting. The boat sprung a leak when we were but a short way up the river. We had to put into shore while the crew tried to fix the vessel.

Meanwhile the season had moved well into September. There was a frosty chill to the night air. Geese were moving south. The leaves of the trees and bushes along shore had turned yellow and were falling; the landscape was growing bare. All the men went ashore daily to cut wood so we would be less delayed later by stops for fuel.

After a five-day halt for repairs, we were finally able to get under way. Our fingers were crossed. It would have been like a picnic if it hadn't been for the constant strain of uncertainty about reaching Dawson. We just knew that fortunes were slipping through our hands. But the food and accommodations were exceptionally good under the circumstances. In addition, the huge, empty country captivated me. It was so big and awesomely quiet. Somehow it was different from the West — it seemed more remote and withdrawn.

Night navigation was considered too hazardous to risk, so our progress was further slowed by tying up each night. Evening was a time I looked forward to. Then there was a friendly gathering of passengers and crew for supper in the mellow lamplight of the warm, large cabin that passed for the dining salon.

After supper one unforgettable evening, Wyatt and I stood on the deck only a few feet above the murmuring, dark, swirling water, with the gold blush of the setting sun still faintly visible all around. At the same time in the east, a beautiful moon rose over the river. We stood holding hands, thinking private thoughts of what the future might hold.

We remained that way for a long while, as the moon coasted higher. Then, to cap the entire display, the aurora borealis spread its weird rippling rainbow across the whole sky. I had never seen the aurora perform with such versatility and multicolored brilliance before, nor had Wyatt, though we were to see it many times after. But it never again impressed me in the same awe-inspiring fashion. We stood in the crisp, silvery night with our exhaled breath visible on the frosty air and were silent. There was no need to express our thoughts; they could only be the same — "How beautiful!" And how wonderful to be together on an adventure in this best of all lovely worlds. Later we slept like children, clasped warmly close in each others' arms.

The Yukon valley had been aflame with the golds and reds of the aspen and birch. Then suddenly the mornings were white with frost. Snow flurries sifted down through still air or whipped along on the wind. The forest became almost lifeless.

The temperature had been steadily dropping, causing slushy ice to appear in the river for the first time. Now we began to fully realize at last that we would not reach Dawson that year, at least not by boat. It might be possible, we were told, to rent native dog sleds and teams to press on after the river was frozen solid. We discussed the possibility. We hoped, at least, to reach Circle City, which was some considerable distance closer to the gold strikes. Before the news from the Klondike started the stampede, Circle City had been a prosperous mining community. Then the gold rush practically depopulated the town. As a consequence, we expected that housing there would be no problem. But it didn't work out that way. The gathering ice let us get no further than Rampart City. Here the captain drove our trusty paddle-wheeler up a side stream to spend the winter.

There was some grousing, but it was obvious to everyone that further boat travel was impossible. Many of the men announced immediately that they would get dog teams and press on as soon as the condition of the river permitted. We again considered this but rejected the idea — if Wyatt felt that I was holding him back there was no discernible trace of it in his outward actions then or ever. The fact that we found old friends already at Rampart influenced our decision to stay.[5]

We also met new friends such as Tex Rickard,[6] who already had been in Dawson the year before. He and some others congratulated us on our decision to stop. Tex told us, "There's nothing left in Dawson for you unless you want to get into a commercial line. There are plenty of good gold prospects right here in the Rampart country. Besides, it's in the U.S.A."

Rampart sprawled out in the typical mining camp fashion, with cabins unevenly lining the river and scattering helter-skelter back into the hills. Near this point several streams flowed into the Yukon River; the largest of these was Big Minook Creek, at the mouth of which Rampart was located.

The camp was lively. Almost everyone was too new to the country to have lost his optimism and enthusiasm. Everyone we

talked to was brimming over with hopeful, "sure-fire" plans to make a fortune quickly.

As usual the men greatly outnumbered the women, a situation which long continued to exist in Alaska. Even at that, there was a great shortage of cabins considered suitable for a woman to dwell in. They didn't know me very well, or know of similar camps, such as Harqua Hala, to which I had willingly and gladly followed Wyatt.

With the help of Tex Rickard we got a lead on a cabin which a friend of his had used the winter before. The North American Trading Company, or N.A.T. as everyone called it, was acting as agent for Tex's friend, a man named Rex Beach. Later we were to meet the owner, who arrived from upriver in November carrying the mail. This was the man later to gain fame as a writer.[7] We learned from Rex that he had purchased the cabin from the man who had built it, the U.S. deputy marshall[8] who had been wintered in on his way to his Circle City headquarters the year before. Most of the buildings in Rampart dated from just the previous year.

Rampart, Alaska, from the Yukon riverfront. The large Alaska Commercial Company store near the center of the front row of buildings was operated by Al Mayo during the Earps' stay at Rampart.

Our cabin was built of logs chinked with moss, and the roof was covered with a deep layer of dirt. The rent was one hundred dollars a month; we considered ourselves lucky to get anything at any price. It was built by a brook, a fact which was to make me very happy when the spring thaw came and I could hear the water merrily running by.

We had to be ingenious to make our new home cozy and livable because, except for the barest necessities, furniture simply could not be obtained. We had a small iron cookstove that we had brought with us from the boat. Our table was homemade of packing boxes, our bed of spruce poles put together by Wyatt and strung with rope for springs. On this we spread fur robes purchased from the natives for use as a mattress. We had brought comforters and blankets from the states; to these we added more native furs. Carpets seemed indispensable, but there were none to be had. We improvised by using burlap sacks doubled and sewed together, then tacked to the floors. We added layer after layer, whenever we could get them. On top of this were thrown furs purchased from the Tanana Indians.

About all these arrangements I had but one complaint — not much can be said for furs for mattresses, but the ropes had enough spring and give to alleviate their hardness. It *was* warm.

One could get calico in almost unlimited quantities, thank goodness. With this I curtained off one end of our cabin for the bedroom, used the same material for curtains on the single window, and also covered my packing-box cupboard the same way. It added cheer to an otherwise drab home.

Finally we were settled in to my satisfaction. I had a pot of beans going on the stove and was taking my first batch of bread from the oven. I remember that Wyatt came lurching through the door, letting in a gust of wind and flurry of light snow. He stamped his mukluk-clad feet, clapped his mittened hands together, then drew off the mittens and his knee-length hooded fur parka. When his eyes adjusted to the lamplight he pronounced his opinion: "Snug as a bug in a rug!"

It really was too. A housewife used to the conveniences of the states might not think so, but with so little I was happy as a queen because I was with Wyatt. What did I have to complain of — I could stay snugly inside all winter. But poor Wyatt's moustache was frozen stiff as a board from battling the outdoors. "I'll thaw it out in the steam from the cooking pot!" he laughed, leaning over the stove and, like a typical husband, pulling the lid from the pot for a preview of the menu.

During the winter we kept a fire going day and night. Back of the stove we kept a little barrel containing water for our daily use so that it would not freeze. Every night before we went to bed it was our final task to fill our little barrel with ice so that morning would not find us without water for breakfast.

We were lucky to live close to Mrs. Llewellyn from Seattle, who had a small restaurant; I believe it was the only one in Rampart at that time. Her husband, her brother and her younger sister Agnes were with her, so we three women had our coffee klatches.

There wasn't much money in circulation in Rampart; gold dust and nuggets were used. I remember one day in the spring, after navigation had reopened, I happened to be in the restaurant when some miners from the Dawson country stopped off from a passing steamer to get a meal. The men were paying Mrs. Llewellyn, who was weighing out their gold dust. As she handed their pokes back to them, they passed them to Agnes and me and said, "Help yourselves, ladies!" To be polite we each took a dainty pinch.

"Don't be afraid," they said, "take a lot of it, take some of the nuggets!" Then they dropped a nugget in each of our hands. Indeed gold was plentiful if one could find it, but many could not.

As I mentioned before, Rex Beach, who later struck it rich on his stories of Alaskan adventure, was there at Rampart, but I think his gold-seeking was about as unrewarding as our own. Rampart lives again in his book, *The Barrier,* as the town of Flambeau. It's easy to recognize the people I knew in his characters.[9]

Captain Al Mayo operated the Alaska Commercial Company store at Rampart City. He was one of the real old-timers in the country. They were called sourdoughs after their habit of keeping a crock of sourdough on hand as rising for their bread, rather than using baking powder or yeast.

Al was a little man in stature only. He had once been a circus acrobat, but had the itchy foot of the true wandering pioneer. He was fond of practical joking and had the frontiersman's expansive sense of humor and conversational hyperbole. I heard him say he'd been in the north so long that when he first came the Yukon was only a creek and the Chilkoot Pass was a hole in the ground.

Al Mayo was one of the three explorers who had opened the Yukon Valley. The others were Jack McQuesten and Art Harper.[10] When they arrived in 1873, the Yukon was devoid of whites. They roamed it unfettered for years, took Indian wives, and lived the lives of nomads whenever they wished.

However, these explorers generally lived in cabins when they weren't roaming up and down the river in canoes. They educated their children "outside," and lived in every way like white men, raising vegetable gardens, reading books and becoming traders as soon as there were enough people in the country. McQuesten had the trading post upriver at Circle City.

Aggie Mayo was Al's Indian wife. She was a very nice person, and they seemed ideally suited to each other. She kept his house and raised his children in the manner of a typical American housewife, having over the years almost entirely adopted the way of life of her husband.

Wyatt and Captain Mayo, as almost everyone called him, hit it off from the first, while Aggie seemed as fond of me as I was of her. In her hospitable way Aggie made me a beautiful white fur parka with a wolverine-trimmed hood. The wolverine fur hood is much valued in the artic because it is the only type fur on which one's frosty breath does not condense and freeze. I don't know why this is, but nonetheless it's a fact.[11]

Al provided Aggie a good home and was giving their children every advantage possible under the circumstances. Their oldest daughter was married to a young missionary; they lived up the Yukon at Circle City where he was stationed. The next summer, 1899, the Mayos sent their oldest boy and another girl to Detroit to live with Al's sister and get a better education than was available in the mission schools of Alaska.

By the time we were settled in our cabin and had begun to get acquainted with old-timers like the Mayos, we felt we were well on our way to becoming sourdoughs instead of *Cheechakos,*[12] as tenderfeet in the country were called.

HISTORICAL NOTES AND EDITORIAL COMMENTS

1. Jefferson Randolph Smith, Jr., was commonly known as "Soapy" based on a con racket for which he became notorious in Denver in the 1880s. He sold wrapped bars of soap for five dollars; inside some of the wrappers there was supposed to be a hundred-dollar bill, such as the one Soapy's confederate had just ostentatiously won and displayed to the crowd. As it happened, the confederate, or capper as he would be called by the cons, was always the only winner. A man who also possessed great executive ability, Soapy proceeded from this petty racket to organizing the underworld in Creede, Colorado, when it was a boomtown, then went into the same profession in Skagway, Alaska, during the gold rush to the Yukon.

Soapy Smith was an enigma, fleecing all comers, but also being the first to give generously to the down-and-out and to charities. In both Creede and Skagway his persuasive manner for a time enabled him to be a real community leader whose known underworld connections were tolerated in return for his regulating the local swindlers to prey only on transients.

Soapy was born in Noonan, Georgia, in 1860, drifted west and became a cowboy, as many youths did after the Civil War. Soon he shrewdly observed that gambling and racketeering paid more for less effort. (Frank C. Robertson and Beth K. Harris, *Soapy Smith, King of the Frontier Con Men.*)

2. Soapy Smith undertook to break up a meeting of vigilantes gathered to run him and his gang out of Skagway. Overconfident, since he had bluffed out such groups in the past, Soapy went alone. Unfortunately this time he was met by an old Indian fighter, Frank Reid, who would have killed Soapy before he could fire a shot if Reid's pistol had not misfired on the first round. Soapy then managed to shoot Reid in the groin with his rifle, but the Indian fighter's second shot took the con man in the heart, killing him instantly. Reid died twelve days later. (Robertson and Harris, *Soapy Smith,* p. 208 ff.)

3. It is not likely that Wyatt would have had any open trouble with Soapy Smith's fraternity. In addition to knowing Soapy — or perhaps more importantly, the King of the Con Men knowing and fearing Wyatt — Soapy's strong arm sidekick, Big Ed Burns, had been a member of the so-called Earp gang in Tombstone. Wyatt associated with him after Tombstone in Albuquerque and Denver, where Ed was an underworld luminary. His name appears as Ed Barnes in Wyatt Earp's testimony after the O.K. Corral gunfight. (Document 94, Clerk of the Superior Court, Cochise County, 1881.) Stuart Lake refers to him as Ed Byrnes. (*Wyatt Earp, Frontier Marshal,* pp. 275 & 280.) For more information regarding Burns, see Robertson and Harris, *Soapy Smith,* pp. 46, 186, 192, & 208.

4. Wyatt had money; money talks.

5. Josie does not specifically name any of these old friends but Wilson Mizner, who is mentioned later. We may safely assume they were generally gamblers, sporting men or prospectors who the Earps had known in other stampedes, such as the rush to Tombstone, the Coeur d'Alene, Creede and Harqua Hala.

6. G. L. "Tex" Rickard, a very popular small town marshal, left Henrietta, Texas, in 1895 on a leave of absence to see the world. He never returned. He met old sourdough Al Mayo in Juneau in 1895, and Al's tall stories of the Yukon River basin sold Tex on Alaska. He went to Dyea, over the pass and down the Yukon to the diggings in the Birch Creek District. He filed a claim there but made his living bartending and gambling at Circle City. When the big news broke about the Klondike, Tex headed

up the river to Dawson. There he struck it rich in a small way, but still largely gambled for a living.

After going broke at cards, Tex headed back down the Yukon, stopping at Rampart the winter the Earps were there (1898–99). He went to Nome the spring of 1899, then still known as Anvil City, and opened a saloon. He was on the first city council when Nome was incorporated in 1901. Later Tex went to Tonopah, Rawhide, and Goldfield, Nevada, owning the famous Northern Saloon in Goldfield. Mainly to stimulate business he staged the famous "Battle of the Century," featuring boxers Joe Gans and Battling Nelson. Excited by his first flyer into boxing, Tex went on to become the leading fight-promoter of the twentieth century, building Madison Square Garden and making Jack Dempsey famous. He died in December 1928 a few weeks before his friend Wyatt Earp. (*Year, Mid-Century Edition*, p. 97; Wharton, *The Alaska Gold Rush*; Charles Samuels, *The Magnificent Rube*.)

7. Rex Beach was a popular author during the first half of the twentieth century. Born in Atwood, Michigan, September 1, 1877, he was educated at Rollins College, Winter Park, Florida; later in Chicago he studied law briefly, then played pro football. The Klondike gold rush appealed to the adventure in his nature. Beach was in the north for several years, especially at Rampart and Nome. His best known Alaskan books, which achieved his early fame, were *The Spoilers*, set in Nome, and *The Barrier*, about Rampart. The Earps knew him well. (Cason notes, and Stanley J. Kunitz and Howard Haycraft, *Twentieth Century Authors*, p. 91.)

8. This was Frank Canton, deputy U.S. marshal at Circle City for the Yukon District of Alaska. He had acquired his job through the influence of P. B. Weare, general manager of the North American Trading and Transportation Company, trading rival of the Alaska Commercial Company, whose executive Mr. Ling later employed Wyatt at Saint Michael. Canton, who had spent a good part of his life in the cattle business, had operated a packing plant at Nebraska City for Weare and J. Sterling Morton of Morton Salt fame. More important than this influence was Canton's background as a sheriff and stock detective in Wyoming and Montana from the 1870s through the early 1890s and as a deputy U.S. marshal in Oklahoma at its worst period in the mid-1890s.

Canton served in Alaska from 1897 to 1899 and departed for the U.S. on the same S. S. *Cleveland* that almost sunk Wyatt and Josie in a storm as related in Chapter 15. It seems he was relieved as deputy in Alaska when it was discovered by the Justice Department that he was the same Canton who had had some unexplained irregularities in his deputy marshal's accounts in Oklahoma, causing his resignation there. He died in 1927 in

Oklahoma, much respected, having been the first adjutant general of that state.

After Canton's death, his friend and editor Edward Everett Dale thought it rather odd that the old man had left a lacuna in his autobiography from 1871 to 1878. Investigating, he discovered that Frank Canton was an alias for Joe Horner, Texas bank robber, who had been born in Virginia in 1849. As adjutant general of Oklahoma, through his friendship with Texas pioneer millionaire Burk Burnett, Canton in later life was able to obtain a pardon for his former escapades. (Frank M. Canton, *Frontier Trails*; William G. Bell, "*Frontier Lawman*," p. 5ff; Helena H. Smith, *The War on Powder River*; Canton files, libraries of the universities of Oklahoma and Wyoming.)

9. It is quite likely that Wyatt was Rex Beach's prototype for Ben Stark and that Al Mayo was the model for Old Man Gale in *The Barrier*. Beach mentions the gambling equipment Ben Stark brought to Flambeau; Josie doesn't say that Wyatt carried gambling appurtenances to Rampart, but we are safe in assuming he wasn't headed for Dawson to open a grocery. If Wyatt was in fact the prototype for the fictional Ben Stark, then Rex Beach probably knew of Wyatt's having deserted his second wife, since a similar incident figures in the past of the character Ben Stark in the novel. (Rex Beach, *The Barrier*.)

10. In 1861 more than four hundred Americans who had been prospectors in California and the Sierra Nevada went up the Stikine River out of Wrangell, Alaska, and over the border into British Columbia looking for prospects similar to those found in the gold-rush days. Prominent among those were Leroy Napoleon "Jack" McQuesten, Captain Al Mayo and a man listed only as McKrieff. They were in the Caribou excitement in British Columbia when they heard of the U.S. purchase of Alaska. McQuesten later said this decided them to see what the new country was like.

It took the group two years to get financed and equipped to go to the Yukon. They arrived there in 1873. The next year a second party came, of which Art Harper was a member. The three, McQuesten, Harper and Mayo, did more for the opening of the Yukon Basin than any others. Harper was primarily a prospector, but McQuesten and Mayo were traders. In 1875 all three were appointed traders for the Alaska Commercial Company on a percentage basis and assigned the whole upper Yukon River territory.

After moving around the Yukon for years, Al Mayo settled in Rampart and became mayor in 1897, probably by self-appointment. He was something of a character. It is reported that a minister took Mayo to task for the sinful example that Rampart's "palefaces" set for the "innercent injuns," a veritable hell on earth, as he put it. Mayo told him, "Take yer gawddamned injuns across the river where they kin see hell and not be in it." Al had a sign posted in his Florence Hotel that read as follows:

HOUSE RULES — Mayo's Hotel

Craps, Chuckluck, Stud Horse Poker.
Black Jack games run by the management.
Dogs bought and sold.
Insect powder for sale at the bar.
Always notify the bartender the size of your poke.
Spike boots must be removed at night.
Dogs not allowed in bunks.
Every known fluid except water for sale at the bar.
Fire escapes through the chimney.
Special rate to ministers and to the gambling "profesh."

Rampart, Alaska, 1898

(Herbert Heller, *Sourdough Sagas,* p. 127; David Wharton, *The Alaska Gold Rush,* pp. 17, 18, 20, 252 & 259.)

11. In 1948 at Anchorage the arctic explorer Vilhjalmur Stefansson explained this to me as due to the extreme density, hence absolute smoothness, of the surface of the fur, exposing not even minor pores to which frost can adhere. Stefansson, who was the last person I would have expected of an active sense of humor, then added, "At least I've never heard of frost adhering to Wolverine fur — especially in the summer!"

12. *Cheechako* is "Siwash" for greenhorn — one so green he would not smile at the notion of "hitching up one's trusty team of mukluks and mushing across the Williwaw." To become a sourdough one must perform a rather elaborate ritual, according to well-known Alaskan tradition. (Personal experience of editor in Alaska, 1947–49.)

13

Life in an Alaskan Gold Camp

When Thanksgiving came around we invited several people for dinner: Tex Rickard, Mr. and Mrs. Tom Eckert,[1] ex-Governor McGraw[2] of Washington and his partners General Carr[3] and Mr. Brainerd.[4]

Mrs. Eckert pitched in to help me out with dinner. We made fresh doughnuts, pies and cake to top off a meal of roasted ptarmigan, canned meats, vegetables and fruits. McGraw's two partners made it in, but he had sprained his ankle so badly he could barely get around. Wyatt suggested we put up a basket for him and carry it over later.

After dinner Mrs. Eckert and I put the basket together and, to walk off dinner, set out right away while the men were still finishing their cigars. Luckily for us, Wyatt and Mr. Eckert started only a few minutes later.

It was snowing lightly when we left. Before we were halfway there, a regular blizzard started. The path had been fairly clear, but soon it was almost totally covered. The snow, whipped by the driving wind, blinded us, so we strayed from the path. Soon we were completely confused, wandering around and getting tangled in the underbrush. We had both heard of people roaming off to freeze and being found days or weeks later only a short distance from their own doorsteps. Mrs. Eckert was no wiser than I was in the ways of the wild.

I completely panicked. I had visions of packs of wolves. I was sure we'd wandered so far by now that our husbands would never be able to find us. It was really cold, too. Finally we huddled together in an alder thicket, holding each other and alternating between laughing and crying. Finally, after what seemed like hours, we heard men's voices calling our names. We shouted back at the top of our lungs. Soon our husbands were coming through the thicket to meet us. Were we ever glad to see them!

We were nearly frozen. Since we were closest to McGraw's cabin, we went there to thaw out. We learned that Wyatt and Mr. Eckert had gone straight through to McGraw's. Discovering that we hadn't reached there, they backtracked and found us. In all we had been gone less than two hours. It seemed like two days. It was still light, so it could have been no more than two hours, I know.

Besides our little get-togethers, mail from home lightened our long, lonely hours in the arctic. Unfortunately, the last mail we were to see all winter arrived down the Yukon by dog sled in November. Rex Beach and Walter Perry mushed in from Dawson, bringing the last of the mail that had come over Chilkoot Pass. We were almost eight hundred miles down the river from Dawson.

But there were other entertainments, even in Rampart. One of them was provided by a horse owned by a man named Peck. Peck had managed a Seattle store before coming North. He didn't dance or play cards but was interested in athletic pursuits. For this reason he got the nickname "YMCA" Peck. He took it all good naturedly. His horse was the only one in town, and Peck was extremely generous about letting others use old Napoleon, as he called the animal. However, feed was high, and everyone who used the horse always insisted on paying for the service. We went on many a night sleigh ride over the Yukon ice.

Other evenings women gathered in one house or another to embroider, gossip, read aloud from popular books, exchange recipes and enjoy all the other things women do at such gatherings. Often enough the Mayo house was the place chosen for the big gatherings. At such times some of the men generally joined us to hear Al Mayo talk of the early days.

It surprised us both to learn from Captain Mayo that a man well known to both of us from Tombstone days had been to Alaska as early as 1883. This was Ed Schieffelin, the famous founder of Tombstone. Ed brought his own steamboat with him. His prospecting up the Yukon took him almost exactly as far as Big Minook Creek, where we now were at Rampart City. His boat, renamed the *New Racket,* was still on the Yukon in the fleet of the Alaska Commercial Company.

As you can tell by now, we worked at entertaining ourselves. One of the more notable affairs we had was known ever after as the "cookie" dance. This name came from the fact that the principal refreshments were wine punch and cookies. The punch was very popular; I thought it was delicious. The general suspicion later was that someone had "spiked" it with something stronger than wine. In any case, its effect was so quick and pronounced as to make it a great favorite with all the men. They would loudly say to one another, "Let's have another cookie," then go at the refreshments again.

Wyatt, who seldom drank anything but coffee, sampled his share of the "cookies." They made him so brave he actually gave dancing a try when urged to by Mrs. Eckert. It was the only time I ever knew him to attempt dancing. He was a willing pupil but displayed such a remarkable lack of skill that he and Mrs. Eckert drew a running commentary from Governor McGraw and several others on the sidelines. They retired from the field laughing. That night I danced several dances with Tex Rickard, whose talents were just the opposite of Wyatt's so far as dancing went.

Another occasion I recall, partially due to its aftermath, was the entertainment Captain Burke gave to discharge his social obligations to the community. He planned a dinner at Mrs. Llewellyn's and asked some of the ladies to assist in making the affair as "posh" as possible. It was a wonderful dinner, even though largely taken from cans. All of us who were helping him pooled our resources.

The best we could do for a tablecloth was oil cloth, but we made up for it in other areas. Mrs. Morse was a person of no small artistic talent. For example, she made the place cards from the thick red pulp building paper that was characteristically used to line the inside of buildings in those days. She painted miniature snow scenes on the cards, then touched these up with gilt paint so they really looked splendid and professional. The party went off in great style. It was the talk of the community for some days.

Its aftermath created talk for much longer than that. Like all of us, Mrs. Morse had come to Alaska in the hope of striking it rich. She prospected but failed to find the real thing, just as most of us failed. So she decided to create her own bonanza by putting her artistic talents to work. She used her gilt paint to transform small, heavy pebbles into nuggets. After awhile she was caught. It became Captain Burke's unpleasant duty to arrest his former social assistant. There was no jail, so she was only nominally under arrest. If there had been a jail I'm sure he wouldn't have put her in it anyway. She was discovered only shortly before the spring break-up. She was on parole for a brief time, then vanished to return to the "outside."

We also had a second particularly serious crime in which Captain Burke as the only authority in the community had to take a hand. That was the case of "Mose," who worked on one of the riverboats frozen in the ice near Rampart. It came to the attention of the ship's officers that their supply of canned milk was diminishing at an alarming rate. Then they found out that Mose was operating a wholesale canned milk business in town. The case was brought before Captain Burke. The evidence was strong, so Mose admitted the offense.

This posed a real problem with no jail in town. Captain Burke decided to put Mose to work on the government woodpile under the guard of a soldier. The fact that there was almost no entertainment for the soldiers, coupled with Mose being a natural-born comic, led to his having a sizable squad of extra volunteer guards most of the time. He was one of the world's most inept wood-choppers to begin with. Add this to his efforts at clowning and you will begin to get the picture. He was heaven-sent entertainment to break the monotony for the soldiers.

Just before Christmas two young doctors recently graduated from Johns Hopkins took a notion to give a Christmas party for the community. They decided to borrow Mose to liven up the entertainment. They already owned the only phonograph in the community, along with a good supply of records. A phonograph in those days was an extremely rare thing. Mose would have been a very rare thing in any day.

The young medicos contracted for the big room over the post office, installed their phonograph and invited the community to their "affair." The entertaining consisted of phonograph records, the two doctors singing and playing banjos and Mose accompanying one or the other. Mose lived for applause. He never flew so high, danced so fast, grinned so widely or sang so loudly. His entertainment-starved audience was effusively appreciative.

The last entertainment that I remember from Rampart was a dinner party on one of the riverboats frozen in a few miles up river. We went up in a sleigh behind Old Napoleon. Others went by dog sled or on foot.

At the conclusion of a real fine meal the captain announced that a special treat was to be served, the best angel food cake in the world. Sure enough, in it came from the galley, delicately iced in thick vanilla frosting. We all politely sat waiting until the last helping was served, then we pitched right in. Each eater discovered a startling fact. Though he may not have recognized the exact cause of the cake's resistance to the fork, the fact was that the dessert was really a frosted life-preserver. All of the guests, when they recognized that a practical joke was in progress, did their best to keep a straight face so as to rope in those who had not yet been stung. Finally no one could keep a straight face. The captain confessed, told us what the cake really was made of, then served us each a delicious piece of genuine angel food cake.

Folks in the arctic loved a practical joke of almost any sort. Some of them were rougher or potentially more disastrous than this one. For example, a pretty Russian-Indian girl named Babe had a transient love affair with a prospector named Tom. She claimed Tom as the father of her child. By this time her lover had gone outside on another romantic mission; he planned to marry his one-and-only girl back in the states and bring her to the land of the midnight sun. Babe, prompted by Rex Beach, Wyatt and Al Mayo, was on hand to meet Tom's steamer. When it docked she went aboard, carrying her baby. Finding Tom with his new wife, Babe walked up and said her lines: "Here's our baby, Tom, ain't he pretty? We're so glad you're home, honey!"

Tom survived, I know, since some years later we met him on the Colorado River as a riverboat captain. He hadn't forgotten. It must have made a lasting impression on him — probably on his wife too.

HISTORICAL NOTES AND EDITORIAL COMMENTS

1. I have been unable to unearth additional information regarding Tom Eckert. Unfortunately this is likewise true of a number of other persons mentioned by Josie in this chapter, including Walter Perry, Captain Burke, and Mrs. Morse.

2. John H. McGraw (1850–1910) was a self-made man. He left his home state of Maine for Washington Territory in 1876. He was sheriff of King County there in 1882 and 1890, admitted to the bar in 1886, president of the First National Bank of Seattle from 1890–97, territorial governor from 1892–96, investment broker in 1900 and president of the Seattle Chamber of Commerce in 1905. He apparently went to Alaska to repair his fortunes, which had declined during his years as governor, and succeeded. (Seattle Chamber of Commerce, *In Memoriam John Harte McGraw; Who Was Who in America*, vol. 1, p. 813.)

3. E. M. Carr was a brigadier general in the Washington state militia and had a very lucrative law practice. (Letter from Frank L. Green, librarian, Washington Historical Society, to the editor, May 16, 1975.)

4. Josie is undoubtedly referring to Erastus Brainerd of the Seattle Chamber of Commerce. He did an exceptional job of advertising the Alaska/Yukon boom, making it known that Seattle was the northernmost rail terminal and seaport and the most experienced center for northern outfitting. In Illinois, for example, 488 weeklies carried his ads. He also propagandized foreign embassies. He had a special issue of 212,000 copies of the *Seattle Post Intelligencer* sent to other newspapers throughout the country. Probably due to his energy, Seattle far outstripped rival points as a base of departure to Alaska. Perhaps he may take equally as much credit for the town's 88% population growth in the late 1890s. Apparently Brainerd's Alaskan promotion campaign eventually influenced the chief promoter to visit what he was ballyhooing. Like the Earps, he doubtlessly had not expected to end up spending the winter in Rampart. (Frank L. Green to the editor, May 16, 1975.) For more on Brainerd, see Archie Satterfield, "He Sold the Klondike," *Seattle Times Magazine*, January 2, 1972.

14

Spring: The Itchy Foot and Saint Michael

Anyone who has not heard the ice go out of the Yukon in the spring could never imagine the racket. Long cracks are visible in the river for several days. Then comes the shocking event.

The year we were there, at the instigation of Al Mayo, almost everyone guessed a date and hour for the ice to actually break up. We wrote our guesses on slips of paper and dropped them into a large crock at the Alaska Commercial Company store.[1]

Suddenly one day the ice lurched forward and began to upend. A few moments after the first forward motion, the floes began to climb on top of each other. The grinding, booming roar was almost deafening. It sounded like huge explosions of some kind. Some of the pieces were a dozen feet thick and as large as a big city block. As they climbed over each other, they pounded up onto the bank, shattering. The year before, several greenhorns who had built cabins too close to the banks had seen them swept away. No one had repeated this mistake.

The break-up went on all day and night, then something seemed to give way downstream, and the whole mass began moving at once. For several days large ice floes slid past, then the last of them were gone. It was mid-May. Spring was with us in a day.

The money wagered on the ice break-up was won by the Indian girl, Babe. Wyatt and several others had each wagered a dollar and a guess on her behalf. She got around a thousand dollars, more money than she had seen in her life. Al Mayo took care of the fund for her. Almost the first thing it brought her was several offers of marriage. Philosophically she accepted what she considered to be her best bet. They disappeared upriver in a canoe with Tom's baby and a load of supplies purchased from Babe's money. I never saw her again. I hope she has lived a long, happy life.

As the spring advanced Wyatt planted a garden; not in the ground, since that was still frozen, but on top of the house, for our cabin roof was covered with a thick layer of earth. The sun warmed up our little roof-top garden, and it wasn't long until the young lettuce, radish and onion plants were sprouting up.

Wyatt watched and tended the young plants like a nurse. One brilliant moonlit night I found him up on the ladder watching his garden. "What are you doing up there this time of night, Wyatt?" I asked. "Can't you watch those vegetables enough in the day time?"

"Why, honey," he said, "I'm just watching them grow! I do believe they grow as fast in the moonlight as they do in the sun. You can just see them shoot up!"

Wyatt was as elated over our first meal of tiny green onions and radishes from his garden as a miner over a new strike. I must admit that I have never seen anything grow as fast as those vegetables of Wyatt's did. There is an exceedingly short growing season in that section of Alaska, but it's offset by how fast things ripen.

Before I end the story of our stay in Rampart, I've got to tell about one more happening that shows the sly sense of humor so few suspected in Wyatt. The Yukon was a great lane of traffic during the summer. At Rampart it swept around a wide bend above the town, then was soon lost to view behind a wooded point. Thus we were unable to see the approaching steamers until they were close to town. We could hear their distant whistles, but the dogs always heard them before us. Those animals were as interested in the steamer's arrival as we were, since there was a very good prospect of scraps of food the cook had saved for them. For us there were the possibilities of friends, of mail, of new faces to see.

It was on such an arrival that I first met Wilson Mizner, one of the famous "many Mizners" who later became the writer of such successful plays as *Alias Jimmy Valentine*.[2] Wyatt had known him before, and we were to see more of him later in our lives. He and Wyatt recognized each other before the boat had tied up, and they were shouting back and forth across the water.

Wilson stayed with us for several days, which led to the incident I remember best about Rampart. It started with Wilson's offer to hunt up some game for the larder. "Let me use your shotgun, Wyatt," he said, "I'll get us a bag of ptarmigan!"

"Can you hit anything with a shotgun?" Wyatt wanted to know. "Shells are scarce up here, and you should make every shot count."

"Of course I will," Wilson told him. "Why don't you try me and see?"

The upshot was that Wyatt trusted his favorite shotgun and several precious shells to Wilson's unproven hands. We heard him shooting on the slope back of the cabin off and on during the next hour or so. Some time later Wilson returned with half a dozen birds, dumping them proudly before Wyatt. "How many shells did you use?" my husband asked him.

"Only six!" Wilson stated with obvious self-congratulation.

"Where are the rest of the birds?" Wyatt inquired with a perfectly straight face.

"What rest of 'em?" Wilson asked indignantly. "I kicked up six birds — I used six shells, and I got six ptarmigan!"

"I see that," Wyatt agreed, "and I suppose that's O.K., being as you're new to the country. I guess I should have told you how to get the most from each shot before you ever went out."

Wilson looked puzzled. Sensing his confusion, Wyatt went dryly on, setting him up for the old one-two. "You know," he said, "the ptarmigan is a first cousin to the sage hen, or prairie chicken as we used to call them. They were so tame they could be killed with a club. That's why we also called them fool hens. The ptarmigan is the same proposition. We don't kick them up before we shoot them. Being a sport and wing-shooting them doesn't count up here, where shells are so scarce."

Wilson was set up ready for the final blow. He looked truly dismayed. "Howinthehell do you shoot them then?" he blurted.

"Well," Wyatt explained, "You herd no less than half a dozen together in a little bunch, then step back so the shot spreads good and get them all sitting, with one shot."

Wilson wasn't sure whether he was being kidded or not; Wyatt looked so solemn. "Why don't you go out and try it again, kid?" Wyatt suggested. "You'll get the hang of it!" Wilson trudged away for another try.

Sometime later a sourdough stopped by the cabin. He told Wyatt, "I just seen the damnedest sight ever. Some feller is up the trail talking to a bunch of ptarmigan, tellin' 'em he has 'em herded together fair and square, so stay put, dammit! You don't know who he is, do you?"

"I expect I do, Wyatt admitted. Then he told the story. They roared. After the sourdough spread the tale around, the whole community started shouting out whenever they spied Wilson coming, "Stay put, dammit!" He was a good sport. He never visited us afterward in all the years we knew him without mentioning the incident and laughing, "And remember," he would add, "I got exactly twelve more with two shells!"

"And," Wyatt would confess, "you were the first and last man in the country I ever heard of who did!"[3]

Shortly afterward we reluctantly concluded that we would leave Rampart City for Saint Michael on Norton Sound. Before the ice broke up, Wyatt had received a letter from Mr. Ling, who was the manager of the Alaska Commerical Company's store on the island of Saint Michael. Ling wanted him to come to the island and open a canteen. Charley Hoxie, who had been the United States customs officer there, had brought the letter. Eventually, since we weren't making much money in Rampart, Wyatt decided to take Ling up on his offer.

The prospects upriver at Dawson were not bright, with all the creeks already located and the commerce monopolized by the early comers of the year before. The other competition for our attention was on the north end of Norton Sound. There the previous fall (1898), gold had been discovered in Anvil Creek by the three "Lucky Swedes" — Jafet Lindeberg, Erik Lyndebloom and John Brynteson.[4] The name first given to the settlement that sprung up was Anvil City. Later it was to be renamed Nome.[5]

Claims were staked on the creeks and back into the hills. Then gold was discovered in the beach sand. No mining laws covered the finding of gold on such a strip of sand, so new laws had to be made on the spot. The miners got together and ruled that a man could have as much of the shore as he could reach with his shovel from the spot where he started digging. This was called "foot possession."

All this was developing while we were yet in Rampart. In July we left, making our way downstream with thousands returning from Dawson. The boat was jammed to the rails with sun-burned, bearded men in prospector's garb — the mackinaw, boots and hat with fur earflaps.

Most of our Rampart friends were joining us on board the boat, or had already left upstream or down, so there were few on hand to see us off. I do remember that Al Mayo and his wife and children were there to wave and shout goodbye. The boat backed into the channel, then came forward, nosing downstream. We never saw Rampart again. There were tears in my eyes as we left. Wyatt himself looked sober and reflective. It had been a wonderful experience.

Mr. Ling was at the wharf in Saint Michael to welcome us as we landed. Wyatt was still somewhat on the fence regarding what to do. We were both thoroughly infected with "gold fever" and really wanted to go to Nome. However, the offer Mr. Ling made was just too attractive for Wyatt to pass up.

We unpacked our belongings in the Alaska Commercial Company Hotel, which was not far from the canteen Wyatt was to manage. The canteen sold two commodities — beer at a dollar a drink and cigars at fifty cents each. It was a poor day that didn't see two thousand dollars go into the till. Wyatt's share of this was ten percent off the top, generally two hundred dollars per day seven days a week.

Many shiploads of beer and cigars arrived from the states. From our hotel window some days I could see hundreds of barrels of beer rolling by on the boardwalk and as many cases of cigars. Sometimes the rows of beer barrels stretched for several hundred feet and were, in addition, stacked high behind the warehouse.

I was a little ashamed of Wyatt's business, though I can't say why. He'd been in it before and would be again. Perhaps it was seeing that monstrous volume of the brew that was universally condemned as a home-breaker and the ruination of many good men. I took some small comfort from the fact that at least no hard liquor was served — just beer and cigars, but three men were kept busy day and night selling these. I also was pleased that the rules required that the beer be consumed off the premises. This cut down on the need for bouncers, such as were required in Dodge City and Tombstone. I felt Wyatt, at the age of fifty-one, was getting beyond the time when he should engage in such a pro-

Waterfront panorama of the trans-shipping port of Saint Michael at the time of the Earps' stay in 1899. A typical sternwheel Yukon riverboat is tied up on the right.

fession, though he remained in remarkably fine physical condition till only a few months before his death.

The bay town of Saint Michael had some things to be said in its favor over some of the inland settlements. For one, there were almost no mosquitos. For another, it was clean, orderly and law-abiding.

The Alaska Commercial Company had a compound forming one end of Saint Michael. A boardwalk joined it to the North American Trading and Transportation compound at the other end. In between, fronting the boardwalk on both sides, was the bulk of the rest of the town. Saint Michael was a lively place the summer of 1899. It was full of transients heading for Nome or the Klondike, or setting out for the states.

Wyatt stayed busy all day in the canteen, but I was free to roam about town. My most frequent companion was Mrs. Vawter, wife of the U.S. marshal.[6] Sadly, the next year at Nome her husband became a member of the "Spoilers" crowd who tried to take over the town.[7] Their criminal activities when they were finally put out of business not only made world headlines but were the subject of Rex Beach's novel, *The Spoilers*.

One of the fascinating scenes Mrs. Vawter and I used to watch regularly was the arrival of gold dust and nuggets from the Klondike. Bullion was shipped in small cases under the close guard of red-coated Canadian police. They were allowed to operate on U.S. territory in the capacity of bullion guards between Dawson and Saint Michael. We saw hundreds of these cases piled up on small express trucks and rolled down to the waiting steamships.

That was the way our interesting and profitable life at Saint Michael went. But the possibilities at Nome always attracted us. We kept getting letters from both Tex Rickard and Charlie Hoxie urging us to come to the new discovery.

Finally one day when Wyatt was reading another letter from Tex, he looked up in a familiar tricky way and grinned at me. "Tex says we're making chicken feed here," he said. "He has an idea we could triple our take at Nome."

"Did you tell him we're clearing several hundred a day, rain or shine?"

Wyatt nodded. "Let's go over for a day or two and see what's going on. He has some idea for a business."

I had to make at least a gesture along the line of being practical. After all, we were making what came to almost seventy thousand a year, at the rate it was coming in then. When I pointed this out to Wyatt, he said, "That will taper off to nothing by winter. We won't make half that for a whole year."

"Well," I replied, "it's one thing to decide to go and something else again to get a boat."

Wyatt looked innocently toward the ceiling, tilted back in his chair, staring upward with his hands locked behind his head. The pose was pretty familiar.

"What pocket do you have the tickets in?" was all I asked. The old enthusiasm over a pending change of scenery was undoubtedly rising in my breast.

Wyatt pulled two slips of paper from his vest pocket and grinned like a small boy caught in some innocent mischief. "Better throw your trotting harness on, Mrs. Earp," he suggested. "I think we'll leave this evening on the *Saidie*." I threw my things together, as I had so often before.

The *Saidie* was a tubby little side-wheeler. Sometimes in heavy weather it took her three days to reach Nome. We were lucky. It took one night and one day. It was still fairly early in the season, and it never got fully dark all the way. We slept very little, staying up on deck and talking over the prospects.

The sea was glassy. Its color was silvery gold, as though an omen. We were headed toward making the second fortune of our lives, but we didn't know it.

�⌁

HISTORICAL NOTES AND EDITORIAL COMMENTS

1. This appears to be an early-day parallel to the modern Tanana River pool conducted annually at Fairbanks. The 1975 split was eighty thousand dollars. Perhaps Al Mayo's ice pool started the custom, since Rampart is not far from Fairbanks, where the Tanana River pool is conducted.

2. Brothers Wilson and Addison Mizner came to Alaska together. Wilson sang and played piano in Dawson saloons. Apparently he was a little of both con man and lady's man. William Hunt in *North of 53°* cites Wilson as "a leading light of the underworld" in Nome (p. 102) but doesn't go into detail. It appears that he certainly had both lax morals and high spirits.

In Nome, Wilson handled fighters, including "Doc" Kearns, later famous as Jack Dempsey's manager. Undoubtedly Wyatt saw a lot of him in this connection. Although Josie doesn't mention it, many prize fights were staged at Wyatt's Dexter Saloon in Nome. *Who Was Who in America* lists Mizner as a dramatist, and as the author and producer of plays.

Wilson was born May 19, 1876, son of Lansing Bond and Ella Watson Mizner. His father was minister to Guatemala in 1889. Wilson attended Santa Clara College during 1892–97 and went to Alaska for the Alaska Fur Company in the latter year. (Hunt, *North of 53°*, p. 198; *Who Was Who in America*, p. 825; Addison Mizner, *The Many Mizners*; Alva Johnson, *The Legendary Mizners*.)

3. The whole story appears in Wilson Mizner to William S. Hart, February 2, 1929, Cason letters in editor's collection. The anecdote appears to have been recalled as a result of Hart's and Mizner's meeting and conversing after Wyatt's funeral. Apparently either time or circumstances prevented Wilson from finishing the story then, so he did so in a letter.

4. The adjective "lucky" with respect to these three Swedes represents a euphemistic salaam in the direction of their success; it was customary among many to refer to "dumb" Swedes in those days. These men were the end of a chain of individuals involved in the Nome discovery. As events proved, they were far from dumb and certainly were lucky.

Daniel Libbey was the first of a series of people involved, having come to the Seward Peninsula in 1865, when it was still Russian territory, to build a Western Union line to Europe via California, Canada, Alaska and Siberia. He found traces of gold along the Niukluk River, knowledge he didn't capitalize on until thirty years later.

Libbey returned to the Seward Peninsula in 1896, formed the Eldorado Mining District and took out seventy-five thousand dollars in gold. That year one of Libbey's associates, H. L. Blake, accompanied by a Swedish missionary, Nels C. Hultberg, prospected Cape Nome. Hultberg found rich gold deposits on Anvil Creek. For some reason he didn't tell Blake, although two years later he revealed his find to three fellow countrymen — Eric Lindblom, John Brynteson and Jafet Lindeberg. They organized the Cape Nome Mining District with an unusual proviso making it possible to file claims by power of attorney. By this means they filed on most of the rich claims and held them despite later protests of native Americans. In all they filed forty-three claims for themselves and forty-seven for friends, shrewdly including claims for the U.S. commissioner at Saint Michael and the U.S. army commander there. Lindeberg was a former tailor from San Francisco; Brynteson was a coal and iron miner from Michigan. Lindeberg had accompanied reindeer herds imported to Alaska to increase the native food supply. (David Wharton, *The Alaska Gold Rush*, p. 78 ff.)

5. Such names as Anvil Creek and Anvil City and Anvil Mountain undoubtedly came from a large anvil-shaped rock located at the head of Anvil Creek. No record exists of why the name of Anvil City was changed to Nome, but the name Nome itself came from Cape Nome, on which it is located. Speculation is that Nome was a cartographer's misidentification of the word Name, pencilled on the original survey map as a question regarding the identification of the Cape. (*Encyclopedia Britannica*, vol. 16, p. 559.)

6. C. L. Vawter of Montana was appointed U.S. marshal for Alaska upon the recommendation of Senator Thomas H. Carter, also of Montana. Carter was a behind-the-scenes supporter of the Spoilers. (Hunt, *North of*

53°, p. 123.) Apparently Vawter was at Saint Michael for a year, then moved to Nome when the boom started. (Cason ms.)

7. The "Spoilers" is the name applied to the group of claim-jumping conspirators abetted by Judge Arthur E. Noyes at Nome. The original scheme allegedly was developed by three unnamed lawyers with the connivance of high level politicians during the McKinley administration. The Alaska Gold Mining Company was formed to take over several mining claims that had been illegally jumped. When the claim-jumping was quite predictably protested in court, Judge Noyes appointed receivers to operate the contested property. They simply gutted the rich claims while litigation was indefinitely postponed. Judge Noyes and associates were eventually arrested and tried, but only a minor official went to jail, due to the intercession of President McKinley on behalf of the bigger fish. It is this group with whom Josie states Marshal Vawter played ball. Apparently his part was not open or perhaps serious enough to get him in trouble, assuming Josie is not simply offering us baseless gossip. (Wharton, *The Alaska Gold Rush,* citing Thomas A. Rickard, *Through the Yukon and Alaska* [San Francisco: Mining and Scientific Press, 1909], p. 350; see also Hunt, *North of 53°,* pp. 122–128.) Perhaps the best coverage of all is by William Morrow, judge of the U.S. Court of Appeals (San Francisco) who heard the case. See *California Law Review,* Volume IV, Number 2 (January 1916.)

15

The Golden Strand

The little steam packet *Saidie* was dangerously overloaded. Every conveyance going to Nome was in the same precarious condition. Fortunately Norton Sound was as placid as a river during our passage. We came in sight of the rugged north coast of Norton Sound well before we reached Nome. "There she is!" I heard someone exclaim.

All I could see was a string of what appeared to be white blocks running for miles. "What are all those white things — rocks?" I asked Wyatt.

"Tents, I imagine," he replied.

And so they turned out to be. The gold-rich section of beach was about two hundred feet wide and twenty miles long. The whole thing was lined with tents and shacks. The beach was the only dry place to locate them.

Nome had no harbor. The ships stood off at anchor in the "roadstead." Passengers and supplies were "lightered" ashore. I was scared white when it became apparent that the only way to get ashore was by climbing down a rope ladder into a bobbing dory. When we ran aground on the sandy beach, men in rubber hip boots came out to bodily carry the women to dry land through the remaining few feet of surf. The one who snatched me up was literally a Paul Bunyan. He must have been almost seven feet tall. He put me down lightly, saying "There you are, little lady!" I never saw him again, though he'd have been easy enough to spot in any crowd.

The beach was bedlam. Every conceivable type of supply was stacked there somewhere. A broad, muddy track led from the

The Golden Strand, c. 1899; the incredibly busy Nome beach as the Earps knew it. The water is dotted with the small boats mentioned by Josie — all Nome cargo and passengers had to be ferried ashore due to shallows.

landing place to the main drag. The town at that time was only a messy sprinkling of tents and a half dozen very rough lumber shacks. The street was a long, muddy lane, running along the landward side of the string of tents that straggled for miles. A sign some wag posted in the middle of the street read:

> This street is impassable —
> Not even jack-assable.

Even before we went back to Saint Michael for our possessions, Wyatt and Charlie Hoxie bought a large lot right in the middle of the town. As quickly as possible they started building the first two-story structure in the community. It was also the largest, being seventy feet deep. The downstairs was to be the Dexter Saloon, named after nearby Dexter Creek. Upstairs were to be twelve clubrooms.

We rented a shack to live in while the work was in progress. We were lucky to get anything. It was not as nice as our cabin in Rampart, but it was home to us. Wyatt had the lumber for the Dexter shipped in from British Columbia. He also imported many tons of coal from Mr. Ling and the Alaska Commercial Company at Saint Michael.

An amusing thing happened which enabled me to make purchases of some real bargains in woolen goods. Three Irishmen arrived in Nome on their own ship loaded with woolen shawls, robes and blankets. They were so sick of each other's company that they sold off their merchandise at the first price offered so they could dissolve their partnership. They practically gave the articles away, sold their ship and went their three separate ways, apparently rejoicing.

Wyatt had been so busy putting up the Dexter that we had made no provision for adequate living quarters of our own. This was sixty-four degrees north latitude, so it would be necessary to have a good, secure dwelling. Due to inadequate sanitary facilities, a typhoid epidemic broke out. All things considered, Wyatt decided Nome was no place for us to spend that winter. Besides, he wanted to go outside to buy furniture for the Dexter. Charlie Hoxie had agreed to stay for the winter and look after the place.

Our main problem was trying to secure ship passage that late. It developed that the *Cleveland* had space aboard. If we had known what we were getting into on that old ship, we may have tried harder to make winter arrangements in Nome. The *Cleveland* was a long, narrow veteran of service in the Spanish American War as a troop ship in the Philippines. We just did squeak onto the passenger list. As it was, Wyatt had to bargain to get a stateroom. But money, as the saying goes, talks. Two returning prospectors gave up their quarters for a very generous price.

We had a rough trip by dory out to the ship's side. Shortly after boarding her, I began to wonder if we were as lucky as we supposed. The *Cleveland* had come to the Alaska run straight from Manila without cleaning or refitting. The vessel was filthy, to put it mildly.

We were only a short distance out of Nome when we discovered the worst about the old tub. Wyatt was in a bunk trying to read a book. It seemed to me he was having trouble concentrating. Thinking it was the poor light, I got up and lit the reflector lamp fixed to the bulkhead. Wyatt continued to fidget now and then, reaching up under his sweater to scratch his spine.

"Whatever ails you?" I finally inquired, since his squirming was making me nervous. "Look down my back," he said. "I'm beginning to itch like the devil!"

What I saw turned my queasy stomach. "You're covered with little gray bugs!" I told him.

"For God's sake, cooties!" he exclaimed. "I'll bet I got them in that filthy barbershop in Nome. Get 'em off o' me!"

"How?" I wailed. "I won't go near the filthy things!"

He hastily peeled off his sweater, shirt and undershirt, throwing them in the corner. Before long he was out of the rest of his clothing as well, standing there in his birthday suit scratching away. I couldn't help but laugh as I helped him rummage through our trunk for a change of clothing.

"What's so damn funny?" he inquired sourly.

"You!" I giggled. That's when I first noticed that I had started to itch. I scratched tentatively, hoping it was my imagination. But my imagination or not, in a few moments I was scratching as furiously as Wyatt had been.

He stood there in his new underwear, a grin spreading over his face. "Something wrong, Sadie?" he asked.

"Don't laugh!" I pouted.

Wyatt roared. "The whole damn ship is probably lousy!" he observed.

We threw our clothes out the porthole and boiled others, all to no avail. Our little friends were with us the whole trip. But soon enough we had something to drive that small perplexity from our minds.

The north Pacific can be a fright to mariners at any season. With winter approaching it was at its worst. We struck a storm that ultimately caused us to be nine days late. The ship had been given up for lost by the port authorities when we finally reached Seattle.

There was no doubt in my chicken heart that this storm was finally the end. In desperation I dressed to go on deck, begging Wyatt to come with me. "I'm going to stay right in this berth and read," he said calmly.

"But when we sink we may at least be able to get into a lifeboat if we're on deck!" I urged.

"Who's sinking?" Wyatt inquired mildly. "Damn fat chance you'd have on one of those boats in this sea! You'd freeze if you didn't drown." He turned a page, never looking up. "If she goes down, this is as good a place as any. Stay here! I'll shoot us both to spare us the strangling when the time comes."

"Don't try to be funny!" I demanded, stamping my foot.

When we finally reached Seattle, we were so glad to be within reach of shedding our cooties that we eagerly rushed down the gangplank empty-handed. We put up at a hotel, and I headed for the bath. Wyatt went out to a bathhouse. We stopped at McDougall's drygoods to get new outfits on the way to the hotel.

We saw the old year out in San Francisco but visited relatives in many other places. We traveled around considerably and didn't plan our return till late in the summer. We were even following the horse-racing season as far east as Denver when the news reached us that Wyatt's brother Warren had been shot to death in Willcox, Arizona.

As I have said before, the Earp family accepted a death in the family hard. When Wyatt received the word, he immediately telegraphed his brother Virgil that we were leaving Denver and heading West. As I recall, the Virgil Earps were then in Prescott, but they may have been in Vanderbilt, California; I am no longer certain.[1] At any rate, we met Virgil in Phoenix. Wyatt and his brother proceeded at once to Willcox, but Wyatt refused to hear of my accompanying them.

They were gone several days. I went on to San Francisco to await Wyatt's return. We planned to leave as soon as possible for Nome, after he concluded his business.

When Wyatt joined me, he looked grim. "It was a clear case of murder," he stated. "The only thing Warren had that could be called a weapon was his pocketknife, which was in his pocket all the time. He was holding out his hand, asking for the gun of a man called Boyett — simply trying to disarm what he considered a dangerous drunk — when Boyett shot him through the heart. But the coroner's jury released the man."[2]

"Why would they do a thing like that?" I stormed, angry at the injustice of it.

"You know the West!" he said. "There'd been bad blood between them previously. They called it self-defense. I'm satisfied there was more to it than that. Warren was making it hot for the small ranchers who were rustling to build up herds around there. Warren earlier had accused Boyett of being hired to kill him."

"What is going to happen now? Are you just going to let Boyett off?" I asked.

"That's about all we can do now. The man has disappeared."

I thought that over. I have no idea really what happened to Boyett, but I was human enough to hope he had been made to pay for his crime in the same coin he had dished out.[3] I knew better than to try to pry information from Wyatt.

I once tried to pump Virge about what he and Wyatt did at Willcox. I believe it was the last time I saw Virge alive. You'd have to have known him to appreciate what he said. He grinned at me, with those merry, crinkly eyes twinkling, and said, "Have a beer, Sadie!" He was as bad as Wyatt.

Virge's wife Allie had more to say to me about it later. "You know the Earp boys as well as I do," she said with a knowing look. "What happened to Stilwell and Curly Bill and Ringo?"[4]

We took passage back to Nome on the *Alliance*. On board

in the hold were thousands of dollars-worth of accouterments to furnish the Dexter as a luxurious club — such things as thick carpets, fine mirrors, carved sideboards, and draperies. I'd had the time of my life helping Wyatt select these rich furnishings. On board as well were Charlie Asher and John Farley who had leased the upstairs clubrooms of the Dexter from Wyatt.

At Unalaska two honeymooners — my niece Edna and her new husband — joined us for the rest of the way to Nome. Our return to the boomtown seemed like a homecoming. Getting into the dory was old stuff for experienced hands such as we. I showed off a little to Edna with my nonchalance and almost fell in. I was quiet and subdued as a mouse all the way to shore.

Our first problem was a place to live. Wyatt had providently purchased the materials for a good, sound house. Work on this started as soon as we got the things unloaded. While we waited for the construction to be completed, we camped out in a tent like the rest of the boomers. We loved it. So did Edna and her new husband. It was the big adventure of their lives. Edna marveled, "To think you two have lived a whole lifetime like this!"

Nome under the midnight sun July 4, 1901. Wyatt's Dexter Saloon can be seen on the left. When finished in 1899, the Dexter stood alone, the first large structure in the midst of a tent city.

University of Alaska

"On the whole," Wyatt observed dryly, "I preferred the Baldwin Hotel before it burned. Especially in the winter."

"Oh you!" she pouted, "you know what I mean! You never had a cookstove set up in the middle of your parlor at the Baldwin. It's just great!"

"Come to think of it," Wyatt agreed, "we didn't. Or mosquitos either!"

"He's a hopeless case!" Edna dismissed him with a look to me for moral support. She skipped gaily out doors and tra-la-la'ed her way up the beach. I know how she felt. The same feeling still sometimes overcomes me, even at my age. It was a wonderful life. I miss it.

The Dexter was soon finished and furnished. It was the most fashionable saloon in town and would have been a standout even in San Francisco. The crowds thronged to it; the money Tex Rickard had forecast began to roll in. As a typical bit of Wyatt's drollery, he had it advertised all over the territory as "The Only Second-Class Saloon in Alaska." This got results. Newcomers all the way from Dawson would drop in as soon as they hit the beach.[5] "What's second class about this?" they would inquire "Beats anything I ever *seen!*"

One day John Clum blew in on a ship and was looking for a place to stay. Wyatt, of course, brought him straight to our cottage, first arranging for someone to bring along his baggage. John had been sent to straighten out the Alaskan postal system. He did just that, though the task required a couple of years. We had a pleasant visit. John would visit us thereafter whenever he happened to be in Nome.

Other old friends were now in town, among them Wilson Mizner, who had become a real favorite of ours. One day another very old friend arrived. Lucky Baldwin's fortunes had declined somewhat.[6] In an attempt to recoup them, he set afoot an Alaskan venture, intending to build a club and saloon in Nome. He arrived with Dave Unrah,[7] who was to be his local manager.

Wyatt was troubled by the decline of Lucky's fortunes. We both wished there was something we could do to help him. It happened that our chance came the following year. Lucky had instructed Dave to dispose of his property in Nome. By that time the Spoilers Ring was firmly entrenched.[8] They claimed there was a twenty-five-hundred-dollar lien against Lucky's property for taxes and blocked a sale unless a bond of ten thousand dollars was deposited. Dave Unrah put up the money in cashier's checks to satisfy this demand. But Marshal Vawter would not accept this; he demanded gold. Of course, his game was obvious to everyone, but he and the judge were hand-and-glove, and no higher court relief was available within a reasonable distance.

Dave came to Wyatt for help. Wyatt put up the ten thousand in gold, being happy to do so. When the Spoilers discovered that Dave could raise ten thousand in gold, they had the security bond raised to twenty thousand. Wyatt and a couple of friends raised the added amount in a few hours, but my husband was good and mad.

Wyatt hadn't spoken to Vawter since his little game in Nome had become clear. However, he now sent a message to him by Dave Unrah. "You tell that such and so that I raised this gold with the help of a few friends and that if we find it necessary to raise anything more it's going to be on hemp!" They accepted the twenty thousand.[9]

We spent an idyllic summer in Nome. I got my wish to pan gold; indeed I got more than my fill of it.

We were becoming a city by the fall of 1900. Social activities were by now a part of the local scene. Talent groups were formed to put on plays and variety shows, which generally took place in Considine's Hall. A leading spirit was Wilson Mizner, who not only wrote, directed and produced entertainments, but was himself a fine, talented singer and actor.

But despite all that I experienced fits of despondency that only the short dreary arctic days and endless arctic nights could induce. Without our entertainments and the steadfast, cheerful support of my husband, I know that the arctic would have been my undoing.

I lost my head and began to gamble wildly.[10] I never knew when to quit. I bet foolishly, wagered too much money and almost

Wyatt Earp and John Clum on the beach at Nome, 1900; their six-shooters no longer protrude — only the prosperous waistlines of successful business-men.

never won anything. When I did, it simply whetted my appetite for more betting in the vain hope of repeating my coup.

Finally Wyatt felt he had no choice but to call me to account for my wanton conduct. He looked infinitely sad when he finally did so, as though he'd rather have done anything else. "Sadie," he said, "You are gambling us poor."

I decided to put on a bold front and counterattack. "So what? We are making a fortune. What good is money if you can't spend it?"

"You aren't spending it," he countered. "You don't know the first thing about gambling. You're throwing it away!"

"Try and stop me!" It was the first time I'd ever said such a defiant thing to my husband in our whole lives. As soon as it slipped out, I wished I could take it back.

I bit my lip, waiting for the wrathful retort. There was none. Wyatt only looked sadder, ashamed that we had descended to this. And I knew it was all my fault, and that I was as wrong as could be. "I have stopped it," Wyatt told me. "I have put out the word — no one in this place will gamble with you from now on."

"You have shamed me before our friends and the hired help!" I stormed.

"So I have," he agreed quietly. "Only after you did the same yourself to both of us."

I was suddenly sorry and started crying. I've never gambled a cent since.[11]

Aside from the isolation, the arctic climate and boom camp conditions, Nome offered about the same sort of humdrum existence as any town of comparable size in the states. By the summer of 1901, our life had become routine. We were getting rich, but we were also getting bored. We both had an itchy foot till the end. Even now I get the urge to go look over the crest of a new ridge every so often. It's particularly pronounced in the spring and summer.

Somehow we kept down the urge until the fall of 1901, but this was mainly in order to hold out for the best possible deal in the sale of our interests in Nome. We left, having amassed another small fortune.[12]

When the S.S. *Roanoke* pulled away from Nome in the fall of 1901, I looked with moist eyes at the receding beach with its sprawling line of buildings, shacks and tents. "She's been a good old burg," Wyatt observed. "Mighty good to us."

"Do you think we'll ever come back?" I asked with a lump in my throat, thinking of the friends we were leaving.

"I doubt it," he replied.

My lump was unnecessary. Pretty soon we met most of our old Nome friends in Tonapah, Nevada, the current big news in mining camps.

The last we saw of Alaska was Unalaska sinking into the ocean as the *Roanoke* went hull down over the southern horizon. Somehow, there was no place we had ever been that was so much like home.

HISTORICAL NOTES AND EDITORIAL COMMENTS

1. Virgil Earp had a ranch in the Peeple's valley near Prescott at that time. His post office address was Kirkland, Arizona. The deed files of Yavapai County show that he owned 160 acres.

2. It is obvious from the coroner's jury testimony that Warren was killed with little chance to defend himself. Boyett had fired two shots at him across the saloon in which the affair took place, whereupon Warren approached him cautiously, trying to talk him into putting down his pistols. The two were well known to each other; it appears from the circumstances that both had been drinking and that Boyett may have been dangerously drunk — perhaps also afraid that Warren might beat him up if he succeeded in disarming him.

With respect to the report of this shooting attributed to Mrs. Virgil Earp by Frank Waters, it is doubtful that she would have given such an inaccurate account, since she knew the facts. Warren was unarmed, an unlikely condition to put himself in if he had seriously feared that Boyett would shoot. Nonetheless, the coroner's hearing brought out the fact that Warren and Boyett had argued earlier, the former accusing Boyett of having once accepted money to murder him.

There have been persistent rumors that this killing was an aftermath of the events at Tombstone, but no definite connection has been made between Boyett and the associates or relatives of those shot by the Earps in the 1880s vendetta at Tombstone. (Inquest of the Coroner into the Death of Warren Earp, July 1900, filed with the Clerk of the Superior Court, Cochise County; for the rumor of a long-standing feud, see the *San Bernardino Sun,* July 10, 1900, p. 1.)

3. I have been unable to obtain definite information regarding the fate of Boyett. No mention is made in newspapers, and no official documents record his having been found mysteriously killed. It would seem probable that Forrestine Hooker of the Sierra Bonita Ranch, who knew both men well, would have mentioned it in her considerable writings if Boyett had simply disappeared, yet she did not, so far as I have been able to discover. The father of movie actor Rex Allen, an old time Willcox resident, several times confirmed the situation inferred by Josie. (Conversation of editor with Bill Hunley, who knew Mr. Allen, in Tombstone, 1975.)

4. Frank Waters' *Earp Brothers of Tombstone* infers that Allie and Josie didn't speak to each other. This is not true. There was no love lost between them, but they were cordial on the surface. (Mrs. Hildreth Hallowell, Allie's niece, on tape, 1971, in the Turner/Oster collection; conversation of editor with Wyatt's niece, Estelle Miller, San Bernardino, 1965.)

5. The *Nome Nugget,* January 1, 1900, reported: "This property, which is one of the most valuable and largest business blocks in the town of Nome, is owned and occupied by Wyatt Earp and C. E. Hoxsie who, as partners, conduct the Dexter Saloon and Club Rooms therein.... The Dexter is 30 x 70 with 12 ft. ceilings.... The proprietors ... built the Dexter in Sept. 1899."

Charlie Hoxie, as mentioned by Josie, was employed by the customs service when they first met him. This is amusing, if true, since in the 1920s in Juneau he was a bootlegger. (Letter from William Hunt to the editor, April 4, 1975.) Wyatt sold his interest in the Dexter to Hoxie when he left Nome in 1901. The name was then changed to the New Eldorado. (*Nome Semi-Weekly News,* November 3, 1903.) This paper lists C. E. Hoxie as sole proprietor. About 1914 Hoxie had moved on to Iditarod to share in its short boom. (Herbert Heller, *Sourdough Sagas,* p. 155.)

6. The panic of 1893 had adversely affected the Baldwin fortunes, as it had many others. To top that off, Lucky's Baldwin Hotel in San Francisco burned on November 23, 1898; it was valued at three and one-half million dollars and uninsured. (Carl B. Glasscock, *Lucky Baldwin,* pp. 263–275.)

7. Dave Unrah was the son of H. A. Unrah, Baldwin's business manager. (Glasscock, *Lucky Baldwin,* p. 280.)

8. See Chapter 14, note 7.

9. Besides assisting Lucky, apparently Wyatt lent a helping hand to many others he hardly knew. George Parsons wrote: "As to our meeting in Nome, Alaska, in 1900, about twenty years after the Tombstone life,

I will not forget the kindness of Wyatt Earp to one or two who were trying to make a start in a business there at Nome, and how he helped them by giving them quarters in his own big, commodious building." (George Parsons to Stuart Lake, November 6, 1928, Lake collection.)

10. Josie had previously gambled wildly on the horses, frequently borrowing large sums from Lucky Baldwin until Wyatt put a stop to it. (Cason ms.)

11. Josie's complete abstinence from gambling is questionable. When the Casons knew her in the 1930s, she apparently still wagered high stakes at poker on private occasions. (Jeanne Cason Laing on tape, 1975, in the editor's collection.)

12. The Earps' interest in the Dexter, plus returns on the business, netted them eighty-five thousand dollars when they liquidated their Alaskan venture. Newspaper reports exaggerated this to as much as three hundred thousand and referred to the triumphant return to the States of "Colonel Wyatt 'Mazuma' Earp," much to Wyatt's annoyance, since it made him a target for con men and grifters. (Conversation of editor with John Flood, Yuma, Arizona, 1956.)

16

Return to Our Beloved Desert

The years between our return from Alaska in 1901 and
Wyatt's death in 1929 were our happiest years together. Because
so few people ever get to experience their heart's desire, I always
think of them as our stolen years. The thing that made our happiness possible was having made enough money from our Alaskan
adventure to live comfortably for the rest of our lives.[1]

When our ship arrived in the States, there was no disagree-
ment about where we were going. We both loved the desert. Wyatt
still wanted a cattle ranch somewhere in a little-settled part of the
West. My husband had been on the verge of such a venture with
his brother Jim at the time that Virgil's letters lured them west
from Kansas to Arizona in 1879. The idea had never deserted
him, and he often daydreamed about a prosperous cattle-rancher's
life.

I must confess that secretly I harbored misgivings, though
I didn't hint at them openly at all. I thought we were getting on
in years. Wyatt was over fifty; I worried about the effect of a large
business venture on my husband's health. It would be hard work
and a financial risk that was bound to create worries. Besides,
it would tie us down. The plan of action I wanted to undertake
could lead to a big strike. It had happened to others and could
just as well happen to us.

Our final compromise was prospecting while we scouted for
a suitable ranch site. We spent hours planning the outfits we
would get, putting our heads together like a couple of kids hatch-

ing some entertainment project. When that grew tiresome we turned our minds to what we planned to do with all our money when we made our big strike — which we undoubtedly would. Our greatest pleasure, though we didn't realize it just then, was in the anticipation and the seeking. In being able to cut loose from the everyday grind, we had already struck it rich.

At this time we started what became our habitual manner of choosing which way we should go: in the event of a disagreewent we drew straws. This appealed to Wyatt's gambling spirit. The one that drew the longer straw two out of three times had the choice of the direction or activity we were to undertake.

There was no need to draw straws on our first prospecting trip. Mining talk in those days was all Nevada and the new discoveries around Tonopah. When we outfitted for this trip, we entered upon a phase of life we were to pursue together until the end. We would wander over the deserts of Nevada, Arizona and California with a camping outfit during the pleasant fall, winter and spring months. The hot summer months would be spent in Los Angeles.

I want to say a few things before writing of this period in our lives. First, I had no idea then that I would later write about it. If I had, I would have kept some sort of journal. As it is, I cannot exactly recall now all the places we went or the order of our going. The reader who is interested in a lengthy account of the lurid, fast-paced life of boom towns such as Tonopah and Goldfield may be disappointed; I could write a story telling exactly what life there was like,[2] but so could hundreds of people — in fact Mr. C. B. Glasscock has done just that. I can vouch from firsthand experience for the accuracy of the picture he constructed. Reading his book carried me back. I highly recommend reading his *Gold In Them Hills*.[3]

Actually, an exact accounting of our travels doesn't seem important to me. The significant thing is the type of life we lived, a sort of nomadic existence together that would be next to impossible today. The important fact, to my mind, is that hundreds of people cannot write a factual tale of living a roaming life with their husband for twenty years in America's last great empty stretch of the West. That is the exact aspect of those years I think is unique, and therefore that's what I intend to emphasize.

We outfitted for our first trip in Los Angeles. Knowing what to expect of mining camps as thoroughly as he did, Wyatt prepared for any emergency we might encounter. He took plenty of supplies for us and grain for the horses. He bought a large Studebaker wagon suitable for freighting and four draft horses. He hired Al Martin,[4] who had worked for us during our racing days, to drive it. He planned to use that rig for freighting supplies to Tonopah from the railroad at Sodaville and for making the return trip hauling ore.

For our own use he bought a spring wagon with a lighter team of horses. Al was to start ahead of us because he would go slower. We would meet in Tonopah. Wyatt carefully planned what we must carry to meet our essential needs, yet he was careful to keep the load to a minimum to preserve the horses.

I'm afraid I have to confess to trying to sneak in all sorts of extras, such as irons, cooking utensils and dishes. I succeeded in getting many of these hidden away when he was busy elsewhere. It didn't do much good however.

At the first stretch of hard-going Wyatt would insist on our walking to ease the pull. If it was exceptionally slow-going, he would seek to cull down the load even further. Then, invariably, my hidden treasures would come to light. His severe looks of exasperation and short lectures on my folly eventually cured me of this practice. "Sadie," he would say in a tone that left no doubt he really considered the case hopeless, "*when* are you going to learn that we can't risk breaking the team down out here on the desert?"

Disgustedly my efficient husband simply threw my frills to the side of the trail and pressed right on. Sometimes he tossed things out without a word or a look at me. I got the message just as well, and he knew it. I was always duly contrite and bowed before the storm, but before I learned my lesson I had probably supplied more trailside Indian wickiups with household goods than anyone living.

Despite his disdain of nonessentials, Wyatt never forgot anything necessary to make camping easy and comfortable. His outfit always included a tent, folding chairs and a folding table. For sleeping he always carried a mattress and springs. When we were more or less permanently camped, he would set these up on sawhorses in the tent. While on the move, the bedsprings were set across the wagonbed, resting on cleats on either side. This left plenty of room for our supplies underneath. During the day, the springs and mattress were fastened upright to the wagon bows. This allowed easy access to our supplies. A sheet-iron camp stove and a well-arranged box of dishes and utensils made meal preparation fairly simple.

On our first trip Wyatt watched my clumsy attempt at making a bed in close quarters. He finally snickered. "If you think you can do it any better, do it yourself!" I told him.

"Here!" he said, grabbing the bedding from my botched attempt. "You may be able to make a bed in the house, but this job needs working on!" In a short time, with a few deft moves, he had made it up as smooth and neat as a hospital bed.

"There!" he said. From then on Wyatt was official bed-maker in the wagon. In the tent I had no trouble, since there was ample room.

After the wagon was repacked, each morning Wyatt threw a large tarpaulin over the load, fitted it snugly and securely fastened it. He was the soul of neatness.

The day to leave Los Angeles and embark on our first prospecting trip finally came. I took my seat beside Wyatt on the wagon, he slapped the lines lightly on the team's backs and we started smartly on our way. The first part of our journey involved getting out of Los Angeles. This was no real job, since it was then only a sprawling town soon giving way to groves and then open country.

One day after we hit the real desert country we overtook a man trudging along the road in the direction we were traveling. There was no second thought then about picking people up, such as there would be today with a hitchhiker. So we stopped to ask the stranger if he'd like a ride. "I'm headed for the new strike up at Tonopah," he told us.

"Traveling pretty light!" Wyatt observed.

"Have to," he rejoined. "I got back from a construction job in San Diego and found my wife sold us out down to my last pair of trousers, took the kid and ran off with a travelin' revivalist." There didn't seem to be much to say to that, so we rode a long way, each buried deeply in his own thoughts.

Our passenger turned out to be good company. He pitched right in and helped with every job in camp or on the trail. I remember this fellow particularly because the first day he joined us a peculiar incident occurred. We never ran into such an unheard-of thing again in all our travels.

Toward evening, when the horses were spent and thirsty, the welcome sight of a ranch came into view. We were all tired and hungry. The sound of a dog barking told us that the place was lived in and likely had a good well. In desert country such places were welcome havens to travelers. The owners were usually as glad to see company as the wayfarer was to reach an oasis. "Thank God we're near a place to get some water!" I can recall Wyatt commenting.

Shortly we pulled up at a neat, tidily fenced little homestead. Wyatt and our passenger both got down and approached the gate. It was locked. The dog ran along the fence, sniffing the visitors, then ran back to the house, barking furiously. No one made an appearance.

Wyatt yelled to try to raise someone at the house, but there. was no response. He went to another gate near what must have been the kitchen door. It also was locked. We were sure from the way the dog acted that someone was inside. Wyatt yelled several times more until finally an old man, a Frenchman judging from his accent, stuck his head out. He looked us over suspiciously. "What you want?" he asked.

"We want to water the horses," Wyatt told him

"No water! I don't have no water!" the old man replied with poor grace. "You go two more miles. Plenty of water. No water here. Nothing to eat. You can't camp here!"

We couldn't believe our ears. It was the unwritten code of the desert country to give water to travelers and their animals. The written law demanded it.

"We don't want food or a camping spot," Wyatt patiently told him. "We only want water for our horses so we can go on. Surely you don't aim to make a thirsty animal do without a drink. I can see you have plenty of water over there in the tank."

"I don't give no water tonight!" the old man stated positively and started to go back in.

Wyatt jumped over the fence in a flash and kicked the door open. Shortly, the old man came flying back out, propelled by a strong arm. "You'll water our horses or I'll boot your pants off!" Wyatt shouted, giving a sample to start with. "You'll be lucky if I don't burn your blank-dash house down! Don't you know you can be put in jail for refusing water to horses in this country?"

Our hitchhiker looked somewhat amazed at the whole performance. We got our water tout de suite. Wyatt went inside with the crusty old devil while he got the gate keys. "Just to be sure he doesn't get a shotgun instead!" Wyatt growled. "That'd be a helluva way to go after all I've been through in my life!"

We drove to the next ranch to camp, and it was a good sight more than two miles. "You move around right smart for a man your age!" our passenger told Wyatt admiringly.

I thought, "If you only knew the half of it, stranger!" but I kept quiet. The balance of our trip was comparatively uneventful. All told, it took several weeks to go from Los Angeles to Tonopah. All along the trail we had been warned of the atrocious living conditions in Tonopah. But living conditions didn't bother us — we could live in our wagon and be as clean and comfortable as in any miner's cabin.

The town was crawling with old friends from all over the West and Alaska. Tex Rickard was already in business.[5] He urged Wyatt to get into some enterprise or other and start making a mint. I suppose he would have done so if I hadn't raised Cain. It was the very thing we had been trying to escape. But every man finds it hard to resist the lure of success. Wyatt was no exception.

I put my foot down hard for a change. Happily, my husband saw the sense in this. Beyond grubstaking some prospectors and freighting with Al Martin, he did not get deeply embroiled in the commercial life of the place. He and Al carried ore to Soda-ville a few times and returned with hay and grain for the stock in Tonopah. Before we left, Wyatt financed the Northern Saloon, leaving it in Al Martin's hands to operate when we departed.[6]

Wyatt got acquainted with a pleasant, well-educated young fellow named Tasker Oddie. He was then, of course, an unknown. Eventually he represented Nevada in the U.S. Senate.[7]

Wyatt was able to be of some help to the young fellow on a couple of occasions. One day some men tried to jump one of Mr. Oddie's claims. When Tasker caught them at it he couldn't think of anything to do but jump into the shallow prospect hole and defy them to move him. The men showed pistols at this point and ordered him off his own claim. Just then Wyatt and Al Martin happened on the scene, driving a spring wagon.

Wyatt, always quick to size up that sort of situation, told Al what to do. "It looks like Tasker's in trouble!" he said. "You cover us with the shotgun from behind the wagon — but don't show the gun till after I get out and attract their attention. I'll get in the hole with Oddie. Don't shoot unless I shoot. We'll drop down in the hole if I have to shoot, and then you let 'em have it too!"

They drew up some fifty feet from the excitement. Wyatt jumped from the wagon and strode rapidly to the prospect hole. The men saw him coming but were too surprised or too uncertain to do anything to stop him. Wyatt jumped right in the hole with Mr. Oddie. By this time, Al was behind the wagon with the shotgun ready.

"Hey, butinsky!" one of the claim-jumpers called to Wyatt. "You're asking for trouble! Who the hell do you think you are?"

Wyatt hated to trade on his reputation, but he was still well known from his exploits in the West. He would use his name if it saved bloodshed. "I'm Wyatt Earp," he told them.

I can imagine the tone of voice and the look which I'd experienced once or twice myself. Wyatt pointed toward the wagon and Al, who was ominously aiming the double-barrel. "I'd size up the odds if I were you fellows before you head into a lot of trouble you may not be able to handle."

Wyatt's Northern Saloon in Tonopah, probably in the fall of 1902. The people in the foreground have not been identified.

They turned and looked down those twin barrels of Al's shotgun and stood right where they were. The one that had been so lippy, according to what Mr. Oddie later told me, said, "You win *Mr.* Earp. We'll be going along if it's O.K. with you."

Wyatt nodded assent. "First put back those location stakes you kicked down," he ordered them. They did it without complaint. That parting order from Wyatt was typical. I can clearly remember him telling someone or other, "With hard cases, when you get the upper hand, always rub their noses into it. That way they don't forget!"

Mr. Oddie couldn't have been more impressed. "Wyatt didn't even have a pistol," he told me. I knew better. He generally carried a forty-five under his coat somewhere. But he seldom had to get it out. He was too good a tactician and strategist for that.

We actually only spent a few months around Tonopah, though those months were busy enough to have filled a few years of most lives. Soon we were again getting ready to prospect. Wyatt sold our light team and wagon and one team of the heavier horses to Mr. Oddie. We kept the large wagon and one heavy team for our use.

Our prospecting days were well planned, and we worked systematically. After all, it had become our business, and we treated it with the respect due a profession. There were times when we felt sure for a few hours that we had found our bonanza.

We would hurry to camp with some samples of likely looking ore. One of us would break off some pieces and pound them into powder in the mortar. Anxiously, we would pan the result in our horn spoon,[8] washing it with a little water till only the heaviest residue was left. Then came the tense moment of examining it for "color." When there was enough gold to keep up our hopes, we would head for the nearest assay office to have the value estimated in dollars per ton of ore. More often there was nothing, and our spirits would sink.

We wandered many miles and worked on our prospecting most days, till the days became weeks that finally stretched into many months, without finding anything worth developing. After awhile we found our way to Silver Peak. We camped there for a while to rest ourselves and the horses. Actually, we'd been having a harder time of it than the animals.

We camped in the shelter of an old broken-down adobe house, a relic of the town's long-ago boom days. Fall had overtaken us. A nip was in the night air, making a large cheery fire of mesquite or ironwood welcome. Wyatt was turning over in his mind the notion of leaving Nevada for the winter. We would go to Keeler on the railroad by way of Pipers' Ranch. We would sell our outfit there and go by rail to Los Angeles.

The detour to Pipers' ranch was for the express benefit of our kitty. We always had pets. Tony, our white spitz, went with us wherever we went. But cats don't care to be cooped up for traveling. This one was a stray we had adopted since coming to Silver Peak. Even so, we didn't intend to leave without finding a good home for it somewhere. The Pipers had mentioned needing a cat when we had passed through; cats were always good to have around a ranch to keep down the population of rats and mice.

We sold all our camping equipment but a few items to see us through to the railroad. We kept only our prospecting tools, the mattress, bedding and some utensils for cooking and eating. We even had parted with our bedsprings and stove, for we expected to reach Keeler the evening of the second day of travel. We planned to stay our first night at Pipers' Ranch, but you could never be sure in desert travel. There was a ready demand for our camp supplies. Mr. Vollmer, the assayer at Silver Peak, bought them all.

Then we had a sudden dislocation of our plans. I found a likely looking piece of gold ore that assayed so rich we turned back and bought our outfit back. As it was, we spent a couple of weeks fruitlessly prospecting for the source of the sample. We never found it and nearly froze to death trying. Finally we gave up and returned to Los Angeles for the winter.

HISTORICAL NOTES AND EDITORIAL COMMENTS

1. There is some question as to whether this was entirely true. By the 1920s the couple reportedly was living largely on Josie's inheritance from her parents. Bill Miller, husband of Wyatt's niece Estelle, commented during a conversation in 1965, "She was his meal ticket." Also, Mrs. Hildreth Hallowell, Mrs. Virgil Earp's niece, said it was her opinion that in view of Wyatt's high income in the past he found living on Josie's money deeply humiliating. (1971 tape, Turner/Oster collection.) Neither remark should be taken as gospel, but they are given for what they are worth as family opinions. Another source indicates that Wyatt managed a living from his mines and from gambling up to his last year or so. (Barney Roberts of Parker, Arizona, on tape, 1970, Turner/Oster collection.) Roberts said he frequently observed as much as fifteen hundred dollars on the gambling table during games in which Earp participated at Parker in the 1920s. Josephine had income from her family's business in the Bay area and from oil royalties. (Cason notes.)

2. Wyatt seems to have been more involved in some of the active affairs of the Nevada boom camps than Josie's recollections would lead us to believe. After Wyatt rescued Tasker Oddie from claim jumpers on his

Mizpah mine, for example, Oddie had the former marshal hire some twenty mine guards, with Wyatt himself as supervisor, to prevent a recurrence of claim-jumping. (Mrs. Hugh Brown, *Lady in Boomtown*, p. 29.)

3. C. B. Glasscock was writing from firsthand experience about the turn-of-the-century mining boom. He was co-editor of the *Death Valley Chuck-Walla* published at Greenwater, Nevada, in those days and knew most of the principals involved at Tonopah and Goldfield personally, having also been in both those camps during the big boom. In the foreword to *Gold In Them Hills* he acknowledges having interviewed almost everyone of importance in the founding of the Tonopah District. The book is full of colorful, first-person, detailed accounts. See the Reference section of this book for bibliographical information.

4. Wyatt seems to have turned the operation of the Northern over to Al Martin relatively soon after it opened. The *Tonopah Bonanza* for February 1, 1902, announced Wyatt's arrival from Nome. The next month it advertised "*The Northern*, Wyatt Earp prop. A gentleman's resort." Al Martin was alive as late as 1930, since Josie met him in the Oakland depot sometime during that year. Martin had been a horseman who worked for the Earps during the racing days as a trainer. (Cason notes, Lake notes.)

5. Tex Rickard's first Nevada saloon was at Tonopah. Next he opened the huge Northern at Goldfield, which he moved to Rawhide before entering the world of sports as a full-time fight-promoter. (Charles Samuels, *The Magnificent Rube*.) For more details on Rickard, see Chapter 12, note 6.

6. Wyatt sold his Northern Saloon to Al Martin. (Cason notes.)

7. Tasker L. Oddie came to Nevada from his home in New Jersey on legal business for the Anson Phelps Stokes mining interests about 1900. At the time of Jim Butler's discovery, Oddie was a practicing lawyer and district attorney for Nye County. (Brown, *Lady in Boomtown*, p. 25; Glasscock, *Gold in Them Hills*, p. 23.) Oddie made and lost a fortune between 1902 and 1911, ending up as a beans-and-buns prospector once more. Shortly he launched a successful campaign for governor and later for U.S. senator. (Glasscock, *Gold In Them Hills*, pp. 316–318.)

8. A horn spoon is a miniature gold-panning device used in dry country to save water. It is made by cutting a cow's horn diagonally to obtain an oval-shaped spoon. The ore is ground to a powdery consistency, then panned in the horn spoon with only a small quantity of water.

17

Desert Living

The next spring we equipped ourselves as we had previously. With a brief stop in San Bernardino to visit Wyatt's family, we made our way onto the Mojave. "This is the same trail my family and I came down when we moved to San Bernardino from Iowa in 1864," Wyatt told me as we were climbing from San Bernardino up onto the high desert. After the highway to Barstow was built over that route, it took only hours to make the same trip that took us two weeks.

I was thrilled to rejoin the desert land I loved. No air is so crystal clear and invigorating. The sunsets were incomparable, each one different, every one subtly beautiful. Words can't describe them; they must be experienced. Wyatt seemed to understand, perhaps share, my twilight and evening fantasy. If the chores of setting up camp and caring for the team didn't absolutely prevent it, we would walk to a rise together and silently watch the sunsets and moonrises. We must have done so a thousand nights during those years.

After dark the desert came to life. The wild, chilling, yet half-friendly cry of the coyote greeted us almost every night. Owls would glide and flit, hooting mournfully. The night hawk swooped on silent wings, uttering his occasional squawk. Nearby there were little stirrings in the rocks and sand, as small creatures set about making their living.

I am not religious, although my mother was deeply so. Perhaps because of her example the peaceful, yet awesome desert nights never failed to move me to informal prayer directed to my German mother's "Lieber Gott." I talked over my thoughts with Him, my hopes, anxieties, fears. No matter how tired or tense or irritable the day may have left me, when I laid my head down and silently uttered my "Lieber Gott," I relaxed almost at once and could feel peace.

I used to tease Wyatt about the hardship to which he subjected his poor wife, but I loved every second of it. I recall once saying to him, "Wyatt, there aren't many women who would live with you as I do, roughing it in a hard country such as this. You should really appreciate me more. Look what has happened to my complexion and hair!"

He looked me over carefully, even parting my hair and pretending to peer closely into it. I knew better. He couldn't see much at that range any longer without his glasses.[1] "What do you see?" I asked.

"No bugs, if that's what's worrying you. Not much gray hair." He backed away for a longer view. "On the whole, you look pretty healthy to me," he observed. "There aren't many women that keep as well as you do. You never need a doctor. For my money, you suit me pretty well."

That satisfied me. Wyatt wasn't much for pretty talk.

Near where Parker, Arizona, now stands we crossed the Colorado River on a barge operated by a Mojave Indian. We went to Harqua Hala, where we had been for awhile in 1889, and stayed for some time. When we found no land of the type Wyatt was seeking, we returned to a location closer to the river near Cibola. Wyatt's oldest brother Jim[2] joined us there. The two still were thinking of ranching together, as they had been when they left Kansas in 1879.[3]

Near our camp they located land that appeared to be good for a ranch, but they had to find out whether it had enough groundwater. Without almost unlimited sub-surface water, it would have been foolish to try ranching in that dry country. There was plenty of forage, but no springs or waterholes. They hired two Mexicans to sink trial wells.

Our camp was on a high piece of ground overlooking a broad gulch. We kept the horses on the opposite side, where the forage was better. The bank over there was quite a bit lower than our camping spot, and we could see the horses for quite a distance away. Generally they didn't stray far, since the men kept them hobbled.

It was July, much later than we generally stayed on the desert, but the year had been pleasantly cool. We usually left for the Coast no later than May, but this year the work on the wells had caused the men to linger.

July and August are the rainy season in that part of the country, just as they are in Tombstone. One day we spotted a real lulu of a summer storm forming to the southwest of us. These rainstorms are usually accompanied by heavy winds, blowing sand and lightning. We could hear the thunder worrying around, muttering to itself in the canyons west of the river, some time before the first puffs of wind reached us.

"I'll go round up the horses and get them on the high ground," Jim said. "You two had better tie down everything movable, from the looks of this one!" He set out for the opposite bank of the wash at a trot, since the storm was now moving in fast.

The sand was being sucked up into a regular yellow wall. High behind it, an ominously churning black cloud was flashing lightning. We hurried around, weighting down or otherwise securing everything light enough to blow away. Wyatt reinforced the tent stakes with piles of heavy stones.

Tony, our spitz, got under the bed in the tent, scared out of her wits by the roar of the wind and the continuous thunder. I was scared, too, and felt as though I'd like to join her. Typically, Wyatt was unconcerned. He filled his pipe and prepared to watch the spectacle from the front of the tent. "Doesn't all that noise scare you?" I asked him.

"You'll never hear any thunder from the lightning that gets you," he told me. I found that bit of news small consolation — in fact none at all.

The sand hit us first, getting into everything. Very soon it was turned to mud right in the air by the huge drops of rain, the forerunners of the deluge that followed. The wind ripped and tore at everything, but we had succeeded in tying and weighting things so well that very little blew away. The tent whipped, snapped and billowed, but withstood the severest gusts. The worst passed in perhaps ten minutes; after that it was just a heavy downpour. Every depression filled, and streams formed in every gully. Our gulch was rapidly becoming a river, getting wider and wider.

Wyatt wasn't a worrier, but I could tell he was concerned for Jim's safety. Every few minutes he would try to see to the opposite bank through the sheets of rain that were coming down. Once or twice he said, "I hope Jim found the horses and got them on high ground," or, "I hope none of them were hit by lightning!"

By now the water in the gulch was roaring loud enough to hear above the pounding of the rain. Finally, the violent cloudburst phase of the storm let up in favor of a steady rain. We settled down to wait it out. Eventually it tapered off to a light spatter. Up till then I had taken no pleasure in any part of the meteorological display. Now my spirits were lifted by my favorite desert odor — the pungent smell of wet creosote bushes. This is a pleasant, spicy aroma that I never get enough of. To me it's the most typical desert fragrance. I love it.

As soon as the heavier rain stopped, we set out along the bank of the gulch, trying to locate Jim on the other side. I thought I could hear faint shouting from time to time, but the roaring water prevented my telling from which direction it was coming. Then Wyatt heard it too. "It's on the other side somewhere, I think," he said.

We both scrutinized the far side of the gulch. Finally we spotted a movement over there in a large old cottonwood tree some distance above our camp. Jim was safely perched on a branch some twenty feet up. When we got closer, Wyatt yelled, "That water must have been pretty high to wash you way up there!" I could detect relief in his tone.

"Wash, hell!" Jim screamed back. "I had to skin up here damn quick, I'll tell you! You two had it pretty soft!" They were both yelling at the top of their voices to make themselves heard above the torrent rushing along in the gully.

"You got the horses up there with you?" Wyatt hollered.

"Not so's you can notice!" Jim bellowed back. "They're back there!" He motioned toward the hills on the other side. "I got caught trying to make it to camp!"

"I see that! Planning to stay there long?"

'Till that river dries up or freezes over!"

A steady rain kept up almost until dawn, and the water roared by violently. Although Jim was not in any danger, Wyatt sat in his slicker on the bank on a soapbox all night, calling over to his brother occasionally. Surely my husband knew his vigil couldn't help Jim; it was prompted by close Earp family affection.

I'm afraid the excitement did me in. After cooking something for the two of us with wood we had kept dry under the wagon sheet, I went to bed. "These beans are sure good!" was the last thing I heard Wyatt yell to Jim.

"Go to H!" his brother hollered back.

On that note, I went to sleep.

Jim was sixty-two or sixty-three at this time, so his predicament was no joke. Fortunately, he had lived an active life, and the experience did him no harm. It was warm enough that the wetting didn't cause him to get a cold or pneumonia.

We had many good days and nights together on this trip. During the conversations of Wyatt and Jim around the evening campfire I learned many new things about Wyatt's dangerous experiences as a lawman. The men were not talking for my ears, but much of what they said is the basis of what I have told here about my husband's life.

The revelations of those days prompted me to quiz Wyatt for details later, whenever he was in a talkative mood. That wasn't very often. Generally, when someone pumped him for bloody details, he would gently refuse by saying, "I reckon we could talk about something a little more cheerful than that!" That was the end of it, too. He could be extremely uncommunicative and most always was when strangers were around. On only one other occasion in later years did I hear him talk of the old times. That was when Bill Tilghman,[4] a fellow lawman from the Dodge City days, visited him.

It was getting hotter every day, so Wyatt sent me over to the

Coast to escape the heat while he and Jim stayed to work with the Mexicans who were sinking the test wells. Early in September I returned, taking the train from Los Angeles to Yuma. Small river steamers still plied the Colorado at that time to accommodate the isolated mining camps and ranches that the railroad and freight lines did not reach. In fact, they ran intermittently until about 1907, when the Laguna Dam was constructed above Yuma. It was on one of those boats that I left Yuma to travel as far as Ehrenberg, where Wyatt met me with the wagon and took me on to camp.

"I have a surprise for you, honey!" he said shortly before we reached camp. "I built a nice house for you while you were away!"

"A house!" I exclaimed. "Are you going to take up that land where you are?"

"I don't know about that," he said. "But you will have this house I've built while we are here at any rate."

When Jim joined us they spoke a great deal of the house and of how sure they were that I would like it. There seemed to be some joke about it, and I curiously asked a good many questions without finding out a thing except that it was a house, my house, and it seemed to have been built to protect me from snakes.

I was dying of curiosity to see this wonderful construction. When we got to camp I looked around but saw no building. Wyatt led me past the camp to a big mesquite tree that stood close to the gulch. About six or seven feet up, its huge trunk divided into several large branches that held up my "house," almost hidden by the leaves, all secure and snug. The shelter was constructed of packing boxes and wagon canvas, while the ladder climbing up to it was made of poles, Indian fashion. It was no work of art, but I could sleep there without fear of snakes.

Wyatt was obviously waiting for approval. "It's beautiful!" I told him. "Just beautiful!" To my eyes it was. I think I loved my husband more that minute than I ever had.

"You probably couldn't find a better house if you looked around the whole neighborhood," Wyatt said.

At night, when I went up to bed in my "house," I sometimes thought back to all of the fancy places in which we had lived. I knew I wouldn't for the world exchange this simple life for that.

HISTORICAL NOTES AND EDITORIAL COMMENTS

1. This was probably 1903, so we may judge that Wyatt was wearing glasses for close work at least by age fifty-five. One can imagine a parody of the classic Hollywood gunfight in which two old-timers, before drawing their pistols, excuse themselves to get out their specs.

2. See Chapter 8, note 2, for Jim Earp's post-Tombstone peregrinations.

3. Wyatt and Jim may have been planning to preempt, or homestead, public land. This was still being done as late as after World War II in that vicinity, since the editor lived on such a ranch in the Yuma Valley in 1957–58.

4. Bill Tilghman had been a Dodge City acquaintance of Wyatt's in the early days. He was later city marshal of Dodge. In 1889 he made the run into the Cherokee Strip in Oklahoma and remained in there for the rest of his life. He was a lawman during most of that period, being a deputy U.S. marshal (in which capacity he captured the famous outlaw Bill Doolin), a county sheriff, then chief of police of Oklahoma City. He was shot and killed as the marshall of Cromwell, Oklahoma, still in harness at age seventy-two in 1926. (Letters of his wife, Zoe Tilghman, to the editor, 1962–64.) Mrs. Tilghman did not hold Wyatt or Bat in very high esteem as lawmen compared to her husband. In terms of years of experience, Tilghman indeed made them both appear amateurs.

18

We Find a Roost at Last

The test wells at Cibola didn't pan out for Wyatt and Jim. If I'm not mistaken, this was the end of Wyatt's lifelong ambition to own a ranch. I did my best to talk him out of the idea. It was, I argued, risky, time-consuming and too hard for a man his age. That last argument probably wasn't too smart. "I'm as good as I ever was!" he told me.

What I had to say to that was, "And you'll stay that way for another twenty years if you don't do anything foolish!" Whatever Wyatt thought, the subject of a ranch was dropped and never came up seriously again.

The dream of a ranch had been realized, however, by our good old friend from Tombstone, John Clum. He owned a nice piece of land near Indio, where he raised dates along with a few cattle. One time during World War I we went there to visit John in our first automobile.

Knowing his love of horses, I had been surprised when Wyatt bought the contraption. But he took to it with enthusiasm. With his usual grace and coordination, learning to drive, even at nearly seventy years old, was no problem for Wyatt.

The roads in those days were not what they are today. In dry weather the dust was almost suffocating, so we wore what were called dusters. They were the same kind of linen overcoats we wore for stagecoach travel in the old days. We also had goggles, such as aviators wear, and donned caps and scarfs to keep our hair in place. In wet weather there were also problems with mud.

It was hardly worth trying to travel by auto under such conditions, since there were almost no good roads except in the cities. When we traveled any distance it was usually by train if we expected to be relatively certain of arriving on time. But on this occasion Wyatt was proud of our new auto, and I'm sure he wanted to show it off to John Clum, who also had recently purchased a flivver of some sort.

We were rolling confidently along at the breath-taking speed of thirty mph when a huge bull rushed into our path. Wyatt braked abruptly and swung the wheel to avoid the animal, but it was mad at us. It ran full tilt into our radiator. Fortunately, by this time we were hardly in motion at all, but even at that I can remember the jolt when the beast hit us. It brought us to a full stop.

Wyatt said something unprintable. The bull shook its head and backed away, then lowered its head to attack again. "Do something, Wyatt!" I cried hysterically. "He'll kill us!"

Wyatt reached into the back seat where a forty-five caliber six-shooter was shoved down among our luggage within ready reach. He fired a shot in an attempt to scare the animal away. It didn't even seem to notice. Instead it rushed to my side of the car and lowered its head for another charge at us, bellowing fiercely. I screamed, sure it would climb right into the seat and gore me to death.

The roar of the six-shooter rang in my ear. It was the first time I'd seen anything killed directly under my nose. The sight of such a mammoth warm-blooded creature losing its life sickened me. I must have fainted. The next thing I knew Wyatt was swabbing my face with a wet cloth.

"It's all right, honey!" he reassured me. "The bull is dead."

"I know," I said. I still felt weak and trembly. "Our poor new car!" I moaned.

At this point a man rode up on a horse. "Did you plug that bull, mister?" he asked.

"You damn betcha I did!" Wyatt told him.

"You'll pay for him!" the man stated positively.

"Before you get hot under the collar," Wyatt advised, "look at what he did to the front of our car. And he was just ready to gore my wife when I shot him. You ought to be arrested for letting a critter like that run loose!"

The man rode around to the front of the car and looked it over. We got out and walked around front ourselves. Little streams of water were running out into the dust. "See what I mean?" Wyatt asked.

"That don't amount to much," the man observed. "Five dollars will fix it. That bull was worth five hundred. You're gonna have to pay too!"

"We'll see about that," Wyatt told him in a level voice — too level. I could see the symptoms of trouble brewing.

"You're G. D. right we'll see about it!" the man hollered. "We're gonna see about it right now! You greenhorns are gonna stay here till I call the sheriff!"

Wyatt laughed. "The sheriff is two days away in San Bernardino," he observed.

"There's a deputy up the road," the man retorted. Wyatt ignored the bluster. "How far is John Clum's place?" he asked the fellow.

"You a friend of Mr. Clum's?" the man inquired, some of the hostility dropping from his voice.

"You bet!" Wyatt told him.

The man laughed. "I'm Mr. Clum's foreman. That's his bull you just shot."

Wyatt's expression was worth a hundred dollars. "I'll be damned!" he said.

The man hooked his lariat to our bumper, and his horse towed us the two miles that remained to the Clum ranch. When John heard what happened he just roared. "That damn bull wasn't worth ten cents anyway!" he observed.

Visits with old friends like John were just interludes in our winter wanderings up and down across the Mojave, sometimes in California, sometimes in Nevada or Arizona. We prospected on and off, hoping to make the big find. In the course of our travels we met a good many original characters. In that sense, we struck it rich almost every year.

For example, we went from Cibola back to Harqua Hala, as I recall. There was an old Chilean woman there who was perhaps eighty, in partnership with an American we knew as "Pete." Pete was a product of the times and had obviously played hooky more than he went to school. She, on the other hand, had not only come from a rich Chilean family, but was the widow of a wealthy American businessman. She was now as poor as Pete. No telling where her former fortune went.

This old woman and Pete lived together and worked the claims that gave them a living. She was never found without a Bull Durham cigarette hanging from her lips. In cold weather, she would fill a gold pan with hot coals, place a board over it and sit with her feet on the board. A blanket wrapped her legs, holding in the heat. Sitting in this manner, she played solitaire and smoked for hours on end. She was always cheerful. From her looks and attitude you'd never know she'd had bad luck.

We met another woman at Las Vegas, Nevada, when we stopped at her ranch for a meal. She was tall, thin, shriveled like a dry apple, but energetic and capable. I was happy to see that she was neat and clean as well. She served a dandy meal, but I got quite a shock when after dinner I saw her take a large chew from a plug of tobacco.

While we were wandering in the wilderness, we paid careful attention to what we ate. We tried to have as great a variety as in the city, even though much of it had to be in cans. I did the greater part of the cooking. However, when it came to hotcakes, one of Wyatt's favorites, he thought he did a much better job than me. He'd say, none too tactfully, "Let me cook the hotcakes. You don't quite have the hang of it!"

There were other times when he cooked for enjoyment, or as he said "just to keep my hand in at it." He even turned his hand to a new recipe now and then. This reminds me of a story connected with one of his particular cooking triumphs. When we were at Harqua Hala one time, a young Indian began coming to our camp. He was a Mojave, a big, strapping, goodlooking boy, clean and unusually intelligent. He always dressed in bright colors and wore gay feathers in his hair. For this reason, we nicknamed him Dude.

Wyatt took a shine to the boy and did him small favors whenever he could, such as helping him shoe a horse or giving him tobacco. As a result, my husband could do no wrong in Dude's eyes. It was seldom that a day passed without Dude dropping in to give Wyatt a hand with whatever he was doing.

There was a ranch about three miles from our camp where I went every other day on horseback for eggs, milk and fresh vegetables. One day when I was down at the ranch, Wyatt was reading something that gave him a hankering for some lemon pie. He found my recipe for it but could find no lemon extract, so he made his pie using vinegar in place of lemon. About the time the dessert was cool enough to eat, Dude showed up, so he and Wyatt had lemon pie and coffee.

I came back just as Dude was trying to tell Wyatt how good the pie was. He said, "Plenty good! Fine! Wunnaful!" and about there words failed him. I sampled some, and it really was good, so good that I decided to make some a couple days later as a favor for the men — Wyatt and Dude. I thought the piece I sampled was pretty tasty, but Dude was of a different mind. (I think it may have been the cook and not the pie.) "Make me sick," he said, and that was that. It was a long while before I stopped hearing about that incident. It was too much to expect that a husband wouldn't tell that story on his wife!

The years were full of small events such as this. Basically, we had a satisfying and tranquil existence.[1] This is not to say that we didn't encounter our share of difficulties, as does anyone who journeys on the desert by wagon. One warm day we were traveling along, planning to stop for the night at a well we had used on several previous occasions. However, it had been some time since we were there last. The well was in a little-frequented canyon among some rough hills. To get there, we had to leave the road and travel quite a distance.

We planned to reach the water by night, and the sun had just set as we pulled up. The horses were expectantly awaiting a drink, knowing well what we had come for. However, when we pulled up the bucket, it told a sad tale. All it held was two dead rats. With about five gallons of water left in our barrel, we could have been in a bad spot. We gave our last drop to the horses, rested them for awhile, then pulled wearily back to the road and on into the night.

We had no way of knowing if the next well might not be dry also. This was one of the gambles the desert traveler had to take. Sometimes the price of losing was disaster. It would be hours before we reached the next well, but our best course was to keep moving during the cooler night hours while the horses weren't really suffering from thirst yet. To our relief, the well was full. Though we were dead tired, Wyatt rationed out water to the horses a little at a time to prevent their getting sick.

Looking back, I regret that I didn't help more with the little things when it would have been only a minor inconvenience to do so. But Wyatt was so willing, and it was such a blessing to just sink back and collapse on a roll of bedding till camp was set up. By then I was usually restored enough to cook. Wyatt always seemed to have a reservoir with a little extra energy in it that could be called upon when needed. I didn't.

On one of our return trips from the desert to Los Angeles in the spring, for some reason we went by the unaccustomed route through Banning. In the late afternoon our team climbed the last mile of mountain road into Banning in a chilly, drizzly rain. We were cold, wet and weary when we arrived to find there was no room to be had in the only hotel. We did get a meal of beans and spuds at the one restaurant, which was run by a Chinaman. The hot food hit the spot, simple though it was.

Since it was pouring by this time, it was imperative to find some sort of shelter. We were given permission to camp in the shed of the wagon yard. Wyatt stabled and fed the team, then made our bed in the wagon, pulling the tarpaulin snugly over the whole thing for added warmth.

My husband seemed unusually downcast as he worked, so much so I asked what was troubling him. "This is a helluva life to drag a wife into," Wyatt said. "You haven't so much as a fire to warm yourself before climbing in here."

He couldn't have missed my true feelings further. "I'm tickled to death with this arrangement!" I retorted. "I've always loved the sound of rain on a roof and the smell of fresh, damp air. As for wamth — I'm snug as can be!"

He seemed to brighten up a little at this. "Are you sure?" he asked, still uncertain.

"I'm sure," I told him, and meant it. "I'm glad we couldn't get a room. I wouldn't be half so happy if we were at the Palace Hotel tonight!" Wyatt took my hand and held it between his, squeezing it affectionately. I asked, "Do you remember the time years ago when we passed a cabin on the train in Texas and you said I wouldn't be happy living like that?"

"I guess so," he replied.

"You were dead wrong!" I said.

Wyatt squeezed my hand again. "I remember now. That was a long time ago, and we didn't really know each other yet. You're a dead game sport right down to the ground!"

From Wyatt that was the highest praise. I was so happy and proud I felt as if I'd burst. Tears ran down my checks in the dark, but my husband didn't know it till I kissed him. "Honey," he said, "you're crying! You were just saying that to make me cheer up!"

"Oh, no I wasn't!" I desperately assured him, angry because it came out in a sob he'd be sure to misinterpret, just like a leather-headed man. So few of them know that some women cry when they're sublimely happy. Wyatt cradled me close, and I sobbed myself to sleep on his shoulder. I *was* sublimely happy, and I knew it, whether he did or not.

We of course eventually had a permanent home in Los Angeles, where we landed between trips to the desert.[2] But our life there was no different than that of a retired businessman or banker. Therefore, I intend to expand very little literary steam on it.

It was inevitable that Hollywood would discover Wyatt when they started producing what came to be known as the "horse opera." They approached seeking his advice, they said.[3] His experience with Hollywood was like his experience with newspapermen. After he discovered that they paid no attention to what he told them, Wyatt's sly sense of humor was directed toward the movie people. He pulled their legs, telling them the sort of improbable things found in Western fiction stories. To his amazement, they swallowed these tall tales hook, line and sinker, but were always skeptical of the truth.

At this point, my husband gave up in disgust, refusing to have anything further to do with those "damn fool dudes," as he called them. The only good thing to come of Wyatt's Hollywood experiences was that he made two close friends in the movie business. They were William S. Hart and Tom Mix.[4]

But we were always glad to get back to our desert, notwithstanding the fact that we left behind some good friends. We met few people of any kind most days out in the chaparral. This is not to say that we lacked friends in the wilderness community. On the contrary, there were many, but they were, of necessity, widely spaced.

But if we hadn't a single friend on the desert, I wouldn't have been lonely so long as Wyatt was with me. We had grown so close to one another as a result of the life we had led; we were now a little world unto ourselves. Wyatt always tried to arrange our affairs so I wouldn't be left alone. He knew I was a terrible scaredy-cat. I didn't fear the country so much as the thought of falling into the company of some of the few renegade Indians who still were drifting about.[5]

Try though I would to be brave, I always lost my head when left alone. I remember one trip on which we had a load of supplies too heavy for the horses when we reached hilly country. About twenty miles out from Needles, the trail started a steep upgrade. Wyatt decided we would have to divide the load, leaving part behind and coming back for it.

After caching part of our gear behind a little hill near the road, we drove about fifteen miles further, stopping after dark at Hank's Well. I was dog-tired and didn't wish to return that night, although Wyatt was in a hurry, wanting to go right back. "You go ahead," I generously suggested, never thinking he actually would. "I'm tired and the wind has come up. I'm just not up to it tonight."

I was really put out when Wyatt agreed. "I'll pitch the small tent here for you," he said, matter-of-factly. "Tony can stay with you, and I'll leave a gun." A gun! I couldn't have used a gun on a human if my life depended on it!

Wyatt cooked a supper of beans, bacon and coffee, rested awhile then hitched up for the return trip. "If anybody comes, just tell them your husband has gone down the road a ways and will be back soon." I'd have felt better if he hadn't mentioned the possibility of someone coming.

It was a bright, moonlit night. I laid down in the tent, talking to Tony, unable to go to sleep and trying to keep up my nerve by borrowing some from the dog. I knew that the Chemehuevis often used this road, and I had never really gotten over my fear of Indians.

At about two in the morning, when I was almost asleep, Tony jumped up from the bed, barking like crazy. My heart came up into my throat. The wind was blowing, but above the wind I could hear some other noise, a sort of thrashing of a heavy body in the brush. I remember that I could hardly breathe and was literally stiff with fright. Even my feet, normally warm as toast, turned to ice.

Tony was outside the tent, still barking furiously. The thrashing sound was repeated at regular intervals, seeming louder at times. Then Tony gradually stopped barking, although the noise continued. I wondered how the intruder had managed to silence my only protector, the dog.

At last I couldn't bear the suspense. I sneaked to the tent flap to peek out. There was Tony sitting happily beneath a mesquite from which the wind had broken loose a branch. She was now worrying the limb with her teeth, shaking it and trying to back up and pull it down, growling a little as she worked.

"Tony, you dunce!" I shouted. "Shame on you for scaring me to death over nothing!" I was weak, but relieved. Tony was very apologetic, at least outwardly.

Another incident happened when we were passing through Daggett. We met an old prospector who gave me a very rich specimen of gold ore. It was a toy for me. It was fun to chip off small pieces to grind up and pan out the gold. Finally there was but a small sample left. I started to throw it away one day when we were cutting down on excess baggage.

Wyatt stopped me. "Don't do that. Let me bury it! Otherwise somebody might find it and spend a lot of unnecessary time trying to locate the source around here. We don't want to put anyone to that kind of trouble." So Wyatt buried it deeply beneath the road, where the passing traffic would pack down the spot. It was typical of him to do this sort of considerate thing.

One day in May 1905, after wandering here and there prospecting all winter, we set out from Needles southward toward the Colorado River Indian Reservation. For no particular reason, Wyatt drove off the road and several hundred yards up the gulch to make our camp for lunch.

After unbridling the horses and watering them, my husband browsed around, looking at the various rocks, probably from force of prospecting habit, while I set about getting the food ready. He picked up some float rock that showed signs of copper. I noted his obvious interest. "What have you got?" I asked, meaning what kind of mineral did it appear to be.

"I'm not sure," he said. "While you're fixing grub, I think I'll mosey up the gulch and see if I can find the ledge this came from." Before he left, he set out the folding chairs, table and other things to make a comfortable noon camp in the shade of a large mesquite tree. He even started the fire, as he usually did, though I recognized that he was anxious to trace up the source of the sample.

At last he got his sample bag and pick, then set out up the gulch. "We'll have lunch when I get back," he said. "I won't be gone long."

I expected him in a half hour or so, but that stretched into an hour — then two — then three. I began to fret. When I finally spotted him returning at a rapid pace, I thought, "He's found something he thinks is good!" As he drew closer, it was easy to see that his pack was bulging with samples.

"I found the ledge I think our sample came from. It's about a mile and a half up the arroyo. It really looks good to me!" We tested some of the ore with our simple outfit and found free gold mixed with copper. It was also likely to have silver mixed with it, since the three are often found together.

We had been planning to go to Harqua Hala[6] anyhow, so we decided to go at once and have our samples assayed. We carefully observed the location of our camp. It was about six miles from the Colorado River on the California side.

After eating, we repacked and started for the river, hoping to cross it that evening. We were now impatient to reach an assayer. As luck would have it, the ferry barge was on the far side of the river, and no one was there. We knew that it would not come to our side till morning. There was nothing to do but make camp for the night. This was directly across from where Parker, Arizona, now stands. There was no town there then — no highway, no bridge, no large dam. It was a wild, lonesome and beautiful spot. The only life in the scene was the ferry and the camp of the Indians who operated it. The reservation was just a few miles downstream.

There was a thin dawn mist as we ferried across the river. We went down to a store operated by Mrs. Rainy on the reservation. There we replenished our stock of supplies, bought hay for the horses, and filled our waterbarrels.

I was growing more impatient over each delay, but at my age I had to learn to fight off impatience. We moved at the pace of our livestock, and if we failed to consider their welfare we might not move at all. Even the wealthy learned that they must have at least that much patience. We finally got under way, reaching Bouse by nightfall. We camped there, pressing on in the morning for the longest leg of our trip.

This time we both had a strong hunch we had found something worthwhile. It was late afternoon when we reached the Socorro mine near Harqua Hala. We found an assayer there who agreed to test our samples in the morning.

The Earps' cottage in Vidal, California, where they spent happy winters for almost a quarter of a century. Josie called it their "dream come true."

Another wait. I was used to them, but each was hard to bear. What had we found this time? Would it be another disappointment or good news at last? We were quiet that night as we sat around the campfire. I imagine our thoughts were pretty much the same: what will it be — another disappointment? We'd had enough hopes dashed to be used to it!

Then in the morning the report finally came. It was good! Not as rich as my float near Silver Peak,[7] but good enough for a living. The gold assayed twenty-five dollars per ton of ore, plus six percent copper. And better than Silver Peak, we knew where this ledge was located. Our days of wandering were at an end! Here we would build a desert retreat,[8] if only the vein didn't pinch out. Wyatt arranged to file our claim, then we spent a little time building air castles.

We planned to spend the rest of our lives simply, operating our mine and living on the desert in the winter and moving to the

Coast in the summer, just as we had been doing. No visions of luxury, social life or world travel entered into our plans. We were ready to have a home with peace and quiet.

Best of all, the dream came true! We still traveled a little on the desert, prospected for the fun of it[9] and visited our families when the mood took us, but we were the masters of our destiny. Then I thought it would never end. Those were the happy years! If only they could be relived!

We called our mine the "Happy Days." We built our desert retreat nearby and spent almost a quarter of a century[10] coming there in the fall, winter and spring months. I think we earned our rest.

HISTORICAL NOTES AND EDITORIAL COMMENTS

1. The tranquility of the Earps' golden years is typically exaggerated by Josie. Even in his sixties Wyatt continued to be involved in his usual blend of gambling and adventure. For example, in July 1911 Wyatt Earp, Walter Scott and Edward Dean were arraigned in Los Angeles for operating a bunco game. At a justice court hearing Wyatt was absolved of complicity in the case; it appears he may have innocently strolled onto the scene where a couple of men, possibly his acquaintances, were running their racket. This occurred at the Auditorium Hotel, near where the Earps were then living. Wyatt gave the arresting officers the false name of William Stapp (the latter was his third given name). One wonders if the Walter Scott cited was Death Valley Scotty (whose name also was Walter Scott), who was a gambler long before he became famous as an eccentric desert recluse living in his castle in Death Valley. The full record of the arrest and hearing from the Los Angeles Justice Court records is a part of the Turner/Oster collection.

2. The Earp letters contain thirteen separate California addresses between October 1920 and Wyatt's January 1929 death. None of the nine Los Angeles residences were owned by the Earps. The couple appears to have resided mostly in tourist-type, light-housekeeping establishments while there, at least during the 1920s.

3. Josie's remarks in the Cason manuscript seem to be the only existent testimonies to Wyatt's activities as a movie consultant.

4. Both Tom Mix and William S. Hart were idols of Western movie fans of the silent film era. Hart did not click in "talkies" because of his thin,

reedy voice. Tom Mix did. Both were close friends of Wyatt's, probably initially because of the connection between their film portrayals and Wyatt's background, although Mix himself had been a lawman, as well as a member of the Rough Riders and a national champion cowboy. As mentioned in the back section titled "How this Book Came To Be," Hart attempted to help Wyatt market his life story.

5. Undoubtedly Josie's fears of renegade Indians were almost groundless at that late date. One suspects that renegade Anglos would have been a more probable source of danger.

6. It is doubtful that Josie actually means Harqua Hala, which was nine miles south of modern Salome, Arizona, since it was too far away to be reached in the time she allots, or in any reasonable amount of time by horse and wagon. She was probably thinking of the Harcuvar Mountains, where the copper mines undoubtedly had an assayer.

7. Here Josie refers to the discovery she mentioned at the end of Chapter 16. The Earps never were able to locate the original source of Josie's gold-rich sample found near Silver Peak, Nevada.

8. This chapter's 1970 photo of the Earp cottage at Vidal, near their mines, gives some idea of the character of the couple's beloved retreat. Vidal is located in California a few miles west of Parker, Arizona, on the edge of the Whipple Mountains.

9. San Bernardino County records indicate that the Earps eventually filed about one hundred claims in this area.

10. The Happy Days discovery was in 1906; the Earps' last period of living on the desert ended in July 1928.

19

Here Lies a Man

The last trip I remember Wyatt taking outside our little home in Los Angeles was in November 1928. He went out to vote in the election between Herbert Hoover and Al Smith. Although Wyatt was practically a teetotaler, he felt strongly about the corrupting effect Prohibition had on our society. He, a lifelong Republican and Protestant, voted for Democratic and Catholic Al Smith and the repeal of Prohibition. He got out of his sickbed to go downtown to vote. He felt it his duty. This was the kind of man he was.

During Wyatt's final illness, many interesting people came to visit him. One of these was Wilson Mizner. We had last seen Wilson when he was a happy-go-lucky boy in Nome, Alaska. Since then the slender boy had grown into a large, portly man and a famous playwright.[1] I remembered how he used to entertain us in Considine's Hall in Nome and was prompted to ask, "Do you remember how you used to entertain us by singing 'Alice Ben Boldt'?"

Wilson laughed. "Do I ever! And 'Jeanie With The Light Brown Hair' and lots of other old-timers!"

We sat and reminisced for many happy hours. When he left for the last time, there was a look in his eye — the intuition of a perceptive man — that conveyed his feeling it would be the last time he saw Wyatt alive.

During the last weeks a frequent visitor had been Jimmy Mitchell[2] of the *Los Angeles Examiner* staff. One day he was there with Wilson Mizner, who was smoking. "Have a cigarette, Wyatt!" Wilson offered. And to my surprise, Wyatt took one and

The small rented cottage in a Los Angeles tourist court, where Wyatt died.

smoked part of it. To my knowledge he had never smoked a cigarette in his life before.[3]

The three men were discussing Tex Rickard's recent death.
Wyatt and Tex had been close friends for a long time. I remembered that Wyatt and Wilson had sent a floral wreath to the
funeral.

About two weeks before Wyatt's death, when we were alone
one day, something occurred that has puzzled and haunted me
ever since. I have thought about it a great deal, wondering what
Wyatt meant. He had been lying quietly for some time, his eyes
and mind far away. Suddenly he raised up on his elbow, looking
through me rather than at me, and said, "Supposing — supposing —"

"What is it, Wyatt?" I asked, concerned by his appearance.

The light went out of his eyes, and he fell back on the pillow.
"Oh, well!" he said in a resigned fashion.

I wanted to know what was going through his mind, but I
never found out. I wondered if he was reliving the past and if the

thought of how he might have averted his favorite brother Morg's murder at Tombstone still haunted him.

The end came so soon. We had a male nurse who was there during the daytime.[4] I would take over at night. This Saturday evening, January 12, 1929, the nurse, who normally went off duty at six o'clock, lingered. Finally he came out in the kitchen and said, "I haven't anything special to do tonight, Mrs. Earp, and I'll stay if you wish."

Something about the way he said it turned my heart to an icy piece of lead. Wyatt overheard us talking and asked, "What are you two coyotes cooking up?" The nurse made a plausible excuse for his staying on.

That night Mr. Clum made his last call. This faithful, loyal friend of half a century sat for a half hour or more, talking quietly and cheerfully. The two old men looked each other bravely in the eyes, each knowing it was the end.[5] Mr. Clum had but a few years more himself.

Another visitor that night was Mrs. Dorubey. We had known each other since the days of the Alaskan gold rush. I sat there beside the bed while she was there, but the sight of the pinched look around my husband's nose took the heart out of me. We made a desperate effort to chat about a lot of silly little things.

Mrs. Dorubey said with forced gaiety, "Are you still in bed, Wyatt? I'd better come over tomorrow and take over the nursing — these people aren't treating you right!" With that she moved over to the bedside and put her hand on his drawn forehead. She nodded and said, "Wyatt, you will get well soon. Then we'll all go back over the long trail together to Alaska. How about it?"

Wyatt nodded and smiled. After she left she told her daughter he wouldn't live out the night, he looked that bad.

The doctor came then, but I never left Wyatt's side all night. About two o'clock my husband stirred, and I asked him if there was something he wanted. "Water!" he murmured. He drained a whole glass of it. I asked him if he wanted more. He thought he did, but could only down a sip of the second glass. It was the last thing to pass his lips until the end.

Wyatt Earp's last photograph, taken a few weeks before his death. His determined character and iron will are still etched plainly on his countenance.

Our kitty Fluffy seemed to sense what was happening. I had had trouble all evening keeping her off the bed. Although she was Wyatt's inseparable companion, sitting on his lap for hours when he was up, she never had been allowed on the bed before.

As the dawn of January 13 lightened the sky, Jimmy Mitchell came. For hours I had held Wyatt's left hand with my own, his head cradled in the crook of my right arm. I watched the light creep around the shades on the windows with a rising feeling of terror and inadequacy in the face of implacably approaching death. When I sensed that Wyatt was finally going, I somewhat wildly begged of the doctor, "My God, can't you *do* something to save him? Oh please do something!"

But there was nothing that anyone could do. I thought in panic "I'm losing him! I had thought I was prepared for it, but now I know that I am not!" All reason fled. I expected Wyatt to say something to help me, unable to realize that I would never hear his reassuring voice again. The doctor's calm as he held his watch seemed heartless, but it probably did more to balance me than kind solicitousness. I had to realize sooner or later that now it would be up to me alone.

At five minutes past eight on Sunday morning, January 13, 1929, the soul to which Virginia Ann Cooksey Earp had given life at Monmouth, Illinois, March 19, 1848, returned to the God who had made him. I couldn't believe it. My darling had breathed his last, dying peacefully, without a struggle, like a baby going to sleep. I don't know how long I continued to hold him in my arms; I wouldn't let him go. They finally had to drag me away. I had gone with him on every trail he had ever taken since those days at Tombstone so long ago.

I was too completely shattered emotionally to attend the funeral. I was comforted no little by the throng who came by to pay their respects to the old marshal, and who stopped for a reassuring word. I thought "you can judge a man by both his friends and enemies." His friends were here as his pallbearers, a distinguished group: John P. Clum, William S. Hart, Wilson Mizner, Tom Mix, Charlie Welsh,[6] and W. J. Hunsaker.[7] As for the enemies, most of the poison tongues that had made my husband's life miserable in later years had long ago been buried in lost outlaw graves or Boot Hills across the West.

Following the funeral I was adrift — a rudderless ship. I couldn't decide where I should put Wyatt's ashes. For a long time I debated spreading them on the hillside by our mine, a spot that he had loved dearly for the twenty-odd years we had found peace there in the desert solitude. But at last my mind turned to the city of my childhood. Wyatt's family were almost gone,[8] and we had no children. My only home was where my parents rested. So I took Wyatt's ashes to San Francisco.

With eyes blinded by tears, I tenderly wrapped the urn, with its precious contents, in several soft towels and put the package in an overnight satchel. I traveled from Los Angeles to San Francisco on the fast daylight train, the Lark. If other passengers happened to notice the little old lady in the black traveling suit, holding tightly to a satchel too dear to let the porter carry, they probably thought it was just some queer old granny. Little could they divine the heartache I carried in my breast on that last journey of love. I placed the satchel protectively between me and the window. We had spent a lifetime traveling — now we were making our last journey together.

Here beside me were the remains of a man who had suffered much. For having pitted himself against forces of evil on the raw frontier, he had been accused of foul deeds and heinous crimes. He was not demonstrative and did not speak out to defend himself. Yet this was the same man who had reproved me, when I, irritated as housewives become, slammed the door on a peddler: "Never close the door in a peddler's face! He has to make a living somehow. Always listen to what he has to say and be nice to him whether you buy or not."

For the enemies who had made life hard, he bore no malice at the end. He was more prone to say, "Let it go!" and dwell on the thought of the many friends who brought great happiness to our lives. He loved children. He loved flowers and animals. He loved his quiet home life above all. He stayed home as much as possible and read a great deal. He had a much finer education from reading than many people would have given him credit for, in view of his rude and scanty formal schooling.

Wyatt was, toward me, affectionate, but not demonstrative. As I look back I can recall many little acts of thoughtfulness on his part — small things, little gifts to remember occasions, candy and jewelry. But never flowers, except once. He gave me a single rose, all the more dear because not the accustomed thing.

I remember the incident well. I had made a trip to San Diego while he was quite ill. He was not totally confined to bed, however, and was up when I reached home. I could tell something was up from the look on his face, like a little boy who has done something nice and is waiting for praise. I looked around for some surprise. There it was on the mantlepiece: the single, beautiful red rose in a tall vase.

I thought, as the train sped along, "Perhaps I can do something to set the picture straight about a conscientious man who died much saddened over the lies and misunderstandings about his life." And that resolve lingered during the years that followed, when many of Wyatt's enemies — men whom I had known as dangerous outlaws — were donning the snowy vestments of angels in the hands of sensation-seeking writers.

At last I could bear it no longer; it was to uncover their lies that I began to write this story. But it was long after that sad day in 1929 when my two nieces went with me to the little Hills of Eternity Cemetery in Colma to place Wyatt's ashes in their last resting place.

More than ten years have passed since Wyatt's death. I've learned to live alone, but I still painfully miss my husband. I find myself going back in my mind most often to three periods in my life: my youth, the Tombstone years and the time after we discovered our claim.

Sometimes I even make a visit back to our desert retreat, unable to resist the lure of the big, empty country we both loved so well. However, I can't bear to stay at our place alone with the memories it brings back. I put up at the Grandview Hotel in

Parker. But even there I am lonely. Loneliness follows you wherever you go after you've lost the love of your life.

Among the mementos I have been keeping for many years is a newspaper clipping of an article written at the time of Wyatt's death. I have lost the part that says who the writer was or what paper it was in, but it was written by someone who knew Wyatt, offering a last tribute to a friend.[9] It reads:

"Mr. Earp was an exceptionally good friend of the writer, and while many unkind stories have been told about him, the writer never knew him to do an unkind or uncharitable act. He was the soul of honor in his dealings, and his word was as good as a rich man's bond. If the writer could make his epitaph, it would read:

HERE LIES A MAN"

HISTORICAL NOTES AND EDITORIAL COMMENTS

1. Unless Wilson Mizner pulled the wool over Josie's eyes, which is doubtful, she is charitably stressing his good side here. See Chapter 14, note 2, for a short biography of Mizner.

2. Wyatt's friendship with Jimmy Mitchell probably stemmed from an interview, since the old marshal made good newspaper copy then, even as he does today.

3. Wyatt smoked a pipe regularly and cigars occasionally. (Cason ms.)

4. Josie refers to a nameless male nurse, but in fact this was their old family friend John Flood. Flood was a man of all work for the Earps simply because he liked them. He typed their correspondence, ran their errands, loaned them money and even wrote Wyatt's biography as described in the concluding section of this book. (Letter from Flood to the editor, 1956.) Why Josie chose not to give him credit for his nursing efforts can be only conjectured; perhaps it was because Flood preferred anonymity.

5. Although it is obvious from his letters of a few days before his death that Wyatt expected to recover from his fatal illness, on the last day he evidently had a premonition that the end was at hand. (Cason ms.)

6. Charlie Welsh was an old friend from the Earps' days on the desert; he owned a ranch near modern Blythe, California. (Cason ms.)

7. William J. Hunsaker was the Earps' attorney, known as the "dean of the Los Angeles bar." He had first become acquainted with Wyatt in Tombstone, where he had practiced law from January 1, 1880, to March 1, 1881. (William J. Hunsaker to Stuart Lake, October 2, 1928, Lake collection.)

8. Only his sister Adelia outlived Wyatt. Of his brothers, Morg was killed in 1882 and Warren in 1900; Virge died a natural death in 1905, Jim in 1926 and half-brother Newton in 1928 a few weeks before Wyatt. His mother had died in 1893, his father in 1907.

9. Search for the source of this clipping has proved fruitless.

Editor's Epilogue

How This Book Came To Be

In the aging Josie Earp, beneath her sprightly charms and annoying eccentricities, there burned one constant, unwavering desire. More than anything else this old woman wanted to create a book that corrected the distorted popular image of her famous husband Wyatt. But it was not until 1976, thirty-two years after her death, that Josie's consuming ambition was finally fulfilled.

In the light of this woman's impetuosity and dogged determination to be heard, such an inordinate wait seems shocking. To understand why it occurred, one must be aware of the stacks of Earp literature that preceded this book — the writings that created a folk hero and the other volumes that painted a villain. Both irked Josie equally, and both were at the bottom of her drive to write what she knew.

THE MAKING OF A FOLK HERO

The myth-making process that eventually transformed Wyatt Earp into a paladin started with the highly colored contemporary newspaper reports of the Tombstone episode inaccurately known as the gunfight at the O.K. Corral. From 1882 on, throughout his forty-seven years of wandering over the continent, Wyatt was dogged by his unsought renown. Writers across the country continually found an outlet and an audience for lionizing or denigrating accounts of his life.

In her narrative, Josie quotes one such story by reporters who met the couple while traveling over a high pass in the Colorado Rockies on a blustery spring day in 1883: "The prettiest sight we have ever seen — the snowy mountain wilderness, the brown-eyed goddess, the blond Apollo who turned out to be none other than the *famous* Wyatt Earp, tamer of wild-western desperados. . . ."[1]

In hope of counteracting such exaggerated panegyrics, as well as of correcting slanderous lies, Wyatt and Josie had endeavored ever since about 1905 to publish an unembellished, factual account of their adventurous lives. The final result of their efforts was an attempted biography of Wyatt by family friend John Flood, Jr. Wyatt worked in close collaboration with Flood and endorsed the factual accuracy of the narrative;[2] unfortunately Flood did not produce a salable story. Even the marketing efforts of Wyatt's friend, Western film star William S. Hart, could not overcome a writing style that one Bobbs Merrill editor called "stilted and florid and diffuse."[3] The manuscript also was rejected by several other publishers, including Thomas Y. Crowell, Houghton Mifflin, Doubleday, and the *Saturday Evening Post*.

In 1926, shortly after the completion of the Flood manuscript, Wyatt was visited by Walter Noble Burns, author of the popular book *The Saga of Billy The Kid*. When Burns told the aging adventurer of his hope to be allowed to write the Earp story, Wyatt regretfully declined to help on the grounds that Hart was still trying to market the Flood work. Burns, however, smoothly persuaded Wyatt to aid him in constructing a biography of Doc Holliday.

Wyatt helped considerably, but his suspicions were aroused when Burns' queries began to center around the old lawman's own activities rather than those of the homicidal Doc. Bill Hart gave Wyatt further cause for alarm when he wrote him that Burns' *The Saga of Billy the Kid* had been plagiarized in spots from an old story by the actor's cowboy detective friend Charlie Siringo.[4] In the end, of course, Wyatt's uneasiness proved justified: much of Burns' 1927 book *Tombstone* was yet another saga of the gunfighting prowess of the gallant Wyatt Earp. The author's interest in the story of Doc Holliday had been used only as a pretext to pump information from the former marshal.

Sadly for Burns, if he had been a little less impatient, Wyatt would have turned the unsuccessful Flood manuscript over to him to be professionalized.[5] If this had happened, perhaps we would not have the folk hero with us today. As it was, instead of telling

the true story of a man, Burns' book *Tombstone* laid the ground-
work for the Earp plaster-saint image, dubbing Wyatt the "Lion
of Tombstone."

Yet it remained for master story-teller Stuart N. Lake to defin-
itively draw the mythical paladin Wyatt Earp. His first contact
with Wyatt was a letter dated Christmas 1927.[6] It turned out to
be quite a Christmas present, leading ultimately to the old marshal's lasting fame.

Wyatt had been informed shortly prior to that time that Billy
Breakenridge was working on his *Helldorado,* a book in which he
intended to "really burn the Earps up."[7] A desire to counter Breakenridge's bias may have been behind Wyatt's willingness to chance
an association with another commercial writer. In any case, by
late summer of 1928, Lake had met the Earps and was correspond-
ing regularly with them.[8]

This writer took over the Flood manuscript and sought to
professionalize it, starting with several personal interviews with
Wyatt. The old lawman may not have learned caution from the
Burns experience, but Josephine had. She made sure that all her
husband's meetings with Lake were monitored by herself and John
Flood, who took down what was said in shorthand.[9]

By the winter of 1928 the manuscript was nearing completion.[10] At this stage, with Wyatt still living, the work was quite
likely a realistic biography as the former marshal wished it to
appear. But Wyatt Earp died on January 13, 1929, without having
read a single word of it.

With his controlling collaborator gone, Lake was now free
to liven up the story. He embarked on a lengthy period of independent research into the Earps' past, including excursions to
Wyatt's old stamping grounds in Dodge City and Tombstone.
However, when he sought to supplement his findings with information from Josie, he found that the widow persistently evaded
his questions. In time the writer came to feel he had discovered
part of the reason for her reticence. His field investigations were
yielding him at least inklings of the truth about Josephine Earp's
past — a past she was becoming more and more determined to
keep secret.

Lake wrote his publisher that he had discovered that Josie had been a dancehall queen, the "belle of the honkytonks" whom notorious "chaser" Johnny Behan had "set up as his girl."[11] This in fact missed the truth — Josie had danced with the Pauline Markham *H.M.S. Pinafore* company, not in saloons — but it came close enough to the facts of this proper old lady's adventurous youth to make her fearful. She had lived openly in Tombstone under the name Mrs. Johnny Behan, as Johnny's wife, though they never married.[12] Furthermore, she was desperately anxious to hide from Lake a scandal that did not come to light until 1960, sixteen years after her death, when Frank Waters published *The Earp Brothers of Tombstone*. Wyatt had come to Tombstone a married man. When he became enamored of Josephine, he deserted his second wife, who committed suicide in 1888,[13] claiming Wyatt had destroyed her life.

Had Lake been aware of the true nature of what Josie sought to conceal, he very likely would have suppressed it himself. It was not conducive to myth-making. As it was, he merely jumped to the erroneous conclusion that Josephine was trying to conceal the fact that she had been a sort of two-bit Helen of Troy in Tombstone. He asserted to his publisher that in "back of all the fighting, the killing, and even Wyatt's duty as a peace officer, the impelling force of his destiny was the nature of his acquisition . . . of Johnny Behan's girl."[14]

In view of Josie's ultimate obsession with respectability in her later years, her fear of possible revelations about her past was very likely initially at the root of the hard feelings that developed between her and Stuart Lake. She feared this talented author, yet, in spite of that, she sought to curb him from writing a blood-and-thunder yarn that portrayed Wyatt as another Wild Bill Hickok. In the end it was the publisher's discretion that kept the writer's conclusions about Josie's past from appearing in print.[15]

However, Lake's editors seem actually to have encouraged the author's other heroizing ideas and embellishments of fact. The Lake collection in the Huntington Library shows that this man was an adroit writer who did not allow unvarnished facts to diminish drama. The Wyatt Earp finally presented in Lake's manuscript was a paragon of irreproachable purity — a perfect model for a folk hero. Lake's Wyatt was lucrative story material but not the warm, real-life human being Josie had loved.

When the dismayed widow read the developing manuscript, she hurried East to plead her case with Ira Rich Kent of Houghton Mifflin. Kent told Lake about the meeting: "It was plain to see that Mrs. Earp was deeply concerned about the matter. She sat at my desk for the better part of an hour, tears rolling down her cheeks in her emotion."[16]

Lake's reaction to Josie's distress was to allege that she was mentally deranged and soon to be hospitalized for removal of a brain tumor.[17] The former allegation was certainly exaggerated; the latter was apparently untrue,[18] perhaps a misconception on Lake's part. It is nonetheless clear that the writer was ready to go to considerable lengths to prevent Josie from destroying the dramatic, money-making myth he already had well formed.

Due only to the publisher's tact, the book finally appeared in 1931 under the title *Wyatt Earp, Frontier Marshal*; Lake had wanted to call it *Wyatt Earp, Gunfighter*, in total disrespect of Josie's inclination. The preface stated that the entire story was Wyatt's first-person account as told to Lake, a statement which he himself later admitted was untrue.[19]

Lake, if not completely candid, was remarkably astute; the romantic folk hero he created eventually proved a bonanza in reprints, movie rights and a TV series. Josie profited considerably from the success, although it is not clear whether in the end she gained as much as the author. This may have been another rock on which their relations ran aground.

Whatever the reasons, eventually Josie had serious differences with Lake. She even initiated efforts to sue the author for allegedly fictionalizing his account of her husband's life.[20] Her attorneys, Nellie Bush and William J. Hunsaker, both discouraged her efforts as more apt to stir up controversy than restore Wyatt's memory to believable human proportions.

They were probably right. It seems that Lake's highly convincing and colorful prose had by this time irreversibly assured America's eager acceptance of Wyatt Earp as a folk hero. Dismayed though she was, Josie could not halt the myth-making process.

It was not until 1939, in fact, that the persistent Josephine was able to come even close to retaliation. This was the year that *Wyatt Earp, Frontier Marshal* was scheduled to be filmed as a high-budget extravaganza starring Randolph Scott. With characteristic vigor, Josie stormed the producers at Twentieth Century-Fox, threatening law suits and worse. She was able to absolutely halt production, and in the end the intimidated executives transformed the spectacular into a grade-B "oater."[21] Josie didn't even permit the use of Wyatt's name; the picture was titled simply *Frontier Marshal*.[22] When Josephine Earp died on December 19, 1944, she had enjoyed the sweet taste of at least a crumb of revenge.

THE MAKING OF A VILLAIN

In addition to the vast range of literature aimed at the apotheosis of Wyatt Earp, there were always numerous writings that set out to prove that he was an exhibitionistic tinhorn gambler and a cold-blooded killer of the most villainous breed. These condemnatory accounts[23] all have their genesis at least partially with the Earps' Tombstone enemies, such as Ike Clanton, whose brother was killed in the famous shootout.

Ike's original retaliatory court testimony about an Earp gang of stage-robbers was kept alive over the years by Johnny Behan's deputy Billy Breakenridge, who outlived Wyatt. He recited this story to anyone who would listen.

In addition to Breakenridge, numerous yellow journalists were anxious to cash in on the fascination offered by a juicy Western scandal. An example of this sort of Earp smear story is J. M. Scanland's grotesque, garbled potboiler that appeared in a Los Angeles newspaper in 1922.[24] Among other things it had Wyatt killed in Colton, California, after leaving Tombstone. Wyatt was so irritated by the article that he hunted Scanland for several years. When he finally found him, the offender turned out to be a harmless and, under the circumstances, very frightened old man, whom Wyatt let off the hook with a retraction. Another example is the story of an undersized runt of a Canadian mounted policeman disarming a drunken, loudly profane and disorderly Wyatt in a Dawson saloon during the Klondike gold rush.[25] Wyatt had never been within five hundred miles of Dawson, seldom drank and was notoriously quiet. He also forced a retraction of that story.

But perhaps the most pointed-damaging account of the Tombstone episode to appear in Wyatt's lifetime was *Helldorado* by Billy Breakenridge, who, having been on the scene in Tombstone, could claim to be in-the-know. Evidently unaware that Billy was spreading bitter lies about the Earps, Wyatt in 1925 welcomed the stooped old man, who, as an investigator, was hunting facts for an estate litigation. The Earps generously devoted a great deal of their time to helping Billy, who needed the fee badly. They were shocked to discover his ingratitude when his deliberately hostile *Helldorado* was published in 1928, even though a family friend had warned them about what they could expect.

This autobiography, ghosted by William McLeod Raine, has remained basic source material for the many "now-it-can-be-told" potboilers which followed the publication of *Wyatt Earp, Frontier Marshal*. For years there has been a cult dedicated to exposing the allegedly sordid truth about the too-noble folk hero created by Stuart Lake. Probably the classic examples of this sort of rabid debunking are Ed Bartholomew's two books.[26] Like all of the works in this genre, they openly maintain that Wyatt was an egotistical liar; after all, hadn't Lake's preface attributed the flattering narrative directly to personal interviews with the old marshal?

Lake himself initiated legal moves against the most effective and vocal of the debunkers, Frank Waters, whose 1960 book, *The Earp Brothers of Tombstone*, revealed the scandal of Wyatt's desertion of his second wife, Celia Ann (Mattie), for Josephine. According to Waters, Lake dropped the case after his attorneys consulted Waters' basic research material, which *appeared* to originate with Wyatt's sister-in-law, Mrs. Virgil Earp. However, Lake's edifice, *Frontier Marshal*, was apparently not materially damaged by the truth Waters introduced about Wyatt's wife desertion.

Other aspects of Waters' extremely bitter and biased account may not have been so valid. In 1935, when the story was being dictated to him by Virgil Earp's wife, Allie, in Los Angeles, Josie heard of the venture. Determined to stop any revelation of her past, she precipitately stormed over to Waters' home. The writer was in Tucson researching Allie's story, but Josie persisted in trying to extract from Frank's aging mother and his sister a promise that he would write nothing of her. When they quite reasonably would not make such a commitment, Josie flew into a rage. Mrs. Waters, who had a weak heart, had a seizure over this disturbance.[27]

Not surprisingly under the circumstances, Frank's book turned out to be highly critical of Wyatt, but he unwisely also included Virgil in his overdone condemnation of the Earps. Allie, who had adored her husband, repudiated the manuscript as a bunch of lies and threatened to sue if Waters published. Significantly, Waters' book did not appear until thirteen years after Allie had died and sixteen years after Josie had passed away.[28]

THE MEMORY OF A MAN

In the midst of the welter of laudatory and slanderous accounts of the gunplay at Tombstone, Josie Earp's memory of her husband remained clear and cherished. As early as 1929, while Lake was still researching his masterpiece, the widow was beginning to work on a story that would truly depict her husband as she had known him. In this endeavor she was assisted by John Flood; to an indeterminate degree by John Clum, the founder and first editor of the *Tombstone Epitaph*; and George W. Parsons, whose Tombstone journal was frequently quoted in the work. The enterprise went slowly and apparently was abandoned upon Clum's death in May 1932.

Several years later, Josie collaborated with two distant relatives by marriage, Mabel Earp Cason and her sister Vinolia Earp Ackerman. Josie did not tell these writers of the earlier manuscript, which could have saved them much time and trouble. It is clear that the widow was becoming even more squeamish about her past and now wished to suppress many facts she had not been able to conceal from her Tombstone contemporaries Clum and Parsons.

Despite her aggravating evasiveness about Tombstone and how she met Wyatt, the old woman was welcomed into the Cason and Ackerman families, who extended her generous affection in a lonely old age. Still Josie obsessively persisted in concealing from them many of the true facts of her youth. After dictating a fairly frank chapter, she would read it and contrarily announce, "Why, we can't say that! They'd think I was a bad woman!"[29]

As a result of Josie's desire to have a "nice clean story," as opposed to her biographers' desire to have a "nice true story," the Cason/Ackerman effort was left incomplete. The collaboration spanned the years from 1936 till Josie's 1944 death, and the unfinished manuscript of more than four hundred pages remained in the possession of the Cason family until it was given to me in October 1967 accompanied by almost five thousand pages of notes, letters and clippings. By then both Mrs. Cason and Mrs. Ackerman were dead. I am indebted to the generosity of Ernest A. Cason and his daughter Jeanne Cason Laing for my unexpected receipt of the manuscript and the voluminous collection of supporting materials in October 1967.

The first Josephine Earp manuscript, the one prepared with the assistance of Parsons and Clum, had been made available to me earlier by Mrs. Charles A. Colyn, an Earp researcher, collector and genealogist of the first magnitude. Upon her death in 1973, this Earp relative by marriage bequeathed me her whole research collection to perpetuate. Without her generous assistance over the years, I would not have attempted to construct this book. The Cason manuscript alone simply lacked the necessary detail on Tombstone; it was essential to couple it with the earlier, more frank manuscript, before a complete narrative could be achieved.

Merging the two manuscripts, which contained vastly different materials presented in widely varying styles, was a challenging task. To establish a conversational standard for the combined first-person narrative, I interviewed and corresponded with many people who were intimately associated in life with both Wyatt and Josie. In the course of my research, many of them became my warm friends, including the family of Celia Ann Blaylock, Wyatt's second wife. From directions and clues picked up from such informants, I was able to arrive at a vocabulary and syntax that closely approximated the speech of the living Earps.

Josephine's story was naturally biased, and in constructing this book I have retained the occasional prejudices and miscolorings as Josie originally presented them. However, in such instances I have provided annotation pointing out the more probable facts. Such commentary is most prominent in the early chapters of the narrative, where Josie gives us what is obviously a "sanitized" version of the romantic adventures of her youth and presents her view of the controversial Tombstone episode.

To augment the research conducted in connection with my earlier, related books.[30] I spent eighteen months on location in Tombstone investigating Josie's story. I was especially intrigued by her presentation of the famous O.K. Corral gunfight as being the result of a complicated politico-economic struggle, rather than a dramatic confrontation of good and evil. I also engaged in considerable research to further illuminate Josie's version of her forty-seven years with Wyatt after Tombstone — years previously shrouded in mystery simply because they were unknown.

Personally I must confess a preference for these latter chapters, which, by comparison, relegate the short bloody vendetta at Tombstone to its proper perspective as a regrettable interlude in a long, happy, adventurous lifetime. With tenderness and enthusiasm, Josie tells us of Wyatt's real-estate flyer in San Diego, his horse-racing days, his involvement with the sporting game, his undercover work for Wells Fargo, their Alaskan adventure, and finally their golden years of seasonal prospecting in the vast deserts of California, Arizona and Nevada. The story forms a detailed odyssey of a seldom-comprehended Western type — the itinerant boomer who settled the frontier — sometimes lawman, sometimes gambler, townlot speculator, prospector, whatever might turn a profit.

Adventurous Josie loved every minute of her life with this kind of husband. Her depiction of him cuts through the folk-hero mythology, revealing at last a rather complex, brave, and sensitive human being — a likeable real man, Wyatt Earp.

GLENN G. BOYER

NOTES

1. Josephine stated that this article appeared in a Chicago newspaper shortly after the meeting in spring 1883, but I have been unable to locate the paper's name or date. (Statement in Earp memoirs prepared by Mabel Earp Cason and Vinolia Earp Ackerman, henceforth cited as Cason ms.)

2. This Flood manuscript was used in part by Stuart Lake in constructing his book *Wyatt Earp, Frontier Marshal.* As far as I know, there exists no copy of the original Flood work.

3. Anne Johnson to William S. Hart, February 21, 1926. Earp letters in collection of the editor, henceforth cited as Earp letters.

4. William Hart to Wyatt Earp, September 9, 1926, Earp letters. Apparently Hart was unaware that Siringo was equally guilty of borrowing literally from Pat F. Garrett's earlier *Authentic Life of Billy The Kid.*

5. John H. Flood to Walter Noble Burns, March 28, 1927, Earp letters.

6. Stuart N. Lake to Wyatt S. Earp, December 25, 1927, Earp letters.

7. In the Cason ms., Josie states that in fall 1927 Albert Behan, son of her former Tombstone fiancé Johnny, informed the Earps of the malicious intent of Billy's literary endeavor.

8. Earp letters.

9. Verified in the Cason ms.

10. Lake to Earp, October 31, 1928; November 14, 1928; January 10, 1929, Earp letters.

11. Stuart N. Lake to Ira Rich Kent, February 13, 1930. Lake collection, Huntington Library, San Marino, California; henceforth cited as Lake collection.

12. Cason ms. and postal money order dated June 11, 1881 (number 2298) from Mrs. Josephine Behan to Mrs. H. Marcus, San Francisco. Postal Receipt Book, Tombstone, Arizona Territory, 1881, collection of Mrs. Jeanne Devere, Tombstone; photocopy in editor's collection.

13. For confirmation of this event see Glenn G. Boyer, *The Suppressed Murder of Wyatt Earp,* pp. 39 & 15.

14. Lake to Kent, February 13, 1930, Lake collection. In fact Wyatt did not steal Josie from Johnny Behan. Johnny rejected her. It was not until after he refused to go through with a marriage that she became seriously involved with Wyatt, probably about July 1881. (Cason ms.)

15. Kent to Lake, February 19, 1930, Lake collection.

16. Kent to Lake, October 23, 1930, Lake collection.

17. Lake to Kent, October 15, October 30, 1930, Lake collection.

18. There appears to have been some substance to Josie's intent to enter a hospital, but the reason for her plan is not clear. Her letters contain no indication that she ever was in fact hospitalized, an event which certainly would have occurred had a brain tumor existed. (Josephine Earp to Stuart Lake, November 10, 1930, Earp letters.)

19. Stuart N. Lake to Burton Rascoe, January 9, 1941, Lake collection. In part this letter states: "... your suspicions are well founded.... As a matter of cold fact, Wyatt never 'dictated' a word to me.... He was delightfully laconic, or exasperatingly so."

20. Columnist Burr Belden in *Sun-Telegram* (San Bernardino, California) June 25, 1961, p. B-12 and also April 26, 1956.

21. Jeanne Cason Laing, on tape, 1975, in editor's collection.

22. Glenn Shirley, "Cowboy Strongman — Tom Tyler," p. 39.

23. Examples are William Breakenridge's *Helldorado*, Frank Waters' *Earp Brothers of Tombstone* and Ed Bartholomew's *Wyatt Earp: The Man and the Myth* and *Wyatt Earp: The Untold Story*.

24. J. M. Scanland, "Lurid Trails Are Left By Olden Day Bandits," *Times* (Los Angeles), March 12, 1922. Also referred to in Josephine Earp to William S. Hart, March 24, 1922, Earp letters.

25. Unsigned article, "The Taking of Wyatt Earp," *New York Sun*, August 16, 1903.

26. See note 23 above.

27. Interview with Frank Waters, Fort Collins, Colorado, January 1966. Waters avoids the whole truth in his introduction to *The Earp Brothers of Tombstone* and does not mention the heart attack which could have been the prime motive for his otherwise illogical bias.

28. Hildreth Hallowell (Allie's niece with whom she resided at the time of Waters' interviews) to John B. Sullivan, February 21, 1967. Also Mrs. Hallowell on tape, 1971, in an interview by Al Turner and Bill Oster, copies of both in editor's collection.

29. Laing tape, 1975, in editor's collection.

30. *The Suppressed Murder of Wyatt Earp* (the story of the genesis of the Earp myth) and *An Illustrated Life of Doc Holliday*.

References

Note that the following list is neither an exhaustive compendium of Earpiana nor a complete survey of the editor's Earp research. It includes only those items cited in the footnotes of this book.

BOOKS AND ARTICLES

Bartholomew, Ed Ellsworth. *Wyatt Earp, 1848 to 1880, The Untold Story*. Toyahvale, Texas: Frontier Book Company, 1963.

———. *Wyatt Earp, 1879 to 1882, The Man and the Myth*. Toyahvale, Texas: Frontier Book Company, 1964.

Beach, Rex. *The Barrier*. New York: A. L. Burt Company, 1908.

Bell, William G. "Frontier Lawman: Frank Canton." *The American West* 1, Summer 1964.

Bourke, John Gregory. *An Apache Campaign In The Sierra Madres*. New York: Charles Scribner's Sons, 1886.

———. *On The Border With Crook*. New York: Charles Scribner's Sons, 1892.

Boyer, Glenn G. *An Illustrated Life of Doc Holliday*. Glenwood Springs, Colorado: The Reminder Press, 1966.

———. *The Suppressed Murder of Wyatt Earp*. San Antonio: The Naylor Company, 1967.

Breakenridge, William M. *Helldorado*. Boston: Houghton Mifflin Company, 1928.

Brown, Mrs. Hugh. *Lady in Boomtown*. New York: Ballantine Books, 1972.

Burns, Walter Noble. *Tombstone*. New York: Penguin Books, 1942.

Canton, Frank M. *Frontier Trails*. Norman: University of Oklahoma Press, 1966.

Clum, John P. *It All Happened in Tombstone*. Flagstaff: The Northland Press, 1965.

Clum, Woodworth. *Apache Agent*. Boston: Houghton Mifflin, 1936.

Cox, William R. *Luke Short and His Era*. Garden City: Doubleday and Company, 1961.

Dodge, Fred. *Under Cover For Wells Fargo.* Boston: Houghton Mifflin Company, 1969.

Ellis, Amanda M. *Bonanza Towns: Leadville and Cripple Creek.* Colorado Springs: Denton Printing Company, 1954.

Fireman, Bert M. "Frémont's Arizona Adventure." *The American West* 1, Winter 1964.

Garrett, Patrick Floyd. *The Authentic Life of Billy the Kid.* Santa Fe: New Mexican Printing Company, 1882.

Glasscock, Carl Burgess. *Gold In Them Hills.* Indianapolis: Bobbs-Merrill, 1932.

————. *Lucky Baldwin.* Indianapolis: Bobbs-Merrill, 1933.

Heller, Herbert. *Sourdough Sagas.* New York: Ballantine Books, 1972.

Hunt, William R. *North of 53°.* New York: Macmillan Publishing Company, 1974.

Jahns, Pat. *The Frontier World of Doc Holliday.* New York: Hastings House, 1957.

Kunitz, Stanley J. and Harcraft, Howard. *Twentieth Century Authors.* New York: H. W. Wilson Company, 1942.

Lake, Stuart N. *Wyatt Earp: Frontier Marshal.* Boston: Houghton Mifflin, 1931.

Magnuson, Richard G. *Coeur d'Alene Diary.* Seattle: Metropolitan Press, 1968.

Masterson, William Barclay. *Famous Gunfighters of the Western Frontier.* Ruidoso, New Mexico: Frontier Book Company, 1959.

Miller, Joseph Henry. *Arizona: The Last Frontier.* New York: Hastings House, 1956.

Miller, Nyle H. and Snell, Joseph. *Why The West Was Wild.* Topeka: Kansas State Historical Society, 1963.

Mizner, Addison. *The Many Mizners.* New York: Vere Publishing Company, 1932.

Morrow, William. "The Spoilers." *California Law Review* 4, January 1916.

Myers, John Myers. *Tombstone: The Last Chance.* New York: E. P. Dutton, 1950.

Parsons, George W. *The Private Journal of George W. Parsons.* Tombstone: *Tombstone Epitaph*, 1972.

Pendleton, Albert S., Jr., and Thomas, Susan McKey. *In Search of the Hollidays.* Valdosta: Little River Press, 1972.

Raymond, Dora Neill. *Captain Lee Hall of Texas.* Norman: University of Oklahoma Press, 1940.

Roberts, Gary. "The Wells Spicer Decision: 1881." *Montana, the Magazine of Western History* 20, Winter 1970.

Robertson, Frank C. and Harris, Beth K. *Soapy Smith: King of the Frontier Con Men.* New York: Hastings House, 1961.

Ryan, Pat M. "Tombstone Theatre Tonight." *The Smoke Signal* (Tucson) 7, Spring 1966.

Samuels, Charles. *The Magnificent Rube: The Life and Times of Tex Rickard.* New York: McGraw-Hill, 1957.

Seattle Chamber of Commerce. *John Harte McGraw: A Tribute To His Memory.* Seattle: The Chamber of Commerce, 1911.

Shirley, Glenn. "Cowboy Strongman Tom Tyler." In *Old West* 2, Winter 1974.

Smith, Helen Huntington. *The War On Powder River.* New York: McGraw-Hill, 1966.

Theobald, John and Theobald, Lillian. *Arizona Territory: Post Offices and Post Masters.* Phoenix: Arizona Historical Foundation, 1961.

Thrapp, Dan. *Al Sieber: Chief of Scouts.* Norman: University of Oklahoma Press, 1964.

Wagoner, Jay J. *Arizona Territory 1863–1912: A Political History.* Tucson: The University of Arizona Press, 1970.

Waters, Frank. *The Earp Brothers of Tombstone.* New York: Clarkson N. Potter, Inc., 1960.

Wharton, David. *The Alaska Gold Rush.* Bloomington: Indiana University Press, 1972.

Who Was Who In America, Volume I, 1897–1942. Chicago: A. N. Marquis Company, 1942.

Work Projects Administration: Writers' Program. *Arizona: A State Guide.* New York: Hastings House, 1940.

Year: Mid-Century Edition: 1900–1950. Los Angeles: Year Incorporated, 1950.

NEWSPAPERS

Alaska

Nome Semi-Weekly News. November 3, 1903.

Nugget (Nome) January 1, 1900.

Arizona

Arizona Daily Citizen (Tucson), March 27, 1882.

Arizona Daily Star (Tucson), November 16, 1879; June 23, 1881; June 9, 1975.

Arizona Republican (Phoenix), September 26, 1900.

Arizona Weekly Miner (Prescott), December 5, 1879; December 12, 1879; January 2, 1880.

Arizona Weekly Star (Tucson), May 26, 1881; November 16, 1884.

Tombstone Epitaph, July 31, 1880; October 29, 1880; September 10. 1881; March 20, 1882; March 22, 1882; April 4, 1882; December 20, 1974.

Tombstone Nugget, May 13, 1880; June 24, 1880; November 12, 1880; January 27 and 31, 1882.

California

Los Angeles Times, December 3, 4, 5, 11, 18, 1896; March 12, 1922.
San Diego Union, July 6, 1908.
San Francisco Chronicle, December 9, 1896.
San Francisco Examiner, December 4, and 8, 1896; May 19, 1906.
San Francisco Exchange, November 2, 1881.
Sun (San Bernardino), July 10, 1900.
Sun Telegram (San Bernardino), April 26, 1956; June 21, 1961.

Colorado

Denver Republican, May 22, 1882.

Kansas

Dodge City Times, October 14, 1876.
Ellsworth Reporter, August 21, 1873.
Ford County Globe (Dodge City), September 9, 1879.
Wichita Weekly Beacon, May 24, 1876.

Missouri

Lamar Democrat, September 6, 1957. (Centennial Edition)

Nevada

Tonopah Bonanza, February 1, 1902.

New Mexico

Albuquerque Journal (date not given), quoted in the *Arizona Weekly Star* (Tucson), November 16, 1884.

New York

New York Sun, August 16, 1903.

Texas

Dallas Herald, December 22, 1858.
Dallas Herald, January 2, 1875.
Galveston News, August 25, 1877.

Washington

Seattle Times, January 2, 1972.

PUBLIC RECORDS

Bisbee, Arizona. Cochise County. Clerk of the Superior Court: Civil Actions, Minute Book Number 1, a damage suit against John Clum, et al., by the Townlot Company, February 17, 1882.

Criminal Register of Actions, Book number 1, containing references to misdemeanor and felony actions against John H. Behan and John O. Dunbar.

Coroner's inquest into the death of Morgan Earp, March 19, 1882.

Coroner's inquest into the death of Warren Earp, July 12, 1900.

Coroner's inquest, Document number 48, into the death of Billy Clanton et al., filed December 1, 1881.

Document number 94, Territory of Arizona vs. Morgan Earp et al., defendants, filed January 3, 1882 (the so-called O.K. Corral hearing before Justice Wells Spicer). The original of this document disappeared from the county files sometime after 1929 when Stuart Lake examined it; the editor has a complete copy in his collection, as do a few other collectors.

Injunction obtained by John Clum et al., restraining the Tombstone Townlot Company, December 4, 1880.

Marriage records, Book 1, p. 9, Peter Spencer to Maria Duarte, August 13, 1881.

Bisbee, Arizona. Cochise County Recorder.

Great Registers, 1881–1900.

Treasurer's Warrant Register, October 1881–December 1892.

Dodge City, Kansas. Ford County Treasurer's Warrants.

Fort Worth, Texas. Federal Records Center. Records of the U.S. Court for the Western District of Arkansas, 1871; the U.S. vs. Wyatt Earp: horse stealing in the Indian Nations.

Knoxville, Iowa. Marion County. Marriage Records, 1861, recording the wedding of Walter Earp and Ellen Donahoo.

Lamar, Missouri. Barton County. Marriage Records: Wyatt Earp to Urilla Sutherland, January 10, 1870.

Prescott, Arizona. Yavapai County. Clerk of the District Court. Decree of divorce: Victoria F. Behan vs. John H. Behan, June 2, 1875.

Prescott, Arizona. Yavapai County Recorder. Bonds and Oaths file showing political offices held by John H. Behan.

San Bernardino, California. San Bernardino County Supervisors' District 4, Enumerator's District 63a. 1880 Census.

Springfield, Illinois. Illinois Adjutant General's Records of Earps' military service.

Tombstone, Arizona. City Records. Tax Rolls, 1881 and 1882; Map of the town plat.

Washington, D.C. National Archives.

Civil War pension record of James Cooksey Earp.

War with Mexico pension record of Nicholas Porter Earp.

U.S. Army Adjutant General's Office (AGO) Letters received 1882, Sieber to Willcox, June 8, 1882.

LIBRARIES AND HISTORICAL SOCIETIES

Berkeley. University of California, Bancroft Library. Records of G. W. Caldwell's sale of the *Bancroft History* set to Wyatt Earp, 1885.

Colton, California. Public Library. Earp research notes of Melvin Gibson, Captain, USAF.

Laramie. University of Wyoming Library. Canton papers.

Milwaukee. Historical Society. City Directories and Great Registers, c. 1880.

Norman. University of Oklahoma Library. Canton papers.

Prescott, Arizona. Sharlott Hall Museum. Correspondence with Mabel Earp Cason.

San Diego, California. Public Library, California Room. E. B. Gifford obituary.

San Marino, California. The Huntington Library. Lake collection.

Tucson. Arizona Historical Society. John Vosburg interview given to Frank C. Lockwood regarding opening of the Tombstone discovery; Sanborn map of Tombstone, 1882.

Tucson. University of Arizona. Special Collections. The Behan papers; U.S. Census, 1880, including Tombstone.

MAJOR PERSONAL COLLECTIONS AND MANUSCRIPTS

Alexander, Mrs. Kyle, Highland, California. Earp family Bible, with family records in the hand of Nicholas Porter Earp.

Boyer, Glenn G., Bisbee, Arizona (editor's collection). Includes the Cason and Colyn collections and the Rousseau diary, as indicated below.

Cason, Mabel Earp. The collected memoirs of Mrs. Wyatt Earp; includes several thousand pages of manuscript and related notes. In editor's collection.

Colyn, Esther. Genealogy of the Nicholas Porter Earp line, 1950–1973; this with many letters and related research is a part of the editor's collection.

Devere, Jeanne, Tombstone, Arizona. Contains many Earp items. Mrs. Devere is the daughter of Ethel Robertson Macia, who was born in Tombstone in 1881. Mr. and Mrs. Devere are the owners of the Rosetree Inn at Tombstone.

Holladay, Fred, San Bernardino, California. Genealogies, letters, memoirs, and photographs relating to Nicholas Porter Earp and family.

Rousseau, Mrs. J. A. Diary, 1864. Firsthand account of trip from Pella, Iowa, to San Bernardino, California, in the wagon train captained by Nicholas Porter Earp. In editor's collection.

Turner, Alford and Oster, William, Tombstone, Arizona. The Turner/
Oster collection of official documentation on the Earps is the most
extensive in existence.

EARP LETTERS

The following letters are contained in the editor's collection, unless
otherwise indicated.

California State Library to Mabel Earp Cason, June 9, 1937.
Cason, Mabel Earp to Esther Irvine, February 13, 1959.
Coe, Mary to the editor, September 16, 1974.
Earp, Josephine to Stuart N. Lake, November 10, 1930.
Earp, Josephine to William S. Hart, March 24, 1922.
Earp, Nicholas Porter to James Copla, April 2, 1865.
Earp, Wyatt to George W. Earp, February 12, 1928.
Flood, John H. to the editor, 1956.
Flood, John H. to Walter Noble Burns, March 28, 1927.
Hallowell, Hildreth to John B. Sullivan II, February 21, 1967.
Hart, William S. to Wyatt Earp, September 9, 1926.
Hunsaker, William J. to Stuart N. Lake, October 2, 1928, Lake collection.
Hunt, William R. to the editor, April 4, 1975.
Israel, Solomon to Stuart N. Lake, September 21, 1928, Lake collection.
Johnson, Anne to William S. Hart, February 21, 1926.
Kent, Ira Rich to Stuart N. Lake, February 19, 1930; October 23, 1930,
    Lake collection.
Kruse, Rhoda E. to the editor, June 6, 1975.
Lake, Stuart N. to Burton Rascoe, January 9, 1941, Lake collection.
Lake, Stuart N. to Ira Rich Kent, February 13, 1930; October 15, 1930;
    October 30, 1930, Lake collection.
Lake, Stuart N. to Wyatt Earp, December 25, 1927. (Lake's first contact
    with Earp.)
Lake, Stuart N. to Wyatt S. Earp, October 31, 1928; November 14, 1928;
    January 10, 1929.
Llewellen, Sarah to Albert Behan, 1942.
Magnuson, Richard G. to the editor, May 2, 1975.
McLaury, Will to his father, April 13, 1884.
Meeker, Mrs. Behan W. to the editor, August–September 1974.
Milwaukee Historical Society to the editor, July 22, 1975.
Scotten, Frank D., Jr. to Stuart N. Lake, October 10, 1928.
Sharlott Hall Museum to Mabel Earp Cason, undated.

Sieber, Al to General Willcox, June 8, 1882. Adjutant General's Office, Letters Received File, 1882, National Archives.

Thomas, Susan McKey to the editor, August 7, 1974.

Tilghman, Zoe to the editor, 1962–64.

Washington Historical Society to the editor, May 16, 1975.

Yavapai County Recorder to the editor, March 20, 1975.

INTERVIEWS

All interviews were conducted by the editor unless otherwise indicated.

Cason, Ernest, 1966, by phone.

Devere, Jeanne, 1974, 1975, Tombstone, Arizona. (1975 interview on tape; copy in editor's collection.)

Escapule, Ernest, 1969, 1970, 1974, Cochise County, Arizona.

Flood, John, 1956, Yuma, Arizona.

Griffin, LaVonne (Wyatt Earp's grand-niece, daughter of Estelle and William Miller), 1965, 1966, 1967, 1973. (Some of the interviews on tape; copies in editor's collection.)

Hallowell, Hildreth (grand-niece of Mrs. Virgil Earp) interviewed by Earp researchers Alford Turner and William Oster, 1971, Valley Center, California. (Tape in editor's collection.)

Laing, Jeanne Cason (daughter of Mabel Earp Cason), 1975, San Jose, California. (Tapes in editor's collection and in Special Collections, University of Arizona, Tucson.)

Marquis, Florence (wife of the nephew of Wyatt Earp's second wife, Celia Ann Blaylock), 1965, 1966, Colorado.

Mayhew, Carmelita, 1957, Yuma, Arizona.

Miller, Estelle (daughter of Wyatt Earp's sister Adelia), 1965, 1966, 1967; almost daily contacts between April and June 1965, San Bernardino, California. (Some of the interviews on tape; copies in editor's collection.)

Miller, William (husband of Wyatt Earp's niece Estelle), 1965, 1966, 1967, San Bernardino, California. (Some of the interviews on tape; copies in editor's collection.)

Stewart, Harry, 1970, Tombstone.

Waters, Frank, 1966, Fort Collins, Colorado. (Substantial parts of interview on tape in Turner/Oster collection.)

Index

Ackerman, Vinolia Earp, 254

Alaska: Earps' decision to go there, 158–59; first trip, 160–66; second trip, 162–65; stay at Nome, 192–94, 197–205; stay in Rampart, 165–80; stay in St. Michael, 181–91; third trip, 195–98

Alaska Commercial Company, 169

Alhambra Saloon, 55n.3

Allen, William (Rustler sympathizer): fires sneak shot at street fight, 90; shot by Doc Holliday in Leadville, 96n.19

Apache Indians, 6

Arizona Lottery, 75n.16

Asher, Charley, 198

Baldwin, Elias Jackson (Lucky), 142, 199; biographical sketch of, 148n.8

Banning, 229

Barnes, Johnny, 26

Bartholomew, Ed, 253

Beach, Rex, 166, 169, 176, 188

Behan, Albert (son of John Harris Behan), 16n.1, 29, 72, 257n.7

Behan, Henrietta (daughter of John Harris Behan), 16n.1

Behan, John Harris (Johnny), 33, 77, 88, 106; announcement by, as candidate for sheriff, 26; Arizona residence of, first, 16n.1; at Globe, Arizona, 128; biographical sketch of, 15n.1; bribe offered by, 109n.8; called down by Wyatt Earp for deceitfulness, 36; charged with misdemeanors and felonies at Tombstone, 74n.12; cowardly behavior of, 27–28; described, 12, 27, 29, 44n.27, 61; divorce of, 20n.20, 39n.5; evasiveness

with Josephine, 77; eviction attempt on Josephine by, 64; income of, as sheriff of Cochise County, 42n.18; history of, subsequent to Tombstone, 16n.1; house in Tombstone, location of, 41n.15; initial Tombstone residence of, 16n.1; jealous nature of, 30; and Josephine Sarah Marcus (See Marcus, Josephine Sarah and John Harris Behan); knocked down by Morgan Earp, 64; as ladies' man, 22, 39n.5; as law officer, Yavapai County, Arizona, 17n.3; love affair of, probably with Kitty Jones, 43n.22; Morgan Earp murder and motive of, 64, 72n.2; personal rift between, and Wyatt Earp, 33; political promise to Wyatt Earp broken by, 30; relations with Rustler gang, 26, 65, 78; suspicious attitude of, 34; threatened by Wyatt Earp, 129; and Victoria Zaff Behan (wife): children of, 16n.1; divorce of, 16n.1, 20n.20; marriage of, 16n.1; and Wyatt Earp (See Wyatt Earp and John Harris Behan)

Behan, Josephine (common-law wife of John H. Behan). See Marcus, Josephine Sarah

Behan, Peter (father of John Harris Behan), 16n.1

Behan, Sarah Ann Harris (wife of Peter Behan and mother of John Harris Behan), 16n.1

Behan, Victoria Zaff. See Behan, John Harris and Victoria Zaff Behan (wife)

Benson, 6

Biebel, Charlie, 119n.4

Big Minook Creek, 165

[267]